CHEKHOV
AND HIS RUSSIA

CHEKHOV
AND HIS RUSSIA

A Sociological Study

by

W. H. BRUFORD

ARCHON BOOKS
1971

First Published in Great Britain 1948
Reissued 1971
by Archon Books
995 Sherman Avenue
Hamden, Connecticut, 06514

PG
3458
B7
1971

ISBN 0 208 01164 1

To My Wife

Printed in Great Britain

CONTENTS

91223

PREFACE

T HE author of this work was one of the many who were irre-
sistibly attracted by Chekhov when Mrs. Garnett's translations
began to appear some thirty years ago, but his book would not
have been written but for the second world war. While separated
from his books and papers during four years of war work he
found in a collected edition of Chekhov in Russian so much
delight and such a rich source of information about the older
Russia, out of which the world power of to-day has grown, that he
was tempted to play truant for once from the normal field of
his studies, and to attempt to communicate to others some of
the pleasure and the illumination which Chekhov had given
him.

His aim from the outset was to throw light both on Chekhov
and on Russia, by trying to see Russia through Chekhov's eyes
and to see Chekhov as the product of a particular age and
country. This way of approaching literature, which is of course
only one among many, had become habitual with him in German
studies, but it soon became clear that although experience gained
in the one field might be of value in the other, a thorough study
of the Russian background would be a very exacting task. He
has done what he could in a limited time and with limited
resources, but in the main this book attempts to use Chekhov
himself as a source, and to give only so much information from
other sources as will serve to furnish a provisional framework
of reference and prevent gross misinterpretation.

Even if the author had been as well informed about Russian
history as he would wish to be, such an attempt would still be
open to criticism on two counts. One of them could hardly be
put more forcibly than it was by Prince Mirsky when he wrote:
'Only persons ignorant alike of the nature of imaginative literature
and of that of historical evidence will attempt to use Russian
fiction as an historical source, unless its evidence is corroborated
by extra-literary sources, in which case it becomes superfluous.'[1]
The last statement, the only one which may be seriously disputed,
may be countered by a few words from a British historian equally

[1] *History of Russian literature to* 1881, p. 219.

learned and perhaps wiser, the late Sir John Maynard: 'Statistics may (and do) lie. They may be (and are) suppressed. But the picture of manners by the hand of a master outlives brass.'[1] Certainly it has been the universal practice of our historians of Russia to make use of the Russian novelists, and surely quite rightly, just as paintings are used as evidence, in spite of the kind of criticism that is annually made of the Royal Academy by *The Tailor and Cutter*. These vivid symbols may be misleading, but they are less misleading than what our unaided imagination would construct from blue-books and our personal experience as foreigners, though they must be used of course with critical discretion.

A second type of critic might consider it a kind of sacrilege to use such a fine literary artist as Chekhov as a quarry for historical material, and the criticism would be justified if there were not already in existence a large number of purely literary appreciations of his work to restore the balance. It would be the height of philistinism to think of Chekhov merely as a historical source, but it is not even good literary criticism to write of him with as little regard to his historical setting as is displayed by many of our essayists.

A comparison between Russian and English appreciations of Chekhov shows that the former tend to stress the content of his work, and the latter the form. Russian critics, both during his lifetime and later, have almost always insisted on the truth of his picture of Russia, and represented it as a challenge to action. English critics have frequently overlooked his background of experience, so different from their own, and taken as a verdict on life itself what was written as an indictment of Russian conditions in his own time. A Russian refutes for instance the objections raised by De Vogüé and some English critics to the exaggerated gloom of 'the disconsolate Chekhovs and Gorkis', asserting that Russians find in these artists' work a true reflection of the Russian atmosphere. Chekhov, he says, 'showed up all the horror of Russian actuality, and to a society suffering from blindness of the soul, a society which saw and did not understand, he said with unparalleled force: "We cannot go on living like · this".' Another calls him, in 1904, 'the most authoritative historian of the last twenty years'. 'If all the other works of our age were to disappear,' he says, 'a sociologist could paint a picture on a broad canvas of the life of the 'eighties and 'nineties

---

[1] *The Russian Peasant and other studies*, p. 13.

and its background from his writings alone.'[1] Merezhkovsky said exactly the same in his essay *Chekhov and Gorky*.

A book of this kind is meant to point beyond itself. Perhaps it may serve as a brief guide to fascinating country, the daily life of that richly endowed but tragically misgoverned older Russia, as it was seen by the gentle, humorous and understanding eyes of a truly humane spirit and a consummate artist, the last of the Russian classics. No one who knows Chekhov can feel that there is any unsurmountable barrier to understanding between his country and our own, however much the outward forms of life may change, because he will be convinced that the Russian is a human being with joys and sorrows like his own, and that in spite of our very different history, there are, or were, astonishing similarities in our moral outlook, due no doubt in the main to our common Christian inheritance.

This small contribution to Russian studies would have been still more imperfect if the author had not had at his disposal the resources of the London Library, to whose Committee and staff he wishes to express his great indebtedness. It was also a benefit for which he is most grateful to have had the advice on some points of his colleague Professor B. H. Sumner, who is not however to be held responsible for anything but the quotations from his invaluable 'Survey'.

The quotations from Chekhov are in most cases new translations from the Russian text, but Mrs. Garnett's version was frequently consulted, and where, as in many of the letters, it would have been difficult to avoid her phrasing, it has been gratefully adopted. Titles of stories not included in her translation are marked with an asterisk.

Edinburgh, 1947.   W. H. BRUFORD

[1] V. Lvov and P. E. Pavlov, in N. Pokrovsky's collection of essays on Chekhov, Moscow, 1906.

CHAPTER I

CHEKHOV'S AIMS AND OPPORTUNITIES AS A REALIST

When Chekhov published his first work in 1880 in Moscow comic papers like the *Dragon Fly* and the *Alarm Clock*, he was a first year medical student of twenty, desperately in need of money, both for his own maintenance and that of his family. He had supported himself by coaching ever since his bankrupt father had left his grocer's shop in Taganrog for Moscow in 1876, but now the literary gift he had discovered in himself at school, where he had written stories for a school magazine, as well as a farce and a play, offered a more promising and congenial means of making money. Even three years later, when, mainly through his work, his home circumstances were easier, and he had been writing for a year for a rather more literary St. Petersburg weekly called *Oskolki* (*Chips!*), we find him complaining to its editor of the overcrowded noisy surroundings in which he is forced to write, and of 'the non-literary work in front of him that is mercilessly whipping his conscience'. He felt that week's story to be particularly slight and unpolished, and his 'Moscow notes' to be flat, and it was probably this he had in mind in the sentence quoted, but medicine was on his conscience too, for he was beginning his final year, and his friends and relations were always urging him not to give up 'real work' for scribbling. It was not until 1886, two years after he had taken his degree, that encouragement from the editor of the *Novoe Vremya*, Suvorin, and the respected writer Grigorovich, led him to think of himself as an artist. He did not at that time remember a single story over which he had spent more than twenty-four hours.

Yet Chekhov did not consider these years lost which he had given to medical studies and literary hack-work. In them he had qualified as a doctor and practised a little, he had found his feet unaided in the literary world and relieved his family from penury, and above all, perhaps, he had achieved a certain personal culture and freedom of mind. His high conception of personal culture is evident from the remarkable letter to his artist-brother

Nicolai, which will be quoted later. The moral and intellectual effort that was necessary for the grandson of a serf to make of himself a spiritual aristocrat on the level of a Tolstoy can be divined from a letter to Suvorin, after *Ivanov* (7/1/1889) in which Chekhov says, feeling *Ivanov* to be still immature: 'I am glad that I did not listen to Grigorovitch two or three years ago and write a novel! I can imagine what a lot of good material I should have spoilt if I had. According to him "freshness and talent overcome all difficulties". It is truer to say that freshness and talent can spoil a great deal. In addition to abundance of material and talent, something else, no less important, is necessary. One needs to be mature in the first place, and further, it is essential to have the feeling of personal freedom, a feeling that has only recently begun to spring up in me. What I had earlier in its place was my light-heartedness, carelessness and lack of respect for my work. What writers belonging to the gentry received from nature for nothing, we others (raznochintsy) have to purchase at the cost of our youth. Write a story of how a young man, the son of a serf, who has served in a shop, sung in a choir, and had a secondary school and university education, who has been brought up to respect rank and office, to kiss priests' hands, to bow to other people's ideas, to say thank you for every piece of bread, who has often been whipped, who has trudged from one pupil to another without galoshes, who has been used to fighting, and tormenting animals, who has been glad to be asked to dinner by rich relations and been hypocritical before God and men without any necessity, simply from the consciousness of his own insignificance—write how this young man squeezes the slave out of himself drop by drop until, waking one fine morning, he feels that he has no longer slave's blood flowing in his veins, but a real man's.'

This letter is purely autobiographical, though it gives a less favourable picture of Chekhov's youth than that drawn by his brother Michael in his biographical sketch. It shows in particular how Chekhov had set himself from early manhood to realize in his own life that ideal of a free personality, avoiding any encroachment on the personal life of others and permitting none on his own, which the great Russian authors, following in part the liberal tradition of the West, had by now established. His gentleness, his habit of self-depreciation and of self-sacrifice for others were, as Chukovsky[1] convincingly proves, the result of sustained moral effort, not of indifference and inertia.

[1] *Chekhov the Man*, London 1945.

Anton Chekhov's father Paul had been brought up as a serf in a village in the province of Voronezh, until in 1841, twenty years before the general Emancipation, his own father, an able and energetic peasant who had been able to save, bought freedom for his whole family at 700 roubles a head, a small daughter being thrown in for nothing. Later, Chekhov's grandfather became steward to Count Platov, a hero of the war of 1812, on his estates not far from Taganrog on the sea of Azov. On his visits as a boy to his grandfather, Anton saw something of the life on a big estate, sometimes sitting by the great steam threshing machine checking the corn sacks from dawn till dusk, and hearing tales of peasant life of that day and the preceding age. Paul Chekhov worked as a clerk in Taganrog, until in 1857 he had saved up enough money to open a grocer's shop. He belonged now to the second gild of merchants of Taganrog and had recently married the daughter of a cloth merchant, a man of some education, whose affairs had taken him all over Russia. From his earliest days Paul Chekhov had had a passion for church music and choral singing. He had learnt to sing from music and to play the violin even as a serf boy. In Taganrog he gave rather too much time to town affairs and to music, conducting a church choir, playing the violin and, as his family grew up, teaching them to sing too. Church on Saturday evening and Sunday morning was always followed by hymns sung in parts at home, and sometimes the Chekhov boys would sing trios in church. Everyone envied their parents then, Chekhov said later, but the boys themselves felt like little convicts. An overdose of compulsory religion in youth probably helped to turn them against it later, especially as they associated it with their father's general 'despotism', scenes at table because the soup was oversalted, free use of the rod and the like (cf. *Difficult People*). Meanwhile business in Taganrog was not too bad, until most of the trade of the port was attracted to Rostov-on-Don through railway developments in the 'seventies, and in 1876 Paul Chekhov became bankrupt.

At this time Anton was a healthy and remarkably cheerful schoolboy of sixteen, attending the town grammar school. He had been brought up rather strictly but with real affection in a large family, in which there were two brothers older and two brothers and a sister younger than himself. The patriarchal family life and the example of a stern father and devoted mother had not only helped to form his character—he was unselfish and attached to his family in a rare degree—but he had also unconsciously learnt from them a good deal about life in serf days and about other regions of Russia beside the south where they lived. He was soaked in the music and liturgy of the Orthodox Church, he knew something about merchants and shopkeepers and the life of a port, and he had worked and played and caught fish with peasant boys on a great country estate. After the family's departure for Moscow he lived on in the old house, now taken over by one of the creditors, and gave lessons to the Cossack nephew of the new owner. On holiday visits to this boy's home in the steppe he got to know the Cossack country and the life of its landowners, and learned from his companions to ride and shoot, while in town, in spite of his poverty, he worked and played with the best, flirted with the high school girls, frequented the local theatre and read everything he could lay his hands on. It was not a bad foundation of experience for a future writer.

In Moscow he had not only to maintain himself as a student; he had already serious family responsibilities. His two older brothers had already left home. Alexander, after studying at Moscow, became first a customs official in Taganrog, writing stories in his spare time, and then a journalist in Moscow. Nicolai studied art; he had talent but insufficient strength of character and constitution, and died at an early age of consumption. Anton had their artistic gifts in a much higher degree, together with a moral integrity and buoyancy which they lacked. As their father, when he at last found employment as a poorly-paid clerk in a warehouse, was obliged to live in, like the assistants in *Three years*, the mother and younger children turned to Anton in all their difficulties as the virtual head of the family. He had brought a couple of school-friends to Moscow with him as boarders, and in one way or another the family contrived to live, and to live quite cheerfully, if not in ideal surroundings at first, in the succession of old houses where they found quarters (cf. *The old house*). Anton was extremely gay and sociable. He soon had friends not only in the university, but among the intelligentsia of Moscow, and, soon after graduation, in St. Petersburg as well. In the intervals of writing, and finding a market for, two or three comic stories or feuilletons a week, he worked hard at medicine, which interested him deeply and influenced from an early date both his attitude to life and art, and his subjects.

Before Anton graduated his younger brother Ivan had become the schoolmaster of a parish school at Voskresensk, a sleepy little town in fine country in the Moscow province, and there any of the family who were free joined him in the summer months. Anton went there after graduation in 1884. He was soon on friendly terms with the officers of the battery stationed there and their families (cf. *Three Sisters*), he visited the New Jerusalem monastery near the town, and he acquired some clinical experience under the capable head of the Zemstvo hospital at Chikino, a few miles away, sometimes helping his feldscher assistants with their peasant patients. In the same summer he took the place for a month or two of the Zemstvo doctor at Zvenigorod, about twelve miles away, received thirty to forty patients every morning, accompanied the examining magistrate to a post-mortem or two, attended various zemstvo meetings and gained some knowledge of the life and the administration of the whole region. In a single letter (27 June 1884, to Leikin) we have glimpses of the real experience behind at least three of his early stories, when he tells of his journey with an old examining magistrate to hold a post-mortem on a stranger found dead in a field. Two muzhiks, sitting beside a little fire, have been watching the body since it was found, as they were bound to do until the authorities arrived (cf. *A dead body*). The villagers beg them not to bring it into the village, or 'the women and children won't sleep for fright' (cf. *On official duty*), so the post-mortem is held under an oak tree. Chekhov sees that many ribs are broken, but is not surprised when he learns that on finding the body the peasants had tossed it twice in a mat by way of first aid (cf. *Speedy help**). Amongst other stories that go back to the experiences of that time are *Surgery,** *The run-away, Sorrow*, etc.

In the same eventful summer he first became intimately acquainted with the country-house life of a cultivated family, at Babkino, the estate of the Kiselyovs, three miles from Voskresensk. For the next three years the Chekhovs had the use of a bungalow on this estate for the summer, and became close personal friends of a well-connected family who had great charm, good taste in music and literature, and a host of friends in artistic circles. The father of Mme. Kiselyov, who lived with her and her husband in retirement, was a much-travelled man who had been director of the imperial theatres in Moscow. She herself was a writer and she shared Chekhov's passion for fishing. His letters to her and her family are amongst the best even of Chekhov's letters. They include amusing stories with his own illustrations for the children.

In April and May of 1887 Chekhov found a flood of new impressions on the journey which he made, mainly for reasons of health (he had been spitting blood since 1885, though he would not yet believe that he was consumptive) to the south of Russia. He went by rail through Tula, Orel, Kursk, Byelgorod, Kharkov, Slavyansk to his old home Taganrog, where he stayed with his uncle and renewed old acquaintances. After a fortnight there he went as best man to a Cossack wedding at Novocherkask in the Don valley, east of Rostov, and from there north to a remote Cossack farm on the Donetz road beyond Zvyerevo, where one had to drive fifteen miles for letters to the nearest post-office. He was living, he told Leikin, in the heart of the Donetz hills, amongst 'mountains, ravines, little woods, little streams, and steppe, steppe, steppe', with a retired Cossack cornet. In the thatched farm-house of three rooms, with clay floors, he was wakened in the morning by shots—that was their way of killing the hens and geese which were his main diet—and the chief occupation was rational farming on the basis of wholesale slaughter. 'They kill sparrows, bumble-bees, ants, magpies, crows, so that they won't eat the bees; to prevent bees from spoiling the flowers on the fruit-trees, they kill the bees, and to prevent the trees from exhausting the soil, they uproot them. This highly original cycle is founded on the latest discoveries of science.' This part of his journey clearly gave him ideas for *The Steppe, The Pechenyeg, Happiness*, etc. Chekhov returned to Taganrog by way of Slavyansk and the Holy Mountains monastery, where he spent two nights in the guest-house. Slavyansk was a quiet little provincial town, like Gogol's south Russian town Mirgorod, he said. 'In its dusty and grass-grown streets, pigs, cows and other domestic animals wander about. The houses have an inviting and kindly air, like benign grandmothers, the pavements are soft to walk on, the streets wide, the air is scented with lilac and acacia; in the distance you hear nightingales singing, frogs croaking, dogs barking, the notes of an accordion, and a woman's high-pitched voice.' The Svyatogorsky (Holy Mountains) monastery on the Donets, at the foot of steep pine-clad hills, he described at length in *Uprooted*. After a few more days in Taganrog he returned to Moscow.

In the autumn of this year Chekhov wrote in a fortnight his first big play, *Ivanov*, for a Moscow theatre, where a rather indifferent performance aroused the liveliest interest among the public. It was much discussed even in St. Petersburg because of its striking pre-sentation of contemporary types of character. After this production and the publication of his first long story, *The Steppe*, in the leading monthly magazine, the *Severny Vyestnik*, Chekhov considered himself a professional writer, and though he was still frequently in temporary difficulties, his financial position was much easier. The *Novoe Vremya* and the monthlies could afford to pay him well, his older stories were appearing in book form and *Ivanov* and one or two one-act plays helped to keep the pot boiling. The following summer (1888) he spent chiefly in the Ukraine, at Luka on the Psyol, in the province of Kharkov. His parents were longing for the south after so many years in Moscow, and an acquaintance recommended to them as a 'dacha' a lodge on the old and neglected estate of the Lintvaryovs. Here they found beautiful country, excellent fishing, congenial company at the manor-house, and round about 'sad and poetical estates shut up and deserted where live the souls of beautiful women; old footmen, relics of serfdom, with one foot in the grave; young ladies, longing for the most conventional love'. From there he visited the neighbouring province of Poltava, staying with the Smagins on another old estate, where the doors would not shut, and suckers from the roots of cherry and plum trees came up through cracks in the floor. Here were some more models for his numerous pictures of the country gentry. The old poet Pleshcheyev, the novelist Barantsevich, and Suvorin visited him at Luka. In July he went, through Kiev and down the Dnieper, to Feodosia in the Crimea, to spend a fortnight with the Suvorins. He saw Sevastopol with its sea 'like blue copperas', Yalta, where he was to settle in his later years, 'a mixture of something European that reminds one of views of Nice, with something plebeian, something of the country fair'. From Feodosia he started off with one of Suvorin's sons on what was intended to be a journey through the Caucasus to Persia. They went from Kerch by small steamers to the monastery New Athos, Sukhum and Poti, and then by the Georgian military road through Tiflis to Batum, but here they received news of the death of the younger brother of Chekhov's companion, and had to return.

Next year (1889) Chekhov did not see much new country. He was so tired of Moscow now and his new fame—in the autumn of 1888 he had been awarded the Pushkin prize—that he was looking out for a small farm in the south where he could live permanently. He went back to Luka for the summer, but after the death of his brother Nicolai there he felt so depressed and incapable of work that he determined to go abroad. Suvorin was in the Tyrol, and he went as far as Odessa intending to join him there, but lost touch with him through some misunderstanding and went to the Crimea again instead, to Yalta. A busy winter in Moscow followed, and from January 1890 he was planning the most surprising and adventurous journey of his life, right across Siberia to the penal settlement on the island of Sakhalin. It was through his brother Michael, who was studying law, that he suddenly became intensely interested from the human angle in prison management. His reasons for undertaking the journey, and the objections raised by his friends, are to be found in his long letter to Suvorin of 9th March 1890. It seemed to them a sudden craze, which would make great inroads on his time, his money and his health, and would only lead to a book of no interest to anyone, but though Chekhov did not expect to make any contribution to science or literature through his visit, it is clear that he was bent on discharging a debt of conscience. He had come to realise that the famous reforms of the 'sixties had done nothing for the sick and nothing for those in prison. The first omission was to some extent being made good in his own time, and as doctor-author he had long been concerned with it. But the second still remained, and the first step towards reform was knowledge of the facts. His aim was to get to know all he could about this new Australia, this colony of convicts, 'a place of unbearable suffering, such as only man, free and unfree, was capable of experiencing'. The administration of it was a fearful responsibility, one which, like the responsibility for the fate of those millions who had in the past been sent to rot in Russian prisons, did not fall simply on the shoulders of 'gaolers and red-nosed superintendents', but on them all.

Nothing could show more clearly than this journey, and the book *Sakhalin Island* which resulted from it, that Chekhov was not an artist in an ivory tower, or a mere observer, indifferent to the sufferings of Russia. His social conscience is evident in all his later work, but it is only in *Sakhalin Island* that he is purely the sociologist. This work took the place of the medical thesis that he had always intended to write, proving how much his mind was drawn towards the study of everything that had some bearing on man's happiness in society. It was a straightforward account, in over 400 pages, of his investigations at the penal settlement, containing many striking details, but anything but sensational in tone. It was based on house to house visits and the methodical filling in, at every house in the island, of a questionnaire with twelve headings (age, status, confession, birthplace, date of arrival, occupation, etc.). The analysis of this information was supplemented by a general description of the island and the approach to it, of the daily life, houses, food and clothing of the settlers, their churches and schools, the state of morality, social statistics, and medical services. Chekhov often found whole villages where no one was legally married, irregular unions being the rule everywhere rather than the exception. Venereal disease was exceedingly common, and the principal hospital was far below even Russian standards. There were a few fairly prosperous free men and 'settlers' (who had served their time), but in the usual izba he found just the barest necessities and listless, unhealthy people. Chekhov found the authorities on the island on the whole friendly and helpful; the articles he wrote for *Russkaya Myssl* on his return and the subsequent book were well received in official circles, and may have had some influence on the reforms which followed in the 'nineties, though to judge by Tolstoy's *Resurrection* much still remained to be done in 1899.

Apart from its main purpose, this journey greatly increased Chekhov's knowledge of the Russian Empire and gave him some acquaintance with many other lands. Its effect is to be seen not only in the few stories which it directly inspired, such as *Gusev* and *In Exile*, but in the general broadening of his horizon. No wonder that on his return, his Moscow life seemed to him 'petty, bourgeois and dull'. It put western Europe too in a different perspective. 'After being in India and China,' he wrote, 'I did not see a great difference between Russia and other European countries.' To cross Siberia before the railway was built was a really formidable undertaking, especially for one in his already rather uncertain state of health. He took leave of his friends in Yaroslavl on the Volga on 21st April, sailed down the river to Kazan, and up the Kama to Perm. From here the railway took him through Ekaterinburg to Tyumen, but no further. The next 3000 miles or so to Sryetensk on the Shilka, a tributary of the Amur, he covered by road, except when he had to take to a boat because of the flooding of the roads, and to cross rivers and the great Lake Baikal, where 'the poetry of Siberia began'. The roads were either indescribably muddy or dusty, and accommodation and food on the way very bad. The chief stopping-places were Tomsk, Krasnoyarsk, Irkutsk and a village on Lake Baikal, and the journey took two months. From Sryetensk he travelled by steamer in comparative comfort, first down the Amur, the boundary between China and Siberia, through the most beautiful country he had ever seen. On the steamer the air was 'positively

red-hot' with liberalism, because in those remote parts the people
were not afraid to think aloud. 'The lowest convict breathes
more freely on the Amur,' he wrote, giving us for once a glimpse
of political conditions in Russia, 'than the highest general in
Russia.' He arrived in Sakhalin on 11th July, spent three months
there and returned by sea, with halts at Hong-Kong, Singapore
and Ceylon, a paradise for him after the hell of Sakhalin. He
reached Moscow via Odessa on 9th December.

In March and April of the following year Chekhov was again
abroad, this time with Suvorin, in Austria, Italy and France.
He was delighted with Vienna, Venice and Florence. In Vienna
he wrote: 'It is strange that here one is free to read anything and
to say what one likes,' and looking back on his stay in Venice and
Florence he said that on arriving there for the first time, 'one
would have to be a bull to "turn away from the West",' as
Grigorovitch thought Chekhov and his generation were doing.
The grand tour continued through Rome, Naples, Pompeii, Nice
and Paris. From Nice Chekhov visited Monte Carlo, and in one
evening lost 500 francs at roulette, but without regret, because
now he knew what a gambler felt like. But the general atmosphere
of Monte Carlo disgusted him. 'How contemptible and loath-
some this life is, with its artichokes, its palms and its scent of
orange blossom. I love wealth and luxury, but the luxury here,
this roulette luxury, reminds me of a luxurious water-closet.
There is something in the atmosphere that offends one's sense of
decency, and vulgarises the scenery, the sound of the sea, the
moon.' The summer brought him more country-house impressions, of which he made use particularly in *An artist's story*,
The Chekhovs took part of an old mansion in a fine park, near
Alexin on the Oka, a hundred miles south of Moscow. Michael
was now an inspector of taxes in these parts. Chekhov got up
very early in the morning and worked at his *Sakhalin* three days
a week, another three days at his long story *The duel*, and on
Sunday at short stories, yet he still found time to fish and to
entertain visitors.

The year 1892 and the following years brought him into closer
touch with peasant life than ever before. In the winter 1891–92
there was a serious famine in many parts of Russia owing to the
failure of the harvest. Chekhov threw himself with great energy
into relief work, and came into particularly close relations with a
district in the Nizhegorod province, west of Moscow, where
Yegorov, a friend of his from Voskresensk days, was now a land

captain. Chekhov and he collected money, chiefly from middle-class circles by means of an appeal in the press, and used it principally to save the next year's crops by buying up horses from the peasants, who found themselves forced to sell them for next to nothing in this crisis, feeding them and giving them back the next spring to their owners, to ensure that the fields would be ploughed for the spring corn. *The wife*, with its description of a collection for starving peasants, drew on memories of this time, and expresses Chekhov's disappointment with the results of work such as he did. He visited the district himself in January, and nearly lost his life in a snow-storm. In February he visited with Suvorin another of the hardest hit districts, in the province of Voronezh in the black earth zone south of Moscow, where similar work was being done.

In the same month Chekhov bought a farm at Melikhovo in the district of Serpukhov, about sixty miles due south of Moscow and within fairly easy reach of Alexin, where Michael was still living. He had long wished to settle in the country, partly to have quiet for his work and partly no doubt for reasons of health, for an obstinate cough was now giving him much trouble. Unpractical and impulsive as usual, he took this farm in winter without even seeing it, and when he arrived there, he found the property to be by no means an ideal home. It was eight miles by a vile road from the nearest station, the house was unattractive and the farm buildings badly arranged, there was far too much land to be looked after, some 600 acres of neglected fields and woods, and it was badly stocked in every way. There was no hay to feed the three wretched horses, one of which was lame, while another was soon exchanged by some one in the village for a dead horse which he left in the field. However, with the help of the latest books on agriculture Michael took charge of the farming, coming over from Alexin every week end, new stock and machinery were acquired, the house was repaired and decorated and its surroundings were made presentable, improvements being planned constantly by Anton himself. Labour was cheap—a reliable young labourer was paid five roubles a month—and the Chekhovs began, as he said, 'to understand the attractions of capitalism'. A new well was sunk, a pond was constructed, surrounded with newly planted trees and stocked with all kinds of fish, which Chekhov brought in pails from Moscow, no doubt from the Sunday market on the Truba Square (*The bird market*). This pond was his special plaything, but he took a delighted interest in everything. 'Creative activity,' Michael writes, 'was his passion. He was not satisfied with the ready made, he wanted to bring something new into existence. . . . He planted young trees, grew firs and pines from seed, tended them as if they had been his own children and, like Colonel Vershinin in his *Three sisters*, looking at them he wondered what they would be like in two or three hundred years.'

It was soon found of course that farming did not pay, and most of the land was apparently let to peasants. The farm became a country house with a big garden, before long a very attractive place. Its greatest attraction of course was Chekhov himself. In spite of the bad road, a constant stream of visitors descended upon him in the summer, and in self-defence he had to retire to a small lodge he had built after reconstructing the farm buildings. But before the great world knew about his country retreat, the country people had discovered that he was a doctor and came to him from fifteen miles around for treatment, which he gladly gave them for nothing, though he had no time to spare to visit them in their homes and did so unwillingly. He became a member of the Sanitary Council of the district, and gained a first-hand acquaintance with its hospitals and medical conditions generally. When there was a threat of cholera following the famine, he was asked to organise precautionary measures in a group of about twenty-five villages, and spent weeks in the winter of 1892 visiting them all, persuading factory owners to build isolation huts, acquiring stocks of disinfectants, and so on. Following this activity he was elected a member of the zemstvo of the district, attended its meetings regularly and took a special interest in medical and educational affairs. In his own village and two near by he built schools at his own expense and supervised every step in their construction. He presented to his village also a fire-station and a belfry for the church. One of the first things that had helped to break the ice for the Chekhovs in the village, apart from Anton's medical help, was the choir they had formed among themselves and their visitors, conducted by Paul Chekhov as of old, to sing the Easter services at the village church. In every way Chekhov entered with the greatest public spirit into the regional life, did what he could to raise it materially and spiritually, and of course came to know it through and through, with results which are obvious from his stories. Even in his last winter at Melikhovo, in 1896, he added to his knowledge of the peasantry by taking an active personal part in the census, going from cottage to cottage in a number of villages just as he had done in Sakhalin. Characteristically, the land captains who were supposed to be responsible for this census left nearly all the work to private individuals.

During the five years of constant residence at Melikhovo Chekhov made only one long journey, though he paid frequent visits to Moscow and St. Petersburg. In 1894 he had to spend some wearisome weeks at Yalta in the spring for his health, and in the autumn he again went south, but further afield, from Feodosia to Odessa by sea, and then, after a trip to Lvov, for a Polish exhibition, he revisited Vienna and spent a week or so in Abbazia, returning by way of Trieste, Venice, Milan, Genoa, Nice and Paris. Then in the spring of 1897, after a sudden and serious haemorrhage in Moscow, he could not conceal from himself that tuberculosis had got a hold on him, and went abroad for a whole year. After a short stay at Biarritz he spent the autumn and winter in Nice, where he found congenial Russian company at the Pension Russe, and the spring in Paris. It was while he was in France that the Dreyfus case was being hotly debated. Chekhov's warm championship of Dreyfus led to the rupture for a few years of his long friendship with Suvorin. He had never agreed with the political views of the *Novoe Vremya*, but liked Suvorin personally, as an intelligent and original man who owed his success to his own good qualities and, being like Chekhov the grandson of a serf, shared much of his outlook on society, but in this crisis he could no longer separate the man and his office. After his return to Russia he had to live for most of the year in the Crimea, and presently he gave up Melikhovo and built himself a villa at Yalta. Yet even now he could not reconcile himself to living in one place, as the doctors advised. Whenever he felt a little better he rushed up to Moscow, where he was keenly interested in the Art Theatre (founded in 1898), the theatre where he met the actress Olga Knipper, whom he married in 1901, and where his own plays were performed with so much enthusiasm and understanding. He spent the last month of his life in Germany, a country which he had never visited before, though he had found much to admire in the Germans. On a closer view they hardly came up to his expectations. He died at Badenweiler on 2nd July 1904.

This sketch of Chekhov's life will perhaps suffice to indicate the extent of his first-hand knowledge of Russia and the Russians. He was himself one of the intelligentsia, a professional writer from his student days. He had innumerable friends and acquaintances in this class, in Moscow and St. Petersburg, writers, journalists, artists and actors. He knew the merchant class and the peasantry intimately through his own family and through years of residence in Taganrog and Melikhovo. As a doctor he was thoroughly at home in the medical world and keenly interested in science in general. He had been brought up as a good Orthodox Christian and did not lose his love for the music and ritual of the Church even when he had ceased to believe in its message. He had many friends among the landed gentry and the official class through his summers spent in the country and his years as a modest landed proprietor and member of the zemstvo. If we remember too the contacts he made through his university friends, for he was a very loyal graduate of Moscow university, through his brothers and sister, and through his wide travels in the whole Russian empire, it is clear that few sides of Russian life can have escaped him. We shall not expect to find in him detailed pictures of the high nobility such as Tolstoy could paint, or of factory workers and the town proletariate such as are drawn by Gorky. He was not very intimately acquainted with the law or the army, and he took no part in the revolutionary movement. But he had the seeing eye that could learn much even from brief glimpses, and he had unbounded human sympathy, that 'talent for humanity' which he ascribes to the hero of *A nervous breakdown.*

Before we can be sure that Chekhov tried in his work to hold the mirror up to this Russia that he knew so well, we need to inquire into his temper of mind and his artistic aims. He was of course strongly predisposed towards realism by coming where he did in the development of the Russian novel, after S. T. Aksakov, Goncharov, Turgeniev and Tolstoy. He inherited from them first of all their humane attitude to their subjects. 'People are not good or bad; they are only more or less unhappy and deserving of sympathy—this may be taken as the formula of all the Russian novelists from Turgeniev to Chekhov' (Mirsky). Like them he chose his subjects exclusively from contemporary life, with some bearing on social issues of the day, and he avoided any tendency towards distortion in the pursuit of fine writing. This influence was reinforced by the example of western European literature in general, and above all by his medical and scientific training. As a university man in that triumphantly scientific age, he could not have escaped the effects of the scientific outlook, and as a doctor he was doubly impressed by the enormous progress made by scientific medicine in the 'seventies and 'eighties. As a writer he did not see the necessity of any conflict between science and literature. 'Goethe the poet lives amicably side by side with the scientist.' In fact Chekhov was conscious of owing much to science even in his literary work. 'I have no doubt,' he wrote in 1899, 'that the study of medicine has had an important influence on my literary work; it has considerably enlarged the sphere of my observations. . . . It has also had a directive influence. . . . Familiarity with the natural sciences and with scientific method has always kept me on my guard, and I have always tried where it was possible to be consistent with the facts of science, and where it was impossible I have preferred not to write at all. . . . I do not belong to the class of literary men who take up a sceptical attitude towards science, and to the class of those who rush into anything with only their own imagination to go upon, I should not like to belong.'

The last remark gives a clue to Chekhov's individual make-up. There is nothing luxuriant or flamboyant in his type of imagination. He does not delight in escaping from the world about him into fantastic realms, or in translating into musical words every nuance of feeling aroused in him by persons or places—though some of his landscape descriptions may perhaps be regarded as exceptions to this rule. If he resembles Goethe, it is the mature Goethe, the author of Wilhelm Meister, not the author of Werther and the Friederike songs. Not that Chekhov was never young, but the expression of his youthfulness was not lyricism, but light-hearted humour, a humour which was always ready to emerge in his maturity too, especially in conversation and in letters, but which in his art usually gave way to a graver mood. The phrase applied to Goethe 'ins Reale verliebt', in love with the real, is true of both of them. That is why they see no conflict between science, the study of concrete reality, and literature, regarded as the recording of the truth of things, especially the truth about the different types of men, their background and their relationships, in an imaginative form.

The kind of thing Chekhov aimed at is made clear by some remarks in a letter to Gorky, in which he says that usually in Gorky's stories only two or three figures seem as if they were living in his imagination, but the mass is not grasped, and goes on: 'I except from this criticism your Crimean things, in which, besides the figures, there is a feeling of the human mass out of which they have come, and atmosphere and background—everything, in fact.' In his own best work it is just this power of suggesting a world around his characters which gives it its poetic quality. A human situation is completely realised, a 'psychological volume' has been shaped by the author's imagination and is reconstructed in ours by his words. In the later plays words and action are reinforced by symbolism and other means. 'The dialogue, so to speak, never stops; it is transferred from human beings to objects, from objects back to human beings and from human beings to time, to stillness or noise, to the cricket or to voices round a fire' (Leonid Andreyev). But the effect is essentially the same as in the stories, and it is an effect which depends, according to Chekhov, on their truth.

Because of the scientific age in which he was born, and his own training, he is perhaps inclined, when discussing literature in his letters, to overstress the element of observation, and to give the imagination and insight of the artist too modest a rôle. He might seem to be advocating a merely photographic realism for instance when he says that the artist 'must conquer his squeamishness and soil his imagination with the dirt of life. He is just like an ordinary reporter' who may not, to please his readers, 'describe only honest mayors, high-minded ladies and virtuous railway-contractors'. But the point here is his opposition to the pretty-pretty, his determination to see life whole. His mature work proves on every page that the 'absolute and honest truth' which he considers to be the aim of fiction is not attained by reporting his observations of individual real-life models and casual incidents. The artist observes, but he also 'selects, guesses, combines—and this in itself presupposes a question; unless he had set himself a question from the very first there would be nothing to conjecture and nothing to select'. By 'question' Chekhov means here no doubt the motif or idea round which a work is built and from which it derives its unity. In merely photographic realism there is no such ideal pattern, and it is the absence of it which chiefly distinguishes the work of some of the imitators of Chekhov from that of the master himself, who was, as we have seen, creative to his finger-tips.

In the letters we are sometimes able to find the first un-retouched account of an experience which was later worked up into a story. Here for instance is an extract from a letter of Chekhov's to his sister (2/4/1887) written during a journey to the south. 'At the station I have a helping of remarkably good and rich sorrel soup. Then I walk along the platform. Young ladies.

At an upper window at the far end of the station sits a young girl (or a married lady, goodness knows which) in a white blouse, beautiful and languid. I look at her, she looks at me. . . . I put on my pince-nez, she does the same. . . . Oh, lovely vision! I caught a catarrh of the heart and continued my journey.' The experience half-jestingly reported here was no doubt the germ of the second half of the story *The beauties* published in the following year. It would be tedious to analyse this well-known prose-poem in detail, but no reader of it will fail to see how immeasurably the artist's mind, pondering over this memory, has enriched it in the telling. He has shown us the girl, not sitting at a window, but constantly in movement, the embodiment of youthful grace. He has elaborated the surroundings, so that we see the little station with its whole atmosphere, and even the last sunlight on the steam from the railway engine, enhancing the feeling of transience. The girl's beauty is shown in its effect on a group of passengers, and particularly on a young officer and on the old guard of the train, as well as on the narrator (Lessing would have approved of this Homeric touch), while the feeling which suffuses the whole and gives it unity is brought out by placing alongside this vision another of a very different type. Instead of a blonde Russian girl, whose beauty lay not in the regularity but in the play of her features and her air of freshness and grace, it is an Armenian brunette with features of classic perfection, also seen in continual movement against an ugly commonplace background. The feeling produced on outside beholders is in both instances one of inexplicable sadness. 'Did I dimly feel that her rare beauty was a product of chance, serving no purpose, and like everything in the world, of brief duration?' the narrator reflects, in the first encounter, and in the second: 'This was a butterfly beauty . . . and it seemed as if it was only necessary for a wind to blow on the platform, or rain to fall, for the frail body suddenly to wither and the volatile beauty to shed itself like pollen.' It is the tragic sense of 'beauty that must die', of the passing of time and opportunity, so often expressed in Chekhov, above all in his *Three sisters*. He has conveyed to us something of his sense of values, of his attitude to life.

Though Chekhov's art is far removed from mere photography, he was often criticised even by his friends for what seemed to them his 'indifference to good and evil, lack of ideals and ideas', and so forth. A Russian writer was expected, especially by the progressives, to make clear his attitude to current questions, to be something of a propagandist or a prophet, but Chekhov did not pretend to have a religious message, or to know how to solve the peasant problem, and he did not think it was the business of a writer to give answers to such problems, but only to state them correctly. Sometimes he says that it is his stylistic objectivity which gives him the appearance of indifference. He writes to Suvorin, for instance: 'You would have me, when I describe horse-thieves, say "it is wrong to steal horses". But that has been known for ages without my saying so. Let the jury judge them; it is my job simply to show what sort of people they are. . . . Of course it would be pleasant to combine art with a sermon,' but his technique makes it almost impossible for him, aiming as he does at the utmost conciseness and economy of style, and therefore avoiding subjective asides by the author. The same kind of criticism has been brought against the greatest 'objective' artists, of course, against a Shakespeare or a Goethe. The discussion about the sensual Jewess in his *Mire* was exactly like the old one about Philine in *Wilhelm Meister*. 'A writer,' Chekhov replies to Mme Kiselyov, 'must be as objective as a chemist' and recognise that 'the evil passions are as inherent in life as the good ones'.

But at other times Chekhov felt that there was perhaps something lacking in his art and in that of his contemporaries, something that more fortunate ages had possessed. 'Science and technical knowledge are passing through a great period now,' he wrote, 'but for our sort it is a flabby, stale and dull time. . . . Let me remind you that the writers, who we say are for all time or are simply good, and who intoxicate us, have one common and very important characteristic: they are going towards something and are summoning you towards it, too, and you feel, not with your mind but with your whole being, that they have some object. . . . Some have more immediate objects—the abolition of serfdom, the liberation of their country, politics, beauty, or simply vodka, like Denis Davydov; others have remote objects—God, life beyond the grave, the happiness of humanity, and so on. The best of them are realists and paint life as it is, but, through every line's being soaked in the consciousness of an object, you feel, besides life as it is, the life which ought to be, and that captivates you. And we? We! We paint life as it is, but beyond that— nothing at all. . . . Flog us, and we can do no more! We have neither immediate nor remote aims, and in our soul there is a great empty space. We have no politics, we do not believe in revolution, we have no God, we are not afraid of ghosts, and I personally am not afraid even of death and blindness. One who wants nothing, hopes for nothing, and fears nothing cannot be an artist' (25/11/1892). We shall see in the last chapter how far this statement must be qualified for Chekhov himself. He was indeed a 'man of the 'eighties' and shared the disillusionment of that time, but he had a coherent system of values for all that, a 'Weltanschauung' if not a religion, and although it might be held, if one follows Professor Alexander in distinguishing greatness from beauty in art, that because of the age he lived in, his subject was not profound or large enough for the greatest art, he was undoubtedly an artist, and one who delighted in the pursuit of that 'difficult' beauty which arises from a subject not naturally attractive.

CHAPTER II

CHEKHOV'S RUSSIA—THE LAND AND THE PEOPLE—THE SCOPE OF HIS PICTURE

Chekhov's first published work consisted of feuilletons which were sketches from the life of his time, and his later work developed out of them. With hardly any exceptions he took his subjects from contemporary Russia, and aimed at making his pictures completely convincing in their representative quality. His fellow-countrymen agree that he succeeded, but it does not follow that foreign readers will always take away from his works impressions which closely correspond to the Russian realities of that time. We can only see what our previous experience has made us capable of seeing, and in the mind of a foreign reader quite different impressions will be built up at first from those obtained from his works by Chekhov's contemporaries. To come nearer to the truth we need to acquaint ourselves not with fragments, but with a great deal of his work, and to find out from other sources a number of things, knowledge of which would be taken for granted in a contemporary Russian reader, not merely matters of fact, such as, say, the relative importance of Moscow and Odessa, the social significance of the beard, or what happens on a particular church feast day, but also emotional attitudes habitual in Russians then, towards an official of the fourth class, perhaps, to church bells, or to the first snow. The following chapters are an attempt by the author to overcome some of these difficulties for himself, by bringing the various parts of Chekhov's work together so that they throw light on each other, and by supplementing or interpreting them through information drawn from leading authorities on the Russia of his day.

'The great danger in studying Russian life,' says Mr. Maurice Baring in his *Mainsprings of Russia*, 'is to pay so much importance to the trees that the wood escapes notice,' and he reminds us of some of the great creations of the Russian masters of literature, none of which, he says, though intensely interesting and nothing but Russian, are average Russians, because the man of genius, in creating great types such as Lear or Faust, is not trying to portray the average man, but making a synthesis of the whole range of possibilities of the human soul. A minor classic like Chekhov or Leskov, painting usually less ambitious subjects on a smaller canvas, is surely less open to misunderstanding in this respect by foreigners. Russians felt the very atmosphere of everyday Russia in Chekhov's pages, and he seems to have aimed precisely at this representative quality as his kind of truth, for consciously or not, he was always on the look-out, as his note-books prove, not so much for the heights and depths of human nature as for the typically Russian, the typical magistrate, or village priest, or shop assistant, seen in a particular situation.

To begin with what he tells us about the basic factors, the land and the people, it is characteristic that even the scene of the action is usually not given a name, or not a real one. It is simply in the country, or in a small or large town, and in the absence of other indications it is apparently to be taken as in the heart of Russia. If the scene is laid in other parts of Russia, as sometimes happens, much of the interest lies in their strangeness, as in the stories from the Steppe or the Caucasus, and it is naturally in these that we find the most elaborate landscape painting. But generally speaking there is a marked absence of fine writing in Chekhov's descriptions, for he did not wish to rival Turgeniev. His landscapes are seldom or never there for their own sake, but play a vital part in evoking the total situation, as a background to human beings. The descriptions are brief, but rich in suggestive details, like those of Trigorin, according to Treplev (*The Seagull*, IV): 'He will say that the neck of a broken bottle flashes on the mill dam, and the mill-wheel throws a black shadow—and there you have already the feeling of a moonlit night.' Part of the same illustration had been used by Chekhov himself in advice to his brother Alexander in 1886 (10/5/1886).

The natural descriptions then have the aim of making us feel what it was like to be there, generally from the point of view of the central figure, and particular stress is laid on the weather and the time of year. Nothing brings home to us better the Russian character of the scenes than these frequent pictures of the seasons. The most striking of the many evocations of winter is perhaps the one in *Frost*, which is about a Twelfth Night charity sports day on a frozen river. The temperature was unusually low, there were twenty-eight degrees of frost (Réaumur, equal to $-31°$ Fahrenheit) and a wind blowing, yet the people would not hear of a postponement. 'Frost whitened the trees, the horses, men's beards; it

seemed as if the air itself was trembling with the cold, but in spite
of that, immediately after the blessing of the waters, the police
with chattering teeth were already on the skating rink, and
exactly at one o'clock the military band began to play.' When
some of the notables were assembled later in the governor's
pavilion on the bank to warm themselves, they were joined by the
local millionaire, a self-made old merchant, and it is his reminiscences, so boring to the company, which bring home to us what
a Russian winter can mean. The cold might be healthy, he told
them, as some said, but Russia would be far better without it.
The well fed and warmly clothed could bear it, and enjoy their
sports, but it was often torture for the poor, as he knew well from
his own boyhood and youth, when he had led a blind man about
all day in the snow, 'with an unbearable pain at his heart and
his whole body in agony, as if he were leading not an old man,
but death itself by the hand', or later stood all day at work in a
draughty fish shop. Elsewhere we read of the bonfires at street
crossings in St. Petersburg in the frost, of sleigh drivers sitting
motionless under the falling snow, waiting for a fare, of innumerable adventures on winter journeys, and of the tireless village
policeman trudging miles through snowdrifts to serve official
notices.

After such winters, the coming of spring is even more welcome
in Russia than in our temperate climate, and it is often celebrated
in Chekhov's pages. An early sketch, *In spring,** gives an impression of a spring day, and of its effect on different types of men.
Nature seems to be smiling without any reason, like a man recovering from a serious illness (an example of the personification
of natural processes which Chekhov also recommended to his
brother). The gardener is full of a happy confidence, for he
commands nature, feeling he knows her secrets. The sportsman
is happy beyond measure in anticipation of the shooting season.
In other tales a score of graphic touches bring before us some
aspect of spring in Russia. In one the thaw has set in in early
March, wet snow is falling and the cabbies are driving on wheels
again. In another, again in town, 'The roads are covered with
brown slush, in which future paths are beginning to show; the
roofs and pavements are dry; under the fences fresh green is
springing up through the rotting grass of last year. In the gutters
muddy water, in which the sunbeams do not disdain to bathe, is
gurgling and foaming. Chips, straws, the husks of sunflower
seeds float past rapidly on the water, whirling round and sticking

together in the dirty foam' (*In Passion Week*). Or in the country, the sun becomes friendlier in March, the artificial ice mountain made for sledging loses its glitter and at last thaws, and though there is still snow in the shade of the dunghill and the trees show no sign of life, the earth smells of spring, and the rooks chatter noisily as they fly to their roosting place (*A joke*). Or again, the highroad is dry, the April sun is shining warmly from a fathomless sky, but snow is still lying in the ditches and the woods. Spring has come all of a sudden. The woods, warmed by the breath of spring, are languid and transparent, black flocks of birds are flying over huge pools like lakes in the fields, and a small stream that dries up in August is now, after the spring floods, a fast flowing river, forty feet across (*The schoolmistress*). The reawakening of nature contributes much to the background of emotion of the great feast of Easter, as is finely suggested in *Easter Eve*. 'Yes, it is a joyful day to-day,' says the monastery ferryman, as they cross the river under a star-lit sky, 'the heavens and the earth and the regions under the earth rejoice together. All living creatures hold holiday.'

There is perhaps less that is specifically Russian in the descriptions of summer. It is the dry continental summer, short and very hot. On many days the still sultry air makes any work a burden and a siesta a necessity. The summer scenes that remain longest in the memory are those of summer days and nights in the feather-grass steppe of the south (*The Steppe*), but there is a delightful summer morning by the river in *The fish:* 'A summer morning. There is not a sound in the still air but the gentle creaking of a grasshopper on the river bank, and somewhere the timid purring of a turtle-dove. Feathery clouds float motionless in the sky, looking like sprinkled snow.' Nothing could be more evocative of carefree summer days in Russia than the pages which follow, on the catching of the slippery burbot, a gem that recalls S. T. Aksakov's rapturous descriptions of fishing at Bagrovo, but equally enchanting are the summer nights in some other stories, in *Agafya* for instance. 'The afterglow had not quite vanished yet, but the summer night was already taking nature into its tender soothing embrace. Everything was sinking into its first deep sleep, except some night-bird unfamiliar to me, which slowly and lazily uttered in the thicket a long, clearly articulated cry like the words "Where's Nikita, have you seen him?" and immediately answered itself with "Seen him, seen him, seen him." "Why aren't the nightingales singing to-night?" I asked.' It is May,

2

and in spring and early summer the nightingale is heard all over central and southern Russia, so that, rather surprisingly to the English reader, it plays a much bigger part in Russian than in English literature.

Though Gorky has spoken with truth of the autumnal atmosphere which prevails in Chekhov's works, there are comparatively few pictures of the season itself. Perhaps the most striking is the description of the first snow in *A nervous breakdown*. 'The first snow had recently fallen, and everything in nature was under the spell of this fresh snow. There was a smell of snow in the air, snow crunched softly under one's feet, the ground, the roofs, the trees, the benches on the boulevards—everything was soft, white, young, the houses looked different from yesterday, the street-lamps burned more brightly, the atmosphere was clearer, the carriage wheels made a more muffled sound as they rolled, and as one breathed the fresh, light, frosty air, a feeling that somehow resembled the white, youthful, feathery snow took hold of the heart.' To the hero it seemed as if there were only two periods in the year when such transparent, tender, naive and as it were virginal tints were to be seen in nature, when all was covered in snow, and on bright days or moonlit evenings in spring when the ice was breaking up on the rivers. It is not necessary for Chekhov to underline the contrast between Vassiliev's sense of the purity of nature and his later experiences that night with his student friends in a certain notorious Moscow street.

The scenes quoted so far are all, it would seem, such as were considered by Chekhov typically Russian, the truth of which would be confirmed by his average reader's own experience, and a foreigner needs some guidance before he can form any idea of what a Russian of that age would consider typical. He needs to know something about the average Russian's notions of geography. Here the ingenious diagrammatic map of Russia devised by M. Lucien Tesnière may be of service, a map in which he has tried to put down on paper an 'anthropocentric scheme of the countries of Russian speech', to reproduce, that is, the pattern that arose in a Russian's mind when he thought of the geography of his country. Imagine a pattern like a target, with a bull's eye enclosed within three outer rings. The bull's eye represents Moscow, of course on a disproportionately large scale, corresponding to its importance; in the whole diagram the scale becomes smaller as one proceeds out from the centre, in an attempt to represent what we may call psychological distances. The bull's eye has in its centre a small triangle, the Kremlin, with a rectangle drawn on its north-eastern side to stand for the Kitai Gorod, the old fortress, and this triangle abuts to the south on the Moscow River, which cuts off a southern segment of the bull's eye, 'Moscow beyond the river'. Round the Kremlin is an inner circle, the 'White Town', extending to the boulevards, round that again another belt, the 'Earth Town', reaching to the outer boulevards, and finally on the outer fringe of the bull's eye come the suburbs.

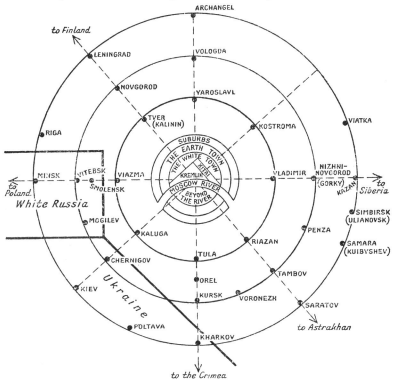

The Old Russia, as a Russian thought of it (*from Lucien Tesnière, Petite Grammaire Russe*). *By permission of Henri Didier of Paris.*

The principal towns of Russia are thought of as situated for the most part on one or other of the three rings surrounding the bull's eye. Going north from Moscow one comes to Yaroslavl on the first ring, Vologda on the second and Archangel on the third, Going south, the three towns are Tula, Kursk and Kharkov, on the main southern railway line leading to the Crimea. Chekhov's farm at Melikhovo was about half-way from Moscow to Tula, Tolstoy's town, and between Tula and Kursk is Orel, Turgeniev's home. The country along this line, the route from Moscow to his birthplace, was very familiar to Chekhov, and it figures prominently in his stories and letters. Going east from Moscow, on the way to Siberia, the key towns are Vladimir, Nizhny-Novgorod (now Gorky) and Kazan, the last two on the Volga, and going west they are Viazma, Vitebsk and Minsk, on the way to Poland, with Smolensk in between Viazma and Vitebsk. Beyond Viazma one comes to White Russia, represented in the diagram by a rectangle jutting into the two outer bands of the target, and a line running south-east from its lower right-hand corner to just above Kharkov is the northern border of the Ukraine, or Little Russia.

The diagram is completed by two intermediate axes, between the north-south and the east-west axes already described. Going north-west from Moscow we find Tver (now Kalinin), Novgorod and St. Petersburg (Leningrad), on the way to Finland, while to the south-east of Moscow come successively Riazan, Tambov and Saratov. The last named is on the Volga well below Kazan, and proceeding downstream, to the south, one comes to what is now Stalingrad and to Astrakhan, on the Caspian, both outside the diagram proper. To the north-east the only town of note is Kostroma, on the first ring, while to the south-west we come successively to Kaluga, Chernigov and Kiev, the last two in the Ukraine.

It will be noted that while Leningrad and Archangel are naturally peripheral in the north, being on the sea, Kharkov and Saratov are also thought of as peripheral in the south, being on the northern boundary of the grassy steppe, which may be imagined as following the course of the outermost circle in the south from near Poltava, intermediate between Kiev and Kharkov, through Kharkov and Saratov to Samara, half-way between Saratov and Kazan. The natural region to the north of this is the wooded steppe, with its northern limit on a line from Kiev through Tula and Riazan to Kazan, so roughly in the two outer bands in the lower half of our diagram. This is the good hunting and farming country familiar from Turgeniev's *Sportsman's Sketches*. The soil here, as in the grassy steppe to the south of it, is the fertile black earth. North of the wooded steppe is the mixed forest zone, a great triangle with its base on the Kiev-Kazan line, its right hand corner at Kazan and its upper corner near Leningrad, a triangle enclosing the whole Moscow region, the heart of old Muscovy. The soil here is far less fertile than the black soil, consisting of 'grey sands and clays with a very low humus content, with much bog and lake' (Sumner). North of this region again comes one of conifer forests, in the remaining north-eastern segment of our circular diagram.

This then was Russia proper for the Russian of Chekhov's day and some time later, though the Russia that has become part of the common consciousness to-day would no doubt call for a considerably extended and more complex diagram, for quite apart from the general consolidation of Russia in Asia and the vast development of heavy industry beyond the Urals which have taken place since the Revolution, the diagram omits the whole of the Donetz Basin and the Krivoi Rog area in the Dniepr bend, which even before 1914 produced about two-thirds of Russia's coal and iron. As we shall see, these regions were constantly growing in importance in Chekhov's day, but as the development had only begun in 1869, in a few centres in a vast area of steppe, it took a long time before the old idea was displaced, according to which the Black Sea steppes were 'New Russia', a border region where Tatars and Cossacks had only comparatively recently been finally brought under control by the central government. Even after this had happened in Catherine II's time, it remained for the Russians colonial land, where Ukrainians and a whole host of foreigners, Germans, Greeks, Armenians and so on, were the principal settlers.

It seems therefore that Chekhov's pictures of typical Russian scenery should be taken to apply to central Russia, especially to that region south and south-east of Moscow which he knew best, where there was enough resemblance between the various parts to allow of a generalised description. Historically too it was the heart of Russia, and the whole area within the outer circle, except the White Russian rectangle and the Ukrainian segment, was 'Great Russian' in speech, with only slight dialectal differences. Chekhov is always careful to distinguish the Little Russian or Ukrainian from the Great Russian, though he does not tell us very much about him in his stories except that he spoke differently and combed his hair over his forehead. Coming as he did from the southern edge of the steppe area just described, where Ukrainian was spoken in all the country districts at least, he had a fellow feeling for these southerners, and he and his family were not happy if they were too long away from the south. We have already seen something of his impressions of Luka in the Ukraine, where he spent the summers of 1888 and 1889. Here is a glimpse of the people, from a letter of the same period. 'Around us in their white cottages live the tufty-heads (the nick-name of the Low Russians). A well-fed, cheerful, talkative, quick-witted people. The peasants here do not sell either meat, or milk or eggs, but consume it all themselves—a good sign.' This was the black-soil area at its most favourable. Something of Chekhov's love of the south comes out in *Ivan Matveyich*, where an old scholar is charmed by his secretary's tales of the warm spring in the Don country, and how they used to play with tarantulas and catch goldfinches, and it is characteristic that he even built part of his Melikhovo farm in the Little Russian style.

For a native of Moscow, Taganrog would no doubt seem at least as remote as Inverness to a Londoner, and Chekhov's steppe country would have a romantic appeal which one might compare with that of Caledonia stern and wild, if there were not a closer parallel between the Highlands and the Caucasus, romanticised half a century earlier by Lermontov. The steppe of the Don region, as Chekhov describes it in *Happiness*, is a vast silent expanse, where only prehistoric burial mounds, the 'kurgany', stand out, indifferent, mysterious, eternal, and man is dwarfed by the elemental, as an old shepherd and a friend talk about treasures hidden in the time of the French invasion, or even of Peter the Great. In *At home*, in the Donetz country, there is the same peace, the same 'kurgany', but ox-carts pass with loads of coal, and we hear soon of mines and factories, and card-playing engineers and doctors. In the longest study, *The Steppe*, we see the steppe in the constantly changing atmosphere of summer days and nights, as a slow caravan of carts moves across it to the market town. We hear of a fabulously rich wool-merchant, a sort of king of the steppe, who puts even a rich countess into the shade, and we visit a lonely inn kept by a kindly Jewish family. But again, all the works of man are as nothing to the feast of beauty in surrounding nature, a beauty which, like 'things' for Rilke, calls out to be celebrated, that it may not perish unnoticed by the world. It is the same idea of the transitoriness of beauty, and the tantalising mystery of its emergence in nature, that we have found already in *The beauties*. When Ivanov-Razumnik took this story as a symbol of the dreary monotony of Russian life, he cannot have read it very recently, because it is the beauty and variety of the steppe on which Chekhov insists, and that, no doubt, was in part a literary discovery of his, for he expresses surprise in a letter at the neglect of this subject by earlier writers.

Apart from the numerous impressions of the steppe, we do not hear very much about the country outside the above mentioned circle, something about a seaside holiday resort in the Caucasus and its neighbourhood in *The duel*, about the Crimea (Yalta) in *The lady with a dog*, and about Siberia, from memories of his own journey to Sakhalin, in *In exile*, *The murder*, and *Dreams*. Within the circle, few towns or villages except Moscow and St. Petersburg are given names in the stories, unless they are invented ones, for provincial Russian towns, as Chekhov says somewhere, are all alike.

Moscow and St. Petersburg are of course frequently mentioned by name, and we gain a clear idea of the physiognomy of Moscow at least, to which as we have seen Chekhov was devoted, from stories like *Three years*, *A nervous breakdown* and *The bird market*. Whoever has lived there, we learn, is never happy for long away from it. Like the *Three sisters* he will have only one thought, to return. Yulia in *Three years*, who had been educated there, thought of it as the capital, the centre of civilized life in Russia, where there lots of clever distinguished people, noise and bustle, splendid theatres and concerts, first-rate dressmakers and confectioners, and she married Laptev principally in order to escape from the provinces and to live in Moscow again. We hear in this story of symphony concerts at the Hall of the Nobility, conducted by Rubinstein, of exhibitions of pictures at the School of Painting, visited 'in the Moscow fashion' by whole families, children and all, and of gay restaurants like Yar's, with electric light, loud music, a 'coupletist' singing his gibes, a smell of face powder, and rows of 'chambres séparées'. The lower haunts frequented by students on the spree in *A nervous breakdown* will be mentioned later. Moscow was of course the Mecca of the intelligentsia. All Laptev's friends have studied at the University, the Conservatory or the School of Painting and Sculpture and have intellectual interests, but for the average citizen there were innumerable card parties, and evening 'At homes' like the *Grasshopper's*, where the same singers were constantly heard because there were not enough to go round. In May prosperous families retired to their dachas at Sokolniki or Butovo, where the ladies were joined from time to time by their men folk.

The typical Muscovite was ill at ease in other towns, and thought even the grey Moscow weather very pleasant and healthy. In the same way some, like Laevsky in *The duel*, longed for St. Petersburg. After years in the Caucasus, he pictured to himself how delightful it would be to find oneself on the southern railway again, heading north, through colder and colder air, past birches and firs, to Kursk, to Moscow. 'At the station restaurants cabbage soup, mutton with kasha, sturgeon, beer, out of the Asiatic, in a word, into Russia, real Russia. The passengers in the train would be talking about business, the new singers, Franco-Russian approaches. On all sides there would be the feeling of keen, cultured, intelligent, bracing life. On, on! At last the Nevsky Prospekt, and Great Morskaya Street, and then Kovensky Lane, where he had lived once with other students, the dear grey sky, the drizzle, the dripping cabmen.' About St. Petersburg itself we hear less in Chekhov than about Moscow. We learn something of its psychological atmosphere from *An anonymous story*. We come to associate it with the thought of high officials, financiers, lawyers. It produces engineers, doctors and technicians rather than writers and artists. But it remains for us rather shadowy and distant, with none of the warm intimacy of Moscow.

Turning from the geographical location of 'Chekhov's Russia' to its place in history, we may note a few landmarks at least by which to take our bearings. It is the Russia of the 'eighties and 'nineties of the nineteenth century, an empire with an unbroken tradition of autocratic rule extending back for centuries. The kingdom of northern slavs, founded upon trade and war under Viking leaders, brought into intimate contact with Byzantine civilisation before 1000 A.D. and converted to the Greek Orthodox form of Christianity, had been paying tribute for two and a half centuries to asiatic nomad invaders, the Mongols or Tatars, when Ivan the Great finally shook off the yoke in 1480. The Golden Horde, which had controlled Russia from headquarters in the lower Volga region, had by now split up into several rival khanates, the nearest of which, the Kazan, Astrakhan and Crimean hordes, were roughly speaking at the eastern, south-eastern and southern extremities respectively of our diagrammatic map. The continual threat which they constituted called for strong centralised control by the founders of Tsarism, Ivan the Great and his two immediate successors. The forefathers of these monarchs had been trained in asiatic administrative methods by Tatar khans, and their ambitions were actively encouraged by the Orthodox Church, with its Byzantine ideals. After the fall of Constantinople (1453), following close upon the nominal reunion of the eastern and western churches, they came to think of themselves as the only defenders of the eastern faith, Orthodoxy, and the heirs of the Eastern Empire, just as Charlemagne, and then the Saxon Emperors, had considered themselves the heirs of Rome in the West. The name, and more than the name, of Imperious Caesar lived on alike in Kaiser and in Tsar.

The civilising influence of Byzantium did not however survive the end of the Eastern Empire, as that of Rome lived on in the West, and Russia was relatively isolated culturally during the first centuries of the Tsardom of Muscovy. The Tsars brought their aristocracy to heel, and gradually overcoming first the Kazan and then the Astrakhan Tatars, made possible the spread of agricultural settlers to the east and south-east over the steppe, but the struggle with the powers who at various times blocked Russian access to the Baltic, Lithuania and Poland, the Teutonic Order and Sweden, swayed this way and that without decisive results until the time of Peter the Great. After long wars he obtained a firm footing on the Baltic, built St. Petersburg as Russia's window on the west, and put the strength of a giant into the effort to remodel Russia in the shortest possible time after the continental west European fashion, as a strong, efficient, bureaucratically ruled military power. Though his success was necessarily only partial, Russia could never again disinterest herself in the West. In the reign of the third of the 'great' Russian monarchs, Catherine II, the Crimean Tatars were at last conquered, and the door was opened wide by this enlightened empress for the intellectual and artistic culture of the West, especially that of France in the age of the 'philosophes'. The way was thus prepared both for Russia's literary revival, and for the movement towards political and social reform.

From now on, while Russia aspired to the rôle of a European Great Power, her rulers were never free from the fears inspired by the rapid spread in their domains of Western European ideas of political liberty and social justice, in all the various forms they assumed from the French Revolution onwards. Under Catherine's grandson, Alexander I, Russia played a decisive part in the overthrow of Napoleon, but at home, in spite of his early democratic leanings, Alexander reverted to reaction in the end, and became the chief prop of the Holy Alliance of sovereigns against aspiring peoples. The short-lived revolutionary movement of liberal-minded officers, the Decembrists, which broke out immediately after his death in 1825, gave his brother Nicholas I an excuse, if he needed one, for severe repressive measures, and for thirty years Russia was ruled by just such a conscientious, lonely autocrat as Schiller had imagined in his Philip II (*Don Carlos*). He worked unceasingly, with the best of intentions, but jealousy of any interference with his divinely imposed task made him regard the secret police as his principal tool of government. The impossibility of efficiency under this system was proved by the Crimean War. Meanwhile, in spite of the strictest censorship, liberal ideas had continued to spread, and for a decade under his successor, Alexander II, in the 'age of the great reforms', even the highest bureaucratic circles, convinced of the necessity of drastic changes, began to entertain hopes of beating the West at its own game.

It was in this spirit that the serfs were emancipated (1861), the administration of justice was completely reorganised and a large measure of local self-government was introduced. But these reforms were all imposed from above, with almost excessive zeal and optimism, and the results achieved did not correspond to expectations because the new structures had not been given sufficiently firm foundations, or to vary the metaphor, a few salients had been pushed out, but what was needed was an advance all along the line. Russia had tried to imitate some of the forms of constitutionally governed capitalistic societies without possessing anything that could really be said to correspond to their accumulated capital, their educated middle class, experienced in industry, commerce and self-administration, and their technical skill and resources.

When difficulties accumulated, the more conservative among the ruling class began to say 'I told you so', and to press for a reversion to tried methods, while the progressives in all classes urged that these difficulties were merely the growing pains of the new Russia. A period of comparative freedom of the press had stimulated eager discussion of social and political questions, led by liberals like Herzen, writing from London, slavophils like Ivan Aksakov and radicals like Chernyshevsky, and for the first time a non-aristocratic intelligentsia came to be an important element in Russian life. The type of the rationalistic ultra-radical of that age was drawn by Turgeniev, in the Bazarov of his *Fathers and Children*, the young 'nihilist', who believed in nothing that the older generation held dear. When after the attempted assassination of the Emperor by Karakozov (1866) the government's policy became more and more reactionary, the revolutionary movement spread wider and wider. Inspired by Lavrov's *Historical Letters* (1868–69) educated young men and women, the Narodniki, began in the early 'seventies to 'go into the people', living the life of peasants, at first with the humanitarian aim of spreading enlightenment, but before long, under Bakunin's influence, to make revolutionary propaganda. Thousands of them were arrested and sent to Siberia, but in response to persecution organisations soon grew up, in the later 'seventies, which were openly terrorist, especially the 'People's Will', a group of the earlier 'Land and Liberty' party. A rather futile series of assassinations carried out by various little centres culminated in well-planned attempts on the life of the Tsar. In 1881, when Chekhov was a second-year student, one of these was successful.

Such were, in briefest outline, the political events in Russia which determined the general character of Chekhov's age. The 'eighties, under Alexander III, were a time of extreme reaction and police rule, when most of the concessions which had been made in the age of reforms to democratic principles were gradually withdrawn or nullified, and, under the influence of the Tsar's trusted adviser, Pobiedonostsev, and the leading publicist Katkov, the principles that were constantly invoked by the government were those of Nationalism, Orthodoxy and Autocracy. In the name of Nationalism, the forcible Russification of Poles, Jews and Baltic Germans was attempted under Alexander III, and of Finns under his successor Nicholas II (1894–1917), a policy which caused great suffering with no permanent results, and did not succeed in diverting attention from the government's internal difficulties. In the name of Orthodoxy and Autocracy the Secret Police was again given full scope, Land Captains were appointed as a kind of official squires, a new Universities' Statute (1884) destroyed the autonomy of the universities, many of the best professors (including the great biologist Kovalevsky, with whom Chekhov became very friendly at Nice), were summarily dismissed, the higher education of women, which had made a promising start, was again interrupted, and in a score of ways it was made quite plain that nothing but the blackest reaction could be expected for a long time to come.

The outward forms of autocracy survived intact until the 1905 revolution, a year after Chekhov's death, but its foundations were being steadily undermined through the economic development of Russia on Western European lines, and the consequent weakening of the landowning class, the mainstay of the army and the bureaucracy. After the Emancipation, in spite of every effort made by the government to bolster up the gentry, they fell more and more heavily into debt, while bankers and industrialists took their place as masters of Russian economic life. A land of self-sufficient estates worked by serf labour, where only the most primitive communications connected village with village, and the towns required by an undeveloped trade and industry and by administrative needs were few and far between, had been forced by the lessons of the Crimean War in particular to modernise herself, if only for the sake of military security. The state did what it could to reform its finances, and at last under Count Witte's leadership, as Minister of Finance, and of Trade and Communications, Russia was put on to the gold standard (1897). After 1861 Russia offered an attractive field for foreign investment, because of her vast natural resources and inexhaustible supply of 'free' and cheap labour. The government borrowed freely itself, encouraged new industries to do so, and offered every inducement to foreign firms to set up branches in Russia run by their own technicians. As in Germany earlier, railway development, which proceeded at a rapid rate, first in the age of reforms and then in Witte's time (1892–1903), proved a great stimulus to the growth of heavy industry, and all the familiar features of the machine age gradually began to make their appearance, 'The Russia that made possible an autocracy was quietly slipping away. Strategical railways were arousing villages from their sleep, and bringing them to rapidly-growing capitals. Factory chimneys had risen up in clusters at various points on the plain. In the region of the Don there was a Black Country of mines and foundries. During the second half of the century, Poland, the Moscow region, Riga and St. Petersburg had become important manufacturing centres, and millions of peasants were abandoning their homespun for the cheap cotton goods which all kinds of enterprising middlemen, from the anglicised wholesale dealer to the old-fashioned bearded merchant in a caftan and the Tartar pedlar, hawked over the plain from Reval to Vladivostock.'[1]

No less important than the change in material conditions was that in the revolutionary idea. Marxian ideas slowly infiltrated into Russia. By 1887, according to Maynard, *Das Kapital* was the most read book among Russian students, and about 1893 the Russian Marxists began to be called Social Democrats, a name taken from the German party, which served to distinguish them from the Anarchists. They concentrated on agitation among the factory workers, instead of continuing, like the Populists, to combine work among the peasantry with occasional acts of terrorism.

[1]Williams, *Russia of the Russians*, p. 49.

There were still many currents of opinion among the revolutionaries. The ideas of the Populists were taken up again by the Social Revolutionary Party, and the Social Democrats came to be divided into several groups. The largest followed Peter Struve in the direction of Revisionism, the movement started by Eduard Bernstein in Germany, which eventually turned the German Social Democrats into something like mild Liberals by stressing the automatic nature of the coming revolution and so inducing a passive attitude in the party. But in 1902 Lenin was already insisting, in *What is to be done*, on the formation of a 'small compact core', a 'strong and disciplined revolutionary organisation' with determined leadership from above, not on democratic principles. The result was the split in the following year between Bolsheviks and Mensheviks, and ultimately the formation of the Communist Party, 'a disciplined order of devoted adherents . . . resembling the Society of Jesus', probably the only remedy for the Russian weaknesses of perpetual discussion, loose talking and premature action.

Maynard sees the central inspiration of the Bolshevist Revolution in a peculiar feeling of freedom, which its adherents owed ultimately, he thinks, to Marx (though others found something very different in him), the conviction that 'man is not bound to a pitilessly revolving wheel, but can contribute to the making of his own destiny. . . . It is the very essence of the new Russia, of its invincible optimism, of its condemnation of despair, of its readiness to undertake the impossible'. Whether this energy was really Marxian, or the mark of a young nation, as its Nazi imitators were wont to say, or the unreflecting vigour of a social class hitherto repressed and now at last attaining to consciousness of itself, it was the complete antithesis of the Russian attitude of mind in the 'eighties, so frequently presented by Chekhov. We shall find traces in his work in the later 'nineties of a new optimism, based on the belief in man's ability, through the right use of his powers, to become his own providence and to turn the whole earth into a garden, but the spirit of confidence in the New Man is put forward with much greater emphasis in Maxim Gorky's writings of the same period. In *Townsmen*, as Maynard reminds us, he makes his robust engine-driver Nil say to a young lady of the intelligentsia: 'I love to live. I love noise, work, jolly simple people. But do you live? You are perpetually groaning for an unknown reason, and complaining. Against whom, why and for what? I don't understand.' And he describes his joy in forging a red, formless mass of metal. 'It is living, malleable . . . and with mighty blows from the shoulder you make of it what you need.' We shall find in Chekhov similar criticisms of the refinement of the cultured as a concealed fear of life and a sign of lack of vitality, but no parallel to Nil, this 'unmistakable anticipation of the Bolshevik attitude to life.'

In the chapters which follow attention will be drawn however to what *can* be found in Chekhov's pages, an incomparably vivid array of representative though fictitious personages from that society of his day which he was ceaselessly occupied in observing and judging, the foundations on which the makers of modern Russia had to build. Chapter III deals with the life of the great mass of the population, the peasantry, and chapter IV with that of the aristocracy and gentry, the privileged class under the old régime, chiefly in their capacity as land owners after the Emancipation, while chapter V is concerned with the part they played, along with the official class in general, in the government, administration and defence of the country. Chapter VI is devoted to the second pillar of the state, the Church, and its rôle in Russian life. Peasantry, serving aristocracy, clergy and townsfolk (merchants and craftsmen) had constituted the hereditary classes for two hundred years and more. Before the great expansion of the last of these is considered in chapter VIII, the specifically modern development of a class of professional men and intelligentsia, which had largely emancipated itself from the old social divisions, is studied in chapter VII.

In each chapter our aim is to see a particular aspect of Russia in the 'eighties and 'nineties through Chekhov's eyes. To do so, the appropriate portions of his writings will have to be critically examined as sources for this particular purpose, and the difficult distinction will have to be attempted between what may be taken as essentially true to life, as part of 'an invented world, in which the sense of the real world is found', to use Dilthey's formula, and what belongs to the individual pattern of a particular work of art, like the swan necks of Botticelli's ladies. If this somewhat adventurous enquiry is to be fruitful we shall have to interpret our texts as literature and at the same time apply any knowledge we have of the historical background from other sources. In particular we shall be constantly concerned with the personal factor in Chekhov, and must try to discover, and as far as possible explain, how he reacted to the main features in the world about him. The threads of this side of the discussion will be drawn together in a final chapter on Chekhov's values. We shall succeed in our task in so far as we can in imagination place ourselves at Chekhov's standpoint and view the scene through his spectacles, while realising at the same time where we are and what spectacles we are looking through. Complete success will of course be unattainable, but even a partial success will perhaps afford a truer understanding than volumes of statistics with their deceptively scientific air, for we shall have seen at least a part of the old Russia in its concrete completeness, as it appeared to a sane, thoughtful and well-informed contemporary.

CHAPTER III

THE PEASANT

In an undeveloped country like Russia, constantly expanding its frontiers into the wilds, and covered, even in the regions long settled, with vast expanses of forest and steppe, the primitive exploitation of the woods and rivers for game, fish, fur, honey, wax and timber played a considerable part even at the end of the nineteenth century. If the frontiersman took his toll of wild nature's products for a living, in the more settled parts, besides the regular woodmen, beekeepers, foresters and gamekeepers there were many of all classes who fished and hunted for sport. Of the backwoodsman and frontier colonist we have only an occasional glimpse in Chekhov, for instance when the vagabond in *Dreams* talks to the two village policemen who are taking him to gaol about the virgin woods and teeming rivers of Eastern Siberia, and sets them dreaming of how 'in the early morning, before the red of dawn has vanished from the sky, a man, a small moving spot on a lonely steep river bank, makes his way forward; ancient pines high as masts, piled up in terraces on both sides of the stream, look down sternly on the free man and murmur sullenly; roots, great boulders and thorny undergrowth bar his way, but stout-hearted and strong, he fears neither the pines, nor the rocks, nor his loneliness, nor the rumbling echo that repeats his every step'.

A more frequent theme is the disastrous consequences of the reckless policy of exploitation that had been practised for generations in the woods of central Russia. Revisiting the scenes of his youth, the old coffin-maker in *Rothschild's Fiddle* finds the woods cut down and the river too shallow for navigation, and the lugubrious shepherd in *The Pipe* is made to say: 'They cut them down, they burn and wither, and nothing grows in their place, or if anything does, down it has to come at once.' That his lamentations over the drying-up of rivers, the disappearance of birds and fishes, the decadence of men are not entirely the product of a soured mind is suggested by the prominence given to similar views in *Uncle Vanya*, in Dr. Astrov's diatribes against man's passion for destroying, instead of increasing by intelligent planning, the good things which nature has given him. Through his lazy indifference 'thousands of trees perish, the homes of wild creatures are turned into a wilderness, the rivers grow shallow and dry up, glorious landscapes vanish for ever'. It is Chekhov's own passionate love of growing things and his awareness of the problems of soil erosion and the like, created solely by the ignorance, laziness and indifference of those in authority, that we hear in these words. Their truth is confirmed by statements in official reports, such as the following: 'Since the Emancipation, the woods have been cut down (owing to the extension of cultivation), the streams have become shallow or have disappeared, drifting sands have invaded the fields, the hay-fields have been ploughed up, the fields have broken away into ravines . . . the land has lost fertility, the natural wealth is exhausted and the people are impoverished.'[1]

As for sport, there is nothing in the work of Chekhov in the way of hunting scenes to compare with the masterpieces of Turgeniev and Tolstoy, for he had not their aristocratic background. He introduces sportsmen who tell each other stories (*The man in a case*, etc.), and young barbarians on a Cossack farm who shoot at hens (*The Pechenyeg*), or a pampered young keeper, married while drunk to a cattle girl, by a master jealous of his marksmanship (*The huntsman*), but it is always the people who interest him, not hunting, which was outside his world. A particularly good example is the early story, *The twenty-ninth of June*,* about a party of six who set out in high spirits in a small trap but return before they have shot anything. The whole story is taken up with their amusing reactions to each other, and how intolerably they get on each other's nerves. With fishing it was a different matter. He was himself (like the writer Trigorin in his *Sea Gull*) a keen angler, and he shows us people from every class who share his passion, which is of course *the* Russian popular sport, as is clear throughout Russian literature. He even puts little disquisitions on fish and their habits into the mouths of the vagabond in *Dreams* and the peasant in *A malefactor*. When brought before the juge d'instruction for unscrewing bolts from a railway line to act as sinkers for his lines, the peasant, who cannot realize that he has done anything wrong, insists on explaining the habits of the local fish. Carters on a long journey through the steppe borrow a net from villagers and catch fish to flavour their 'kasha' for dinner (*The*

[1] Maynard, *Russ. Peas.* 52, from report on over-cropping in Black Soil area,

Steppe) and there is the delightful picture already mentioned of how the contagion of the chase spreads from two joiners making a bathing-place by a river, and trying in vain to dislodge a burbot from tree roots under the bank, to an old shepherd, a coachman and finally the 'barin' himself. Age and rank are forgotten as they all in turn go into the water to show how to catch a slippery fish (*The Fish*). Even many of the city folk of Moscow, when they cannot go fishing, frequent the lively Sunday '*Bird Market*' in the Truba Square, where all kinds of wild birds in cages, and fish in pails of water, are offered for sale by rows of muzhiks from their carts. It is because so many in the city are still country folk at heart that 'they love wild creatures so tenderly and torture them so much'. An early feuilleton (*Wolf baiting**, 1882) stresses still more strongly the insensitiveness of a Russian crowd to animal suffering, in a description of the hunting down by various kinds of dogs, in a Moscow riding school, of a few trapped wolves, for the amusement of an idle crowd of men, women and children. The author is no hunting man, he explains. He has never killed anything bigger than a flea, 'and that without dogs'. But the jesting tone does not conceal his outraged feelings. 'They say that this is the nineteenth century,' he begins. 'Do not believe it, reader.'

All these however are mere hints that serve to remind us of the survival into this age of the primeval Russia, the cold silence of whose steppes, the swaying of whose boundless woods, and the spring floods of whose rivers, like seas, had been loved by Lermontov. But of the everyday Russia of the great mass of the people, the peasantry, Chekhov gives us, for a townsman, a remarkably detailed and convincing picture, one which startled contemporaries by its outspokenness but was never seriously challenged.

There are, it is true, some idyllic pictures in the stories of the external aspects of Russian villages, usually views by moonlight of a sleeping village, such as this:[1] 'It was midnight. To our right we could see the whole village, the long street stretching far away, for five versts. All was buried in quiet sleep; not a movement, not a sound, it was hard to believe that anything in nature could be so quiet. When one looks down a broad village street by moonlight, with its cottages, haystacks, sleeping willows, then one's mind is quietened too; in its rest, shielded by the shadows of night from its labours, its cares and sorrows, it is gentle, sad, beautiful, and it seems as if the stars too look down on it with

[1] *The man in a case.*

affection and tenderness, that there is no more evil in the world and that all that is is right.' But the point of such a picture lies in the contrast with the waking world, which Chekhov was too honest and serious to idealize. Because of his origin and his many years at Melikhovo, in close everyday contact as a doctor with peasants in their homes, he came to closer grips with Russia's greatest problem than most writers of his own or earlier days. There was nothing of the grand seigneur, the tourist or the theorist about him. He considered it his business as an artist rather to state the problem correctly than to attempt its solution, to state it in his concise and reticent way in fiction that should be truer to type than any individual transcript from life, but it is clear that he looked upon most of the efforts that were being made to ease the peasant's lot, by himself and other enlightened people, as mere palliatives, and believed fundamental social changes to be both necessary and inevitable.

In his principal peasant story of the late nineties, *Peasants*, Chekhov shows us a typical village in central Russia through the eyes of Nicolai, a consumptive waiter, who has come back with his wife and child to his native village in the hope of recovering his health. In his small village, Zhukovo, made up of forty houses, 'the cottages were strung out in a single row and the small village as a whole was a pleasant sight, quiet and pensive, with willows, elderberries, and mountain ash looking out of its courtyards. Immediately behind the cottages and their gardens the land began to slope down to the river, so steeply that big stones were exposed here and there in the clay. Winding down between these stones, and holes made by the potter, were narrow footpaths, with whole heaps of broken crockery beside them, some brown, some red, while down below stretched the broad smooth meadow, bright green, already mown, on which the village cattle were grazing. The river, full of twists in its course, with wonderful leafy banks, was about a verst from the village, and beyond it again was another broad meadow, with grazing cattle, long processions of white geese, and then, just as on this side, a steep ascent and on top of it the village, with a five-domed church and not far away a manor-house'.

The sweet clear air of the country and its natural sights and sounds added their own beauty to the scene for the returning Nicolai. 'Sitting by the edge of the steep slope, Nicolai and Olga watched the sun go down, saw the sky, gold and blood-red, reflected in the river, in the windows of the church and in the whole atmosphere, which was tender, calm, inexpressibly pure, as it never is in Moscow. And when the sun had set, the sheep and cattle came past with bleating and bellowing, and geese arrived from the other side of the river—and all was still, the silent light faded in the atmosphere and the darkness of evening quickly began to fall.'

Looked at more closely, Nicolai's parents' cottage seemed about the oldest and poorest in the row, but the only one which caught his eye as prosperous-looking was the end one, the public-house, which had an iron roof and curtains at the windows. 'In his recollections of his childhood his home was bright, cosy and comfortable, but now, entering the izba, he was taken aback; it was so dark, small and dirty. His wife Olga and daughter Sasha looked with surprise at the big untidy stove, occupying nearly half the room, and black with smoke and flies. The stove was down on one side, the logs of the wall lay all askew, and it seemed as if the whole izba might collapse any minute. In the front corner, beside the ikon, labels from bottles and cuttings from newspapers had been pasted on the walls—as substitutes for pictures. Squalor everywhere! None of the grown-ups were at home, all were busy with the harvest. On top of the stove sat a little girl of eight, fair-haired, unwashed, unperturbed at the sight of the visitors. She did not even look at them. On the floor a white cat was rubbing itself against the oven fork. "Puss, puss!" said Sasha. "Puss." "She can't hear you," said the little girl. "She's deaf." "Why?" "She just is. She's been beaten." Nicolai and Olga understood at the first glance what life was like here.'

This izba was clearly the usual single-roomed thatched log hut, about sixteen to eighteen feet square, with two or three small windows looking on to the street and a huge clumsy stove built of brick or rammed clay. As in most izbas the stove heated the room 'in black fashion', that is, it had no chimney to let out the wood-smoke. The small windows were probably of the commoner type, horizontal slits in the wall, one log deep. Only the richer muzhiks had one or more bigger windows made with a frame, like those of the public-house here, with curtains showing through them. The house was entered from the yard through the 'syena', an unheated vestibule built on behind the main building. The fire described later in the story happened through someone lighting a samovar in their syena and setting fire to the low thatch, for there was no ceiling here as there was in the main room. From its steps the sluttish Fyokla emptied the slops straight into the court-yard. Round the court-yard were the outbuildings, amongst which we hear of a byre and a shed, though there would probably be others.

The 'front corner' mentioned is the corner near one of the windows, where a religious picture (icon) stood on a little high corner shelf, with an oil lamp hanging in front of it. Entering the room from the back one might have the stove on one's left, in the back corner, with a kind of shelf, six or eight feet wide, stretching from its top to the right-hand wall, the so-called 'palati' or sleeping platform. This corner near the door with the 'palati' had also a special name, for it was in effect the bedroom. Along the right-hand wall there would be a wooden bench, with a heavy deal table in front of it, extending to beneath the icon in the right-hand 'front corner', a sort of dining and sitting room. The left-hand front corner opposite the stove would be used as a kitchen, and might be screened off.[1]

In this izba lived Nicolai's father and mother, both bent with age and toothless, their two daughters-in-law Marya and Fyokla and eight grandchildren. One of the husbands was serving his six years in the army, the other also lived away from home, as a watchman. In summer, when Nicolai and his family first arrived, the women slept in a shed. Nicolai, as an invalid, shared the top of the stove with his father, there was a baby in a cradle, and the other children slept in any space they could find on the sleeping-platform, or the bench, or the floor. In winter all crowded into the one room, and they could even find space for a stranger. But 'they always slept badly in the izba. All were disturbed in their sleep by some trouble or other which they could not shake off, the old man by the pain in his back, granny by her worries and bad temper, Marya by her fears, the children by their itching skin and hunger. They were continually turning over from side to side, talking in their sleep, or getting up for a drink'.

Food was scanty and of the plainest, usually black bread, which they dipped in water and ate greedily. The old herdsman in *The Pipe* too said he needed nothing but bread, and the joiner in *In the ravine* could cover enormous distances on foot, taking with him no food but bread and an onion. 'The chief art in eating,' as H. W. Williams says, 'was to find ways of consuming the largest possible quantity of bread. Even potatoes were eaten as a kind of

[1] Mackenzie Wallace I 39 and *Soviet Encyclopedia*.

sauce or condiment to bread.'[1] Potatoes are not mentioned in this story. The family grew cabbages in their garden, and probably also the commonest vegetables in Russia, onions, cucumber and garlic. They lived for as long as possible on their own grain, but in one year it lasted to shrove-tide and the next year only till Christmas. After that they had to tighten their belts and buy or borrow flour, and their one cow in her stall mooed pitiably day and night from hunger. On a feast-day they bought a herring at the public-house and made thin soup from its head to eat with their bread, and for a treat they had tea, which smelt of fish. 'At midday they sat down to drink tea and drank it till they sweated and felt swelled out with it. Only after that they began the soup, all eating from the same dish. But granny hid the rest of the herring.' Granny, who would let no one share her responsi-bilities as effective head of the family, was glad of the numerous fast days because no one but the baby could then touch milk.

The old Russian village before the Emancipation, like any village in medieval England, had been an almost completely self-sufficient unit. Its whole economy was based on that principle, as was also the life of the smaller units, the joint-families, of which it was made up. Even the neighbouring manor-house dispensed as far as it could with things that had to be bought with money, however lavish it might be with eggs and game. The peasant family grew its own food, made its own house, furniture and most agricultural implements, and wore home-spun clothes. In a village eighty miles from Moscow in the 1860's, for instance, 'the men wore blue linen or hempen trousers and shirts with gussets under the arms: red ones for holidays: and the women wore 'sarafans' (sleeveless dresses) of printed linen, without buttons, but fastened by strips of stuff and girdles of coloured yarn: and bodices of home-made stuff, either wool or linen and wool mixed. For winter they wore trousers of the same material. Both men and women wore jackets of untanned sheepskin (the 'tulúp'). The usual footgear was birchbark sandals: leather boots only on holidays, and to church, and a pair lasted more than ten years. In the seventies when the village had taken to flax-growing, felt boots made their appearance. For a long time there was only one cloth coat in the village: it was borrowed by friends for festive occasions.'[2] The picture may be supplemented from Mackenzie Wallace's description: 'Money was required only for

[1] *Russia and the Russians* 339.
[2] Maynard, *Russia in Flux*, 43.

the purchase of a few cheap domestic utensils, such as pots, pans, knives, hatchets, wooden dishes and spoons, and for the payment of taxes. In these circumstances the quantity of money in circulation among the peasants was infinitesimally small, the few exchanges which took place in a village being generally effected by barter. The taxes, and the vodka required for village festivals, weddings, or funerals, were the only large items of expenditure for the year, and they were generally covered by the sums brought home by the members who went to work in the towns.'[1]

How near the villages in these stories are still to self-sufficiency is indicated by the fact that the only village craftsman mentioned in *Peasants* is the potter, from whom the villagers would buy their earthenware cooking pots and crockery, made from the local clay. In *In the Ravine* there is a carpenter, and in *The new villa* a smith, each of whom would serve for several villages—we read of the carpenter's long journeys. Apart from these the villagers would employ occasionally a travelling tailor or tailoress, especially in preparation for a wedding or the like (cf. *In the Ravine*, or *The Privy Councillor*, where the customers are country gentry). Even in *Peasants*, on the day when Nicolai died, 'an old tailor in fearsome spectacles was cutting a vest out of old rags and two youths were rolling out wool for felt boots'. There is no mention of spinning and weaving, for textiles came mostly from factories now. Pedlars would tempt the women-folk with prints for dresses, coloured kerchiefs and so on, and occasional purchases would be made at a fair if there was one within walking distance, but in a small village most of the inhabitants would, like Nicolai's sisters-in-law, not have been as far afield as the chief town of the district. There is no hint among these peasants of traditional costumes or of stores of finery put away by village girls in a marriage chest, as in more prosperous parts of Europe, and of Russia itself, according to other authorities, though the women have Sunday dresses in bright colours. These families have literally no reserves, and the only article resembling a luxury that they possess is a samovar, which appeared in most peasant homes in the course of the second half of the nineteenth century. When this too had been seized by the village elder in an attempt to make a family pay a few roubles of its arrears of dues and taxes 'it was as if they had robbed the izba of its good name. It would have been better if the starost had taken away the table, or the benches and crockery—the room would not have looked as bare as it did now'.

---

[1] Mackenzie Wallace, II, 199.

Being ordinary human creatures and not models of thrift, Chekhov's peasants sometimes kick over the traces. If the women must have their tea, at any rate on special occasions, the men of the village, even the village elder, could not be kept away from the inn on Sundays and feast-days. 'They drank on St. Elijah's Day (20th July, the beginning of the harvest), they drank at the Assumption (15th August, the end of the harvest), they drank at the Exaltation of the Cross (14th September). At the Intercession of the Virgin (1st October) it was the Zhukovo Wakes, which the peasants celebrated by drinking for three days on end. They spent fifty roubles of public money on drink and then made a house to house collection for vodka.' And for once in the year all ate meat and ate their fill. Nicolai's family killed a sheep, and had mutton for breakfast, dinner and supper. Even in the night children kept getting up for another bite. We may note, incidentally, that in Russia, as in Germany, the church saint was fêted in autumn, after the harvest, suggesting that in both countries an older harvest festival had been given a new interpretation.

That the Russian peasant has for centuries been inordinately fond of strong drink seems certain, and his impoverishment after the Emancipation, when he had no longer a master to keep him in check, has often been ascribed to this as a principal cause. It is interesting therefore to note that Chekhov does not share this opinion, though he does not in any way gloss over the drunkenness and moral defects of his peasants. His view of the peasant is not unlike that put forward by his friend Korolenko in 1883, in his moving story *Makar's Dream*. When the deeds of his life are weighed in the balance, the golden scale containing his good works is at first outweighed by the wooden scale, heaped high with his lying and his drunkenness, but Makar, looking back on his life in the light of eternity, is given power to defend himself so convincingly that the court is moved to tears and the golden scale sinks lower and lower, as he tells the story of his sufferings and his wrongs. 'In Russia, as elsewhere,' as Maynard says, 'drink is the refuge of those whom life defeats and puzzles.' H. W. Williams, describing Russia in 1914, said that the peasant drank only at intervals, on Sundays and festival days, and that a very small quantity of vodka was enough to intoxicate him. He only drank heavily on special occasions such as a village wakes. The average consumption of alcohol per head was less then than in Great Britain. In villages where there was no drink-shop it could be very low. In two typical villages in the Voronezh province in the Black Earth zone, investigated by a zemstvo doctor round about 1900, it was two-fifths of a gallon per person per annum, while that of sugar was two and a half ounces, and of tea half an ounce![1] At that rate the peasants described by Chekhov were less wretched than many in real life.

It was drink that gave rise to much of the shouting and quarrelling so prominent in *Peasants*. On the day of Nicolai's arrival 'they had not finished their first cup of tea before a loud drawn-out drunken cry was heard from the yard: "Marya!" "That sounds like Kiryak," said the old man. "Talk of the devil!" There was a general silence. And after a little, the same cry came again, coarse and long drawn-out, as if from under the earth: "Marya!" Marya, the oldest daughter-in-law, turned pale, crouched against the stove, and it was strange to see on the face of this broad-shouldered, strong, plain-featured woman the expression of terror. Her daughter, the little girl sitting so nonchalantly on top of the stove, burst into tears.' As was his habit when drunk, Kiryak came in and struck his wife in the face with his fist, making her nose bleed. On Sunday evenings the men of the village at the inn 'sang in drunken voices, each one his own tune, and they brawled so loudly that Olga was all of a tremble and kept saying "Oh dear, oh dear!" She was surprised at the continual cursing and swearing, and that it was the old men who were the worst. But the children and bigger girls listened to this brawling quite unmoved, and it was obvious that they had been accustomed to it from the cradle.' Their bad-tempered old grandmother ruled them with a rod of iron and did not spare even little Sasha when she let the geese into the cabbage-plot. She had even been turned out of the village-meeting and locked up for a night by the elder for her quarrelsomeness.

The over-crowding and lack of privacy that were unavoidable when a joint-family lived in the traditional way in a one-roomed izba naturally gave rise to constant friction, only kept within bounds by the firm control of the head of the family. In *Peasants*, granny was constantly nagging at her old husband for his drinking and shiftlessness, and the coarse-grained Fyokla, the youngest daughter-in-law, lost no opportunity of showing her dislike for the other two. When things went badly even the dying Nicolai was loudly cursed by her and his mother for inflicting himself and his family upon the over-burdened household, and to his face they discussed what they would do after his death. Similar

[1] Maynard, *Russ. Peas.* 50.

features in *In the ravine, The new villa,* and other stories show that Chekhov considered them typical. In *The duel* he makes the deacon, himself no doubt the son of a village priest, draw a general contrast between the coarse masses and those more favoured by fortune, who do not realize their blessings. If these two who were going to fight each other for a trifle 'had known from childhood the same want as he had, if they had been brought up amongst ignorant, insensitive people, always thinking of money, quarrelling over a crust of bread, coarse and uncouth in their manners, spitting on the floor and belching after meals and during prayers,' they would have valued each other's good qualities, the qualities they had insensibly acquired in a good nursery.

Physically too it was a slum existence they led in this izba, without proper beds or bedding, wearing the same clothes day and night, with a poor supply of water and no notions of sanitation. There is no mention here of the bath-houses which were a common village feature in north and central Russia, and where the Russian peasants (like the Finns) took a weekly Turkish bath. Failing this, we are told, they often took the risk of steaming themselves in their own baking-oven. We hear in various stories of young and old bathing for coolness in the hot summer days, but when the shameless Fyokla bathed, in *Peasants*, it was not wholly from motives of cleanliness, and in fact this virtue is not at all stressed in Chekhov's descriptions of his villagers. The children are dirty, unkempt and troubled by skin diseases, and the poorer houses malodourous and full of vermin. Cockroaches and black beetles were always to be seen crawling over the bread and the tea-things, but the bug, the universal plague of village inns and the like, finds no mention in *Peasants*, no doubt because, as Maynard tells us in another connection, 'the bug is a natural aristocrat. He does not like the miserable bedding of the poor man'. The correctness of Chekhov's observation in this small point is confirmed by scientific reports.

From Chekhov the doctor we naturally learn a good deal about the health of the villagers, and their ideas about health and disease. 'The poorer they were, the less were muzhiks afraid of death. They told the old people to their faces that they had had their day, that their time had come, but they took no notice.' They were all excessively afraid of illness, however. 'A trifling illness, indigestion, a slight chill, were enough to make granny lie down on the stove, wrap herself up and begin to moan loudly and unceasingly: "I'm dying, I'm dying." The old man would

run for the priest, to give granny communion and extreme
unction. They were always talking about colds, worms, tumours
that wander about in the stomach and make their way to the
heart. They were especially afraid of colds, so they dressed in
warm clothes even in summer and roasted themselves on the
stove.'

Ignorance was clearly the cause of much of their suffering and
their fears, for the old traditions and superstitions were strong and
they had little guidance. As will be seen later, hospitals were few
and often very badly staffed. The peasant usually went first to
a feldscher or to a 'wise woman' in some near-by village. 'Granny
knew all the doctors, feldschers and "wise women" for twenty
miles round and didn't like any of them.' 'She often went to the
hospital, where she always gave her age as fifty-eight instead of
seventy, thinking that if the doctor knew her real age he would
tell her it was time for her to think of dying and not of taking
cures'—exactly what the feldscher says to the old coffin-maker in
Rothschild's Fiddle when he takes his seventy-year-old wife to the
hospital. Many mothers took their children to the doctor too
late, like the one in *The Runaway*. 'If you yourself get a pimple on
your nose you run straight to the hospital,' the doctor says to her,
'but you'll let the little boy's elbow fester for six months. That's
how you all are.'

Of the moral character and manners of the peasants Chekhov
gives us an unfavourable picture in *Peasants*, *The new villa*, etc.,
but he implies that they could hardly be expected to be better
in existing conditions. 'In the course of this summer and winter
there were hours and even days when Olga felt that the people
lived worse than cattle, that to live with them was horrible. They
were coarse, dishonest, dirty, drunken, they could not live in
peace with each other and were continually quarrelling, because
they had no respect for each other, merely fear and mistrust.
Who keeps the public-house and makes drunkards of the common
people? A peasant. Who embezzles and spends on drink community, school and church funds? Peasants. Who stole from his
neighbour, burnt his house down, gave false witness at court for
a bottle of vodka? Who is the first to declaim against the peasants
at zemstvo meetings and elsewhere? Peasants. Yes, it was terrible
to live with them, but all the same they were human, they
suffered and wept like other humans, and there was nothing in
their life for which some justification could not be found. Heavy
labour, which made the whole body ache at night, cruel winters,

scanty harvests, overcrowded homes—and no help or prospect of help from any one.'

Natural selection working for generations in the brutalizing conditions of serf life produced in the average man, in the absence of any strong counterbalance, a certain coarseness of grain and insensitiveness which revealed itself in many ways. He could live on the plainest of food, he could bear fatigue to an almost incredible degree for short periods, at harvest for instance, though at other times he had no objection to long spells of idleness, he could bear extremes of heat and cold. Though usually good-natured and neighbourly, he was capable of extreme cruelty when provoked, by horse-thieves for instance, or fire-raisers. To western eyes he seemed in particular extraordinarily unfeeling in his treatment of women.

In Turgeniev's *Khor and Kalinych* (in *A sportsman's sketches*) the wise old serf Khor, when asked what is the use of women, replies with conviction: 'A woman is a labourer. A woman is a muzhik's servant.' His old wife, busy all day at the stove and treated with indifference by Khor and her sons, vented her feelings on her daughters-in-law or the dog. 'It is not for nothing,' Turgeniev comments, 'that the mother-in-law in a Russian ballad sings: "What sort of a son are you, what sort of a family man, who do not beat your wife, your young one!" ' In some parts of Russia a whip was given to the bridegroom after the marriage-feast, as a symbol of authority (possibly the origin of Nietzsche's 'Du gehst zu Weibern? Vergiss die Peitsche nicht!').

Chekhov's picture of the treatment of women in the country shows that these traditions died hard. Quite unreflectingly his peasants and working men treat their wives as beasts of burden, and it is only death that tears down the veil of incomprehension between them. The old coffin-maker (*Rothschild's fiddle*) and the turner in *Sorrow*, both poor muzhiks in their way of life, realise only when their wives are dying what they have meant to them and how badly they have treated them, and to both wives death comes as a friend. 'Her face was rosy with fever, unusually bright and cheerful. The coffin-maker, accustomed to see her face pale, timid and unhappy, was rather put out. It looked as if she was really dying, and was glad to be leaving behind at last, and for ever, this izba, the coffins, and Jacob.' 'He remembered again that in all his life he had never once felt sorry for her, or shown her any affection. The fifty-two years, during which they had lived in this one izba, had seemed a long, long time, yet somehow in all those years he had not once thought of her, never paid any attention to her, as if she had been a dog or a cat. Yet every day she had lit the stove, cooked and baked, fetched the water, chopped the sticks, slept in the same bed with him, and when he had come back drunk from a wedding she had always hung up his fiddle reverently on the wall and put him to bed, and all this without a word, with a timid, solicitous expression in her eyes.'

There was of course no romance about most peasant marriages. Mackenzie Wallace says that as the natural labour unit in a Russian village comprised a man, a woman and a horse, it was the duty of a father to provide a horse for his son when he was fully grown, and of the mother to find him a wife. What she looked for in her search, with the help of friends or a marriage-broker ('svakha'), was not beauty but physical strength and capacity for work. Before the Emancipation the son always brought his wife to live in his father's house, and in this way 'joint-families' arose, consisting of three or even four generations. Even when a married son left the village to work elsewhere his wife remained with her parents-in-law. Though the joint-families gradually broke up after the Emancipation, to the disgust of the Slavophils, there are many examples of them in these stories, in *Peasants*, *In the ravine*, etc. Even the village shopkeeper's family in the latter story, though as rich people they looked for beauty in a bride, always chose hard-working peasant girls with no dowry. The son to be married was a detective in a distant province, but his step-mother expected him to leave his wife at home to help in the household. Though he had a very good opinion of himself the young man allowed everything to be arranged for him as if he were only distantly concerned in it. The wedding was celebrated in great style and after a few days, during which he was never sober, the bridegroom left his terrified little bride behind to the tender mercies of her redoubtable sister-in-law.

Inevitably these marriages of convenience and enforced separations led to many infidelities. In *Agafya* there are indications of the compensations that were sought by young wives for their loveless marriages, in the study of the idler Savka, so irresistible for the young wives that he lived by their bounty, while in *Peasants* Fyokla, the absent soldier's wife slips out at night to her friends across the river. Another soldier's wife is Mashenka in *Peasant Wives*, though the setting

here is not a village but a small town. She had been married off
at seventeen in a week, through the good offices of a 'svakha', to
a young carrier, who after a few months was called up. Before
long she and a young neighbour fell in love with each other and
lived together. On the husband's return she did not wish to go
back to him, but her lover, for whom by this time a desirable
marriage had been arranged, insisted that she should. Neither
his sermons nor her husband's entreaties could shake her determination to follow her heart, but her conduct was so little
approved of by both husband and lover that they beat her black
and blue. A few days later her husband was found poisoned. The
striking point about this excellent story is the refusal of both men
to take the romantic view in spite of Mashenka's obvious sincerity.
They hold fast to the peasant idea of marriage inherited from
their forebears.

Chekhov shows us the peasants in their home life as he himself
had got to know them on his house to house visits. He does not
give us any detailed pictures of their working life, and of the
system of agriculture and land-tenure which underlay it. The
peasants live in villages, not on isolated farms, and each family
has its own strips in the open fields, though, like Savka in *Agafya*,
they might not themselves make use of them. He presumably
let his share of land to others, and he was given the old man's
job of watchman and birdscarer at the kitchen gardens. This
village evidently had a communal kitchen garden as well as the
usual hay-meadow, mentioned for instance in *Peasants* and *The
new villa*. In the latter story we see the peasants going out together
to their wood to divide the hay that they had just cut in the
clearings.   In addition to these clearings they had meadows
divided into individual patches, into one of which the engineer's
horses strayed. They were immediately impounded, and following
village custom the village elder and some witnesses were taken
along to inspect the damage done, though the engineer voluntarily
anticipated their claim for compensation. In *Peasants* we see the
low-lying hay-meadow, which in April after the thaws was under
water, turned over in August, when everyone had made and
carried the hay on his own patch, to the village livestock. Nicolai's
old father, instead of keeping his hay for the winter, was improvident enough to sell some to a neighbouring squire for ready
money. The elder caught him at it and boxed his ears by way of
rebuke (if this is the right interpretation of the incident). In *The
pipe* an old herdsman is found grazing cows, sheep and hobbled

horses on the edge of a birch-wood. For a day and a night on end he earns a twenty-kopeck piece. It was because of the almost complete absence of walls and fences in the open fields, and the necessity of making use of every scrap of grass and stubble, that grazing animals had to be watched so carefully. One of the chief drawbacks of the open-field system was the difficulty of providing fodder crops for winter feeding, and the few cattle that survived the winter, after suffering tortures through hunger, like the cow in *Peasants*, were in terrible condition. All the small points mentioned are characteristic then of the prevailing system, which would be familiar to contemporary Russian readers.

For reasons which will be discussed later, agriculture had failed to keep pace with the growth of the population, and the peasantry as a whole, as well as the landowners, were living through a long drawn-out crisis while Chekhov was writing. The famine of 1892 showed him things at their worst. The only peasants who were fairly prosperous were, generally speaking, those who were not entirely dependent on the produce of their own land. It had long been the custom for some members of the joint families to make their living away from home, in town, or in a factory, or as agricultural labourers. In the days of serfdom, no serf could leave his village unless he paid his master an annual due ('obrok'), but as there were very few alternative sources of labour in the towns such serfs were in great demand, and could both pay their 'obrok' and send something home to their families, besides maintaining themselves. So we hear for instance in *Peasants* that the brighter boys of Nicolai's village had all, like him, gone to work in Moscow hotels and restaurants, following in the footsteps of some enterprising spirits in pre-emancipation times, while those from across the river all went to Moscow bakers. Many left the village for seasonal employment, like the reapers in *In the ravine*, or the cabby in *Misery*. Near some villages there were factories, which, as we shall see, were often in the country (so for instance in *In the ravine*), and the factories might provide part-time work for various members of a household to be done at home, domestic industries. There were some survivals still in the 'nineties of the pre-capitalistic form of domestic industry, under which the head of a household bought his own raw material and marketed the product. In the province of Vladimir, for instance, where the pious Olga in *Peasants* came from, they made icons in this way.[1] But Chekhov only shows us peasants who are sweated by some

[1] Mackenzie Wallace, I, 135.

neighbouring manufacturer. Nicolai's family for instance spent their evenings winding silk, by the light of their smoky lamp, all for twenty kopecks a week.

Ready money from any such source was of particular import-ance to the peasant because, though his farming was still almost entirely on a subsistence basis, providing no surplus for sale, the state had demanded from him since 1861 redemption payments for his land, in addition to the state and provincial taxation which already weighed heavily on the serf before this. It is clear from *Peasants* what an impossible burden these combined demands represented. The village of Zhukovo, the scene of the story, with its forty houses, was over 2000 roubles in debt to state and zemstvo, and Nicolai's family were themselves 119 roubles in arrears. The village commune, with its elected elder ('starosta') at its head, was collectively responsible for these payments, and was regularly reminded of its duty by a visit from the chief of police from the nearest town ('stanovoi pristav'), for it was the police who collected direct taxes until 1899. The village called him 'barin', the word they had used for their former lord, just as they still called the payment 'obrok', formerly the commutation payable to a serf's master in place of personal service. The liability of a commune varied according to the number of 'souls' (in the sense of 'male inhabitants') on its list at the last government 'revision', revisions being made at irregular intervals, on the average every fifteen years or so. The assessment was not therefore reduced when a peasant left his village for a town, and as the commune was still responsible for his share of taxes, he had to continue to pay them to the commune, just as he had payed 'obrok' in similar circumstances to his master. One can easily see why the peasant felt that he had simply exchanged one taskmaster for another since 1861, and still used the old terms.

When the 'barin' came to Zhukovo, peasants in arrears were summoned before him in the elder's cottage. Nicolai's father began a rambling story about how the elder had interfered when he was trying to sell hay (for ready money), but the chief of police was informed by the elder that the real cause of his indebtedness was drink. He wrote something down and said to the peasant without raising his voice, just as if he were asking for a glass of water: "Get out!" Soon afterwards the elder took away the family samovar, with those of several other families. Others lost hens or sheep to the police, and they were particularly indignant at the way in which the creatures were neglected and often allowed to die when they had been seized. It was because the police had misused their power of distraint that the collection of taxes was transferred to special officials in 1899.

There is probably no Russian institution which has come in for such extremes of praise and blame as the village commune or 'mir'. When Bazarov, the 'nihilist' in Turgeniev's *Fathers and children*, challenges the Slavophil Pavel Petrovitch to bring forward a single institution in Russia which does not call for complete and unqualified destruction, the first thing that occurs to his opponent is naturally the Mir, and the second, the peasant joint-family. Chekhov does not join in the battle of words, but he gives us a distinctly unflattering picture of village administration, which tends to confirm Maynard's statement that after the Emancipation there was 'a subtle change in the position of the village elder, who had been the officer, rather than the head, of the Mir'. 'He became an official personage; and cases of whipping for insolence to the elder were not unknown.'

The village elder (starosta) in Zhukovo, we are told, though himself a poor man and in arrears with his taxes, always took the side of the authorities. His cottage was no better than the average, but it was clean and tidy, and its walls were almost covered with pictures from newspapers. They included in the most prominent place a portrait of Alexander of Battenberg, the Prince of Bulgaria who had been forced by Alexander III to abdicate in 1886. If this detail is meant to convey anything beyond the date, it indicates perhaps the elder's ignorance, for one so loyal would not otherwise have given the place of honour to an enemy of his Tsar. His skinny unwashed children were to be seen playing on the floor and his wife was to be found winding silk in the evenings, as in any other izba. He tried to maintain his position in spite of his youth and ignorance (he was thirty, had never lived outside the village and had had no education) by a great display of severity. In a crisis, as when fire broke out in a cottage one evening and the whole village was in danger, he proved a wretched leader to the muzhiks, who were celebrating a saint's day in the inn. The fire was put out by a party of workmen from the big estate across the river, led by a wild student, and village democracy gave a poor account of itself.

We receive an even more unfavourable impression from *In the ravine* of a 'starshina' or cantonal elder, the president of the cantonal meeting, which administered the affairs of the group of villages called a 'volost' or canton. He and his clerk (every starshina was assisted by a permanent secretary) were fat, sleek scoundrels who in the fourteen years they had served together had never signed a single paper or received a single caller without cheating and insulting him if they could. The starshina was almost illiterate. In writing he began every word with a capital letter. In his cantonal offices, not an izba but a house of town type, he had had a telephone installed, imitating the factory owners, and pretended to be seriously inconvenienced when it would no longer function, but the reason was that it had been allowed to become a home for bugs and black beetles. When he and his clerk were invited to a wedding in the village, the clerk's wife brought all their children, seized what she could lay hands on from every plate within reach and filled her pockets and the children's. The whole description is so satirical in tone that it reads like a page of Gogol, and in *Speedy help*,* an early story in which a starshina and clerk appear, the tone is already the same: 'The starshina, strolling round the village, wanted to say something (to a group of muzhiks), but was unable to. He made vague movements with his thumbs, opened his eyes wide and puffed out his swollen red cheeks, as if he were blowing the top note on a big trumpet. The clerk, a stocky little red-nosed man wearing a jockey cap, tried to assume an expression of great energy and went up to the crowd.' A stranger had just been pulled out of the river half-drowned, and the best advice the clerk could give was to toss him in a mat. This strange substitute for artificial respiration was only stopped when the lady of the manor appeared on the scene, but the patient was now beyond help.

Poor, ignorant and badly governed as they knew themselves to be, the peasants were naturally far from content with their lot. According to Chekhov, they were moved to particular indignation by the distraint exercised by the police through the starosta. When they came together in someone's cottage on a holiday to talk over their grievances, 'what they blamed for everything, for their arrears, for the acts of oppression, for the bad harvests, was the zemstvo, although no one really knew what the word meant'. Dissatisfied rich muzhiks who had been members of the zemstvo had abused it in their factories and public-houses and their opinion had spread to the mass. In point of fact of course the Zemstvos, the more or less democratic organs of local government set up in 1864, composed of representatives of the landowners, the smaller towns and the peasantry, usually had the interests of the peasant population very much at heart and accomplished much to ameliorate its condition. Chekhov's references to their work in his letters are uniformly favourable, but the peasants could not appreciate it perhaps because, though they were represented by a small number of members in the zemstvo of the district (uyezd), these peasant members were elected indirectly and would be unknown to the vast majority in such a large area as a district, averaging 7000 square miles. There were provincial zemstvos above the district ones, but no cantonal ones below them.

In the passage quoted above Chekhov referred to rich muzhiks. One of the effects of the emancipation had been to remove the levelling influences and to favour differentiation. Some peasants became still poorer, a few, already called 'kulaks', or 'fists', became quite rich, though never, it would seem, from their land alone. In Chekhov they are village shop-keepers, or they have inns or factories. These village capitalists are represented as being on bad terms with the peasants around them, though they are closely connected with them by blood ties and cannot easily put off their way of life. The most detailed picture is that of Gregory Tsybukin in the village of Ukleevo (in *In the ravine*). Ukleevo was a bigger village than Zhukovo, with three small cotton mills and a tannery, employing between them some 400 people. Tsybukin kept a grocer's shop, but he dealt in more profitable wares when he could, in cattle, pigs, hides, grain, and in fact anything that promised a good return, from acres of uncut timber to magpies for ladies' hats. He did not shrink from a shady deal. He was a money-lender, a receiver of stolen goods on occasion, and he carried on a most profitable but illicit trade in vodka.

He lived in a two-storey stone house of town type, with a painted iron roof, but though his family's way of life was so different from that of the peasant in material comforts, it was not on a higher level in any other respect. It was only after his second marriage late in life that his family began to use individual plates instead of a common dish at dinner. Barbara, his new wife, also introduced lamps everywhere, white tablecloths, geraniums at the windows and flowers in the garden (peasants grew no flowers), and, good Christian soul as she was, she did what she could by acts of charity to make up for the rapacity and cruel indifference to all but family interests of her husband and his daughter-in-law Aksinia. The Tsybukins worked hard but they stinted themselves in nothing. Their cook was kept busy, with four regular meals a day to prepare, and tea with white bread six times.[1] They could allow themselves good middle-class clothes for ordinary wear and elaborate ones for special occasions such as a son's wedding, which was celebrated, as the father told every guest on leaving, to a tune of 2000 roubles. Mr. Tsybukin paid his business calls in a smart horse and trap, while Aksinia sometimes wore a hat, a thing unheard of in a village, and on Sundays and holidays she went for drives with the factory owners.

There was nothing of the muzhik's life in this luxury, and Tsybukin was indeed by origin a townsman, yet it was a peasant mentality that was revealed in most of the Tsybukins' behaviour and that led to the chief events of the story. They lived, in the first place, as a joint-family. The sons, poor creatures themselves, the younger weak in body and mind and the elder ugly, conceited and, though a detective, the accomplice of a forger, were married to healthy, hard working and—as a luxury—good-looking peasant girls without dowries. Aksinia, the younger son's wife, was not content to be an unpaid servant. She had spirit, energy and business ability and was soon in sole charge of the shop, but when she began to have business ambitions of her own, inspired by her factory-owning friends, and wanted to start a brick-works on a piece of her father-in-law's land, he refused permission. 'While I am alive,' he said, 'there shall be no dividing in this family. We must all keep together.' It was this insistence on his rights as head of the family that was so bitterly avenged by Aksinia in the further course of the story. What Maynard says about the women in Tolstoy's *Power of darkness* is true also of her. 'The women show an animal-like unawareness of wrong: but a skill in planning and executing it which no animal could possess. This was one of the unintended revenges which woman took, upon man and his offspring, for domestic slavery and brutal treatment. She became a citadel of darkness in his household, and made a prison for her captor.' In *The murder* too we find the same unwillingness to divide the family inheritance, even when those concerned are two cousins who cannot bear each other, and here again a woman murders a close relative and shows no remorse.

---

[1] cf. the daily routine among landed proprietors described by Mavor, *Economic History of Russia* II, 280, note, 'even in households which pride themselves upon their simplicity'. '8 o'clock, light breakfast—tea, bread and honey, e.g.; 11 o'clock, breakfast *à la fourchette*—a formidable meal; 1 o'clock, lunch of similar character; 4–5 o'clock tea and bread, etc.; 7 o'clock, dinner of numerous courses; 9 o'clock, supper; 11 o'clock, a snack before retiral.'

In this story we see a factory come into being, through the initiative of Aksinia, working in partnership with the owner of an existing factory. Its site was on the land of the family into which she had married as a poor peasant girl. Before long her brick-yard was in full production, bricks being in demand for the new railway, and a number of women and girls were kept busy carting bricks to the station and loading trucks, earning twenty-five kopecks a day, more than Nicolai's family earned in a week from their silk-winding. The factory owners opened a public house near the station, like the village merchant Dyudya in *Peasant wives*, another kulak type. Dyudya dealt like Tsybukin in land, cattle and various natural products, and in addition to keeping a public house on the main road let rooms to travellers in the upper storey of his own house. Even the sanctimonious innkeeper Jacob in *The murder* was a money-lender and sold vodka without a licence. All these village capitalists cheat without remorse when they can, with all the low cunning of a peasant. So do the assistants of the wholesale merchants in *Three years'* but not Lopakhin in *The cherry orchard*, though he was the son of a drunken village shopkeeper of serf origin, who would beat him unmercifully for a trifle. Lopakhin was not a kulak but a respected merchant, 'a very decent person in every sense'.

The attitude of the ordinary peasant to a kulak who robbed him at every turn was naturally hostile, but he displayed a similar hostility and distrust towards all who were not of his class, a reflection of the cold contempt with which he was himself usually treated by the outside world. In spite of emancipation he was, as a peasant, a member of a depressed class of so-called 'black people', disfranchised in law from many privileges enjoyed by citizens and officials, and still frequently regarded as scarcely human. It might be illegal now to beat him as in the old days, but it was usually safe for those in authority to do so, and they did. 'The inn parlours had "black" half, where the "black" people sat, isolated from their superiors, the merchants and officials. The kind of work which peasants did was called "black work", unfit for those of higher status.'[1] Or as Chekhov puts it in *Peasants*: 'Those who were richer and more powerful than they were could not help them, being themselves coarse, dishonest, intemperate and just as noisily quarrelsome. Even a minor official or business employee treated peasants like tramps, and used "thou" to cantonal elders and church elders, thinking it his good right to

[1] Maynard, *Russia in Flux*, 39.

do so. And could any help or good example be expected from grasping, dissolute, lazy people, who only went to the villages to insult, swindle and browbeat?' It was by way of retaliation for such treatment then that the peasants in *The new villa* or *My life* were so suspicious of even friendly townspeople settling in the country, so ready to rob and cheat them and so unresponsive to all their well-meant approaches. There was a kind of fog of misunderstanding between them, Chekhov says, that prevented each from seeing the other's good points. They belonged to different worlds.

It is a gloomy picture that has been drawn above of the state of the Russian peasantry. If we ask what influences were at work that might be expected to bring about some improvement in their state, we find, apart from the government, local and central, three groups of people, village school teachers, village clergy and amateur helpers from the ranks of the 'conscience-stricken gentry'. It was generally agreed in progressive circles that Russia's principal need, after the emancipation of the serfs, was education. Given education it was thought she would soon catch up the western nations. The watchword, as in eighteenth-century Germany, was Enlightenment, and Germany was the model. Chekhov fully shared this view, except that he saw other things to be necessary besides education. 'The mother of all Russian evils,' he wrote to Suvorin in 1889, 'is gross ignorance.' Gorky tells us of Chekhov's enthusiasm for the work of the village schools and his indignation at the lack of respect which teachers encountered even from the lowest officials and police officers. They were paid in farthings and lived like hermits, yet the work they were doing was most important for the country. He was frequently visited by village teachers and was always asking Gorky and other friends to help them. In the stories too it is their poor pay and the thankless nature of their task that is emphasised. *The schoolmistress* (Na podvodye) is a marvellously compact study of a teacher in a zemstvo village school, returning from town in a villager's cart, with her month's pay of 21 roubles and her purchases. She was a stolid middle-class girl who had taken up teaching from necessity, and who stood up to it better than the highly-strung people who talked about the vocation of spreading Enlightenment, but there were times when she was filled with resentment against the lazy school-watchman, the insolent school-guardian, an almost illiterate tanner in the village who cheated her of wood, and the inspector, formerly an excise official, who came every three years and knew nothing at all about schools. After seventeen years she felt that 'this life was aging and coarsening her, making her ugly, angular, awkward, as if she were made of lead'. She was through her isolation growing like the peasants around her, afraid of everyone in authority. Above all, she was lonely, friendless and weary of the monotony of her life. Her male counterpart is the wretched Medvyedyenko in *The Sea-Gull*, who on 23 roubles a month has to support his mother and three younger brothers and sisters, and yet marries the listless intellectual Masha, though he is treated as a nonentity by her and her family.

As the government scarcely concerned itself directly with elementary education in the country, schools had to be provided either by the zemstvos, who spent 15 per cent of their income on popular education, or by private benefactors, or, very occasionally, by the church. To found a village school was one of the favourite forms taken by the benevolence of the 'conscience-stricken gentry' and other well-wishers of the peasants. Chekhov himself built three schools, and he would have liked to build hundreds. In *My life* and other stories we find gentlefolk doing the same thing, though their efforts do not often meet with much response from the peasants. Factories too, which were so often situated in the country, sometimes built and maintained schools for their workmen's children, as in *At home* and *The schoolmaster*. In *A nightmare* there is a reference to a parish school to be founded by the church authorities, though very badly endowed by them. A government official gives it his special attention as a church school, in accordance with the policy of the central government after 1864. The Orthodox Church was little interested in popular education, as Mackenzie Wallace explains, because, unlike the Protestant churches, it did not consider it necessary for its members to read the scriptures. The Church was in fact still opposing compulsory primary education after 1905. That all these efforts only touched the fringe of the problem is proved by the fact that in European Russia, excluding Finland, the Baltic Provinces and Poland, even in 1914 about 80 per cent were illiterate.[1]

About the influence of religion on village life, Chekhov's views seem to agree closely with those of Mackenzie Wallace. The Russian people are religious, the latter says, in the sense that 'they go regularly to church on Sundays and holy-days, cross themselves repeatedly when they pass a church or Icon, take the

---

[1] Sumner, *Survey of Russian History*, 339.

Holy Communion at stated seasons, rigorously abstain from animal food—not only on Wednesdays and Fridays, but also during Lent and the other long fasts—make occasional pilgrimages to holy shrines, and, in a word, fulfil punctiliously the ceremonial observances which they suppose necessary for salvation. But here their religiousness ends. They are generally profoundly ignorant of religious doctrine, and know little or nothing of Holy Writ'.

In *Peasants* we learn that the peasants, especially the women, usually observed the external forms of religion and found comfort in them as a kind of magic. Unconsciously they probably derived from the rites of the church and the little that they heard of the scriptures something of the imaginative relief which the cultured gained from literature and art. On fine Sundays the young girls put on their red, green and yellow dresses and went to morning service at the church across the river, one of the outlying churches of the parish, at which only a small number of services were held. Communion, baptisms, marriages and funeral services were celebrated only at the parish church six versts away, where the priest lived. He came round all the cottages with the cross and fined peasants fifteen kopecks who had not communicated in Lent. Nicolai's old father considered religion a matter for women and never thought about it. Granny had only confused recollections of what she had been told in her youth about sin and death and salvation. At night she would stand before the Icon and repeat meaningless fragments of prayers such as: 'To the Madonna of Kazan, to the Madonna of Smolensk, to the Madonna of Troitsa.' The two daughters-in-law had been christened and took communion every year, but they had not the slightest idea what it all meant, and when Maria went to church with the pious Olga, she would not go beyond the porch. They did not teach their children any prayers or tell them anything about God. The only precept they inculcated was that they must not eat forbidden food on fast-days. It was much the same in all families, but though there were few who truly believed or understood, they all loved to hear the Scriptures read. Olga was for that reason a very welcome visitor and treated with great respect, for they had normally no bibles and no one to read to them. We are shown a number of sectarians among the peasantry, with strong and even fanatical personal beliefs, like the two cousins in *The murder*, but there is nothing in Chekhov resembling the picture drawn by Gorky in *Childhood* of his old grandmother, talking aloud to God every night about her family troubles, with childlike simplicity, as if to a trusted personal friend, a scene unforgettably acted by Massalitinova in Mark Donskoi's film (1942).

The one day in the year when all came under the spell of religion was in August, when an Icon was borne in solemn procession from village to village throughout the district (uyezd). 'The girls set off at dawn in their best dresses to meet it, and accompanied it to the village in the evening, following the cross in procession and singing, while the bells rang out from the church across the river. A great crowd of people from the village and beyond filled the street. It was noisy, dusty, hard to move. The old man, granny, Kiryak and all of them stretched out their hands towards the Icon, fixed their eyes on it appealingly and cried with tears: "Pray for us, Little Mother, pray for us".

It was as if all had suddenly realised that the space between earth and heaven is not empty, that the rich and powerful have not taken possession of it all, that there is a refuge from insult and bondage, from the intolerable burden of poverty, the horrible grip of vodka.

"Pray for us, Little Mother," sobbed Marie, "Little Mother!"

But when the service was over and the Icon had been borne away, everything went on in the old way, and once again coarse, drunken voices were heard from the inn.'

Crude as this religion was in many ways, it formed a framework for the peasant's life and for all but the rich muzhiks it robbed death of its sting. The passage of the weeks was marked by the break on Sunday, of the months and seasons by the fasts and holy-days. As the passage quoted above (p. 46) indicates, the peasant referred to dates not by the Julian calendar but by that of the Orthodox Church. The landmarks in the year were the four great fasts (Lent, St. Peter's Fast, the Fast of the Assumption and Advent), the five lesser fasts (Christmas to Epiphany, Shrovetide or Butter-week, when milk products and eggs might be eaten but no meat, Passion Week, before Easter Sunday, Easter Week and St. Thomas' Week), and a score of isolated Saints' Days.[1] Work ceased on the church holy-days, which, including Sundays, made up almost a third of the year, and it was only a very hardened sinner who did not observe the fasts, which accounted for almost another third. The effect of this was that the working year was about sixty days shorter than in protestant countries. Births, marriages and deaths were always marked by church services, even amongst agnostic educated people. On Nicolai's death, in

[1] See e.g. Boyer and Speranski, *Russian Reader*, 3rd ed., 303.

3*

Peasants, a funeral service was held (and paid for) in front of every cottage as the coffin was carried down the village street. 'The orthodox Russian peasant . . . had the most unbounded, childlike confidence in the saving efficacy of the rites which he practised' (Mackenzie Wallace). It was only the rich muzhiks, according to Chekhov, who lost their belief in God and salvation as they grew richer, and only lit candles before the Icons and paid for prayers to be on the safe side, from fear of their approaching end. The poorer a peasant was, the less he feared death.

But even if the church taught poor peasants what Montaigne held to be the chief aim of philosophy, 'apprendre á mourir', it might have done a great deal more than it did to teach them to live. As Mackenzie Wallace remarks, if the Orthodox Church could have made the peasantry refrain from the inordinate use of strong drink as effectually as it made them refrain during a great part of the year from animal food, and if it could have instilled into their minds a few simple moral principles as successfully as it had inspired them with a belief in the efficacy of the Sacraments, it would certainly have conferred on them an inestimable benefit. But this was neither in the tradition of the Orthodox Church nor within the power of the average parish priest.

In his one full-length study of a parish priest, in *A nightmare*, Chekhov shows us a simple-hearted man, struggling uncomplainingly with bitter poverty. We see the twenty-eight year old priest of the village of Sinkovo through the eyes of a self-satisfied government official of about the same age, who has been instructed in St. Petersburg to do what he can for the new parish school in that village. Sending for the priest, who has to walk in five miles through the mud, he finds him pitifully young and undeveloped, with long lank hair and features that have more of the woman than the man about them. He is painfully shy and awkward, and dressed in an old patched cassock he sits on the edge of his chair and does not seem nearly so much interested in the school as in the tea which a lackey brings in to them. He drinks it greedily and surreptitiously pockets a lump of sugar. The official's unfavourable impression is confirmed when he visits the village on a Sunday. The wooden church looks old and neglected, and dignity and grace are lacking in the priest's manner of 'serving'. He does not sing well, and has no deep-voiced deacon to assist him, only a deaf old parish-clerk. He lives in an ordinary izba with rather better furniture than a peasant's, and when the official calls he is unable, much to his embarrassment, to provide tea for his refreshment. The official is moved to write to the bishop, pointing out what a bad influence such a raw, and, as he suspects, intemperate youth must have on his flock.

Soon afterwards the priest calls three times at the official's house, walking ten miles each time, and on the third occasion he is received. Overcoming his shyness by a great effort, he asks to be considered for the secretaryship which the official has just advertised at a salary of twenty roubles a month. He would be delighted to do the work in addition to his own for ten roubles. And now the astonished official learns how this despised fellow-creature lives. With a salary of a hundred and fifty roubles (about £15) a year he spends forty roubles on the maintenance of his brother at the seminary, ten roubles a month goes to the consistory to pay off the fee of two hundred roubles due on his appointment, and at least three roubles a month to keep his predecessor from starvation. He is too proud to ask neighbouring landowners for help, and the muzhiks and even the doctor are too poor themselves. For the new school their village meeting has only been able to vote thirty kopecks a year from each 'soul'. His young wife, a girl from a cultivated home, lives worse than any maid, her only treat being the odd bits of sugar and apples he can take home. Overcome by shame in face of these revelations of a saintly poverty the official determines to make up for his previous misunderstanding.

Chekhov does not mention in this sketch what every Russian knew, that a village priest had a house and a varying amount of land free, sometimes just a vegetable plot, sometimes enough to keep a horse and a few cows, and to grow food for his family or for sale. The most prosperous were those who were good farmers. The priest asked for fees from his parishioners, which might bring him in £50 to £80 a year according to the size of his parish (H. W. Williams). The exaction of these small fees for christenings, weddings, funeral services and so on was a constant source of friction, a temptation to turn the service of God into a trade. Many stories were told among the peasants of the greed and drunkenness of priests, and they naturally varied much in personal character. There were saints among them and there were reprobates. One of the latter is seen in Chekhov's *The letter*. 'Many sins were laid to his account. He led an intemperate life, could not agree with his assistants and with the Mir, kept his parish registers and accounts carelessly—these were the formal charges, but in addition rumours had long been current of his celebrating forbidden marriages for money and selling communion certificates to officials and officers from the town. These rumours were all the more persistent because he was poor and had nine children at home, all as shiftless as himself. The sons were un-educated, spoilt boys, without any employment, and the plain daughters could not find husbands.' We see him pestering his superintendent (blagochinny), the priest of a big parish, entrusted with the supervision of a number of smaller parishes. His final request is for a glass of vodka.

Since the time of Peter the Great the clergy had been a closed caste. The seminaries for the education of candidates for the priesthood admitted only sons of priests, and in the course of time there were far more of these than could find livings. The surplus ones became minor officials and clerks, or not infrequently rogues and vagabonds like the drunken lackey in *Terror*, a priest's son, who, after expulsion from the seminary, proves a failure in a choir and in a monastery, turns tramp, is put in prison, and tries his hand as lackey, forester, whipper-in, church-watchman and whatever job he can find. The brighter spirits among them went to swell the ranks of the intelligentsia. If a priest's son could not succeed his father, he was frequently married off before ordination—he could not marry afterwards—to the daughter of an old priest or one who had recently died, and he received the living with his bride. Such marriages were often arranged by the church authorities (see Mackenzie Wallace, I, 67 ff). The same happened with deacons and parish-clerks, as in *The witch*. The pretty young wife of a parish-clerk (dyachok) tells a postillion sheltering in her wretched hovel from a snow-storm that her father had been dyachok in the village, and when he was dying the consistory was asked to send an unmarried dyachok to marry her and take over her father's post. The result of this arranged marriage is seen in the story, in the jealous imaginings of the middle-aged dyachok, who thinks his wife uses black arts to attract men to the house, and in the unsatisfied feelings of the young wife, who cannot take her eyes off the handsome young postillion sleeping by her stove.

The question of what was fundamentally wrong with the con-dition of the peasantry is occasionally touched on by Chekhov in stories dealing with the efforts of the 'conscience-stricken gentry' to improve their lot. We may conclude this chapter with a comparison of the views of Chekhov's age, as expressed in these stories, with those of some more recent writers.

In *An artist's story* there is a discussion between a serious minded young lady of means, who teaches in the local village school, gives the villagers medical advice and is in general full of good works, and a landscape painter, whom she, with her social conscience and severely practical mind, considers a rather useless person. Stung by her contemptuous attitude he retorts that under present conditions medical outposts, village schools, libraries and so forth only serve to enslave the peasants further. The real trouble is that these peasant women about whom she is so much concerned are so worn out with physical toil and the fight with hunger and sickness that they never have any leisure, any time to think about those things that distinguish man from the animals. If all would share the hard work of the world, it would be done in three or four hours a day. Then all according to their capacity could devote themselves to creative work in the arts and sciences, and men could live like Gods. One is reminded of *Sur la pierre blanche* or *The intelligent woman's guide to socialism*. Lida replies quite rightly that they cannot meanwhile sit with their hands in their laps. They must do what they can for the relief of their neighbours. Again in *My life*, which is full of Tolstoyan ideas, the hero, who has broken with his father, an architect of good family, to earn his living as an artisan, marries a woman of means and together they run her small country estate for a year and devote themselves to understanding and helping the peasants. At the end of it all the wife comes to the conclusion that they themselves are the only people who have benefitted by this work, not the peasants. Individuals can accomplish so little in the fight against ignorance, dirt, drunkenness, infantile mortality. Even if they were to work all their lives in this way, the result would be as a drop in the ocean. What is needed is something much more far-reaching, a message that will impress itself on great masses of people together. She returns to her music, which gives her at least the emotional satisfaction of moving a great audience as one man. In *At home* a university woman, returning to the family estate with ambitions to 'serve the people', loses heart when she realises how much easier it is to talk about such things, as so many around her do, than to struggle with the obstinate and unpleasant facts. She concludes that most of the talk is a way that people with five or ten thousand desiatins have of assuaging their consciences. If they were really serious about improving education and so on they would not let village teachers starve on fifteen roubles a month. They would not merely build factory schools but recognize that the peasant is a man like themselves, who should have access not merely to second-rate elementary schools, but to universities. In the end however she marries a conventionally liberal factory manager. Finally in *Terror*, a young landowner, who confesses himself to be afraid of life, is made to say: 'It was a regrettable movement that drove so many young people into the country. There is plenty of rye and wheat here in Russia, but there are no cultivated people. We need gifted, healthy young people to occupy themselves with science, art and politics.'

In all these speakers there is, as in *Ivanov*, the fullest study of the type, a good deal of that 'Russian excitability that is always followed by exhaustion'. They aim too high and they lose heart too soon. We are shown a better balanced nature in the heroine of *The wife*, who found happiness and a sense of mission in her charitable work for a village where the peasants had sold all their belongings and set out for the Siberian province of Tomsk, where they had hoped to find a new America, but like many others had had to return to worse misery than before, without ever seeing their promised land. Yet the zemstvo doctor Sobol, one of the 'individuals whose steady work was transforming the country in spite of the intellectuals' with their theories (Letter to Orlov, 22/2/1899), who seems to express Chekhov's own views on the peasant question more directly than any other of his characters, though he had great respect for Mme Asorin's efforts, had little faith in their efficacy. They had still to solve the elemental problems in Russia, he thought, which had existed with little change since the days of Rurik, with their village fires, famine, and ceaseless struggle with nature. Mere philanthropy was not enough, there was too much self-deception in it. The problem needed to be faced in a business-like way, with a full knowledge of the complicated facts. 'Oh, if we only talked less about our humane motives, reasoned and calculated better, and did our duty more conscientiously. How many of these humane men of feeling among us will go round with subscription lists, but fail to pay their tailors and cooks. There is no logic in our life, that's the trouble! No logic!' Logic and hard work were Chekhov's prescription for the fundamental socials ills of Russia, and few would deny that history has proved him right.

Before discussing some more recent views on Russia's peasant problem in the later nineteenth century, it may be useful to recall some of the established facts about the systems of land-tenure and agriculture prevailing there in that age. First as to agricultural technique: it is well known that the system which had prevailed in central Russia for three centuries or more before 1861 was the open field system, known in western Europe at least since Carolingian times and for many centuries the almost universal practice there. The manorial system in England familiar to us from school histories shows all its essential features. Even after enclosures had changed the face of the greater part of England, it prevailed in Scotland as 'run rig' until late in the eighteenth century, in most parts of Germany as the three field system until well into the nineteenth century, and there is even an isolated example of it, recently described most illuminatingly by C. S. and C. S. Orwin,[1] surviving at Laxton in Nottinghamshire to-day.

Under the open field system a certain number of families form a village partnership, to cultivate a stretch of country which in most cases their ancestors had no doubt cleared in the virgin forest. They do not live on scattered farms with their fields around them, but in a 'nucleated village', like the Russian villages described above. The arable land of the village is cultivated on a subsistence basis, not with a view to export, the village being relatively isolated. It is unfenced, except perhaps where it abuts on main roads, and is divided into three big fields. Each field is divided into a small number of 'furlongs', the size and lay-out of which vary with the contour of the land, and each furlong is subdivided into a series of parallel strips, each of a convenient size and shape for ploughing—originally no doubt for one team's work in a day. Each partner's holding in each of the three fields consists of a number of scattered strips from each 'furlong', not a block of contiguous strips. The effect of this is to ensure that all have a fair share of good and bad land, and of strips near to or distant from the village, though it may well be, as Mr. Orwin suggests, that originally 'the alternate strips, the furlongs and the fields themselves grew naturally out of the need to live, the common way of life and the practice of plough-farming'. Crops are raised in a three-year rotation, by which in any given year one of the three fields is under autumn-sown corn (wheat or rye), one under spring-sown corn (barley or oats, or perhaps a fodder crop like beans, peas, etc., and later clover), and the third lies fallow.

The arable land is much the largest part of the whole. A

[1] *The Open Fields*, Oxf., 1938.

smaller portion is permanent pasture, mostly low-lying meadows, and this too is divided up on the same principle of equality, each partner receiving small scattered strips on which to make hay, though after the hay harvest the temporary fences are removed and the village live stock are grazed there in common. A third portion of the land is the common, consisting of untouched woods and moorland, giving some pasturage, timber and fuel, and a reserve for use as arable if needed.

It is clear that under this system the village partners must work in co-operation with each other. There must be common cropping because of the intermingled strips, and a great many field operations must be carried out at agreed times and in an agreed way. Something like the English manorial court is there-fore essential to make the necessary arrangements. The manorial court was presided over by the lord's steward. It appointed officers, admitted new partners and allotted land to them, had boundaries remarked, decided what the common crops should be and when common operations should begin, made grazing rules, arranged for fencing and ditching, and decided a great many other matters concerning the village as a community, provision against fire, theft, vagrancy and so on. The Russian village assembly was exactly the same kind of body in origin, a practical necessity rather than a mystical creation, but it acquired or had thrust upon it functions which were unknown to the manorial court, though they were natural developments under serfdom and a highly centralised despotism.

The Russian village commune or 'Mir', of which this village assembly was the governing organ, was an agricultural workers' community, made up, it is true, of units which were in serf days not single families of two generations, as in England, but joint families of three, but otherwise very like village communities anywhere under the open field system as far as agricultural technique was concerned. But in a large proportion of villages in central Russia almost all the peasants were serfs until 1861, owned by the local landowner and influenced at every point by their obligations to him. A serf may be briefly defined as a superior kind of domestic animal. Some masters are kind to animals, because of their nature or out of self-interest, to get the best use out of them, and some are not. In Russia the only external check on them was the state, acting as a very inefficient and lax R.S.P.C.A. The state in this was also acting partly to guard its own interests, for it needed recruits for its armies and a share of what the peasant produced, in the form of the poll-tax, etc., for its treasury. It suited the government to make the village communes fiscal units, collectively responsible for taxation due to the state. It was this fact, that they were collectively responsible for taxation, and after 1861 for redemption payments on their land, which, as we have seen (p. 54) made the freedom granted in that year largely illusory.

The commune, presided over by its elected elder, if it was to be responsible for taxation and the provision of recruits, had to be given full control over its members' movements. They could not leave the village without a passport granted by it, and they could not evade their financial responsibility even by leaving. Because of the burdens which were thus thrust upon it through the unique social and political conditions obtaining in Russia, the Mir became a very important administrative organ. It still resembled the manorial court in some of its functions, but they were more or less matters of routine, except in regard to the important matter of the distribution of the available land. Whereas in England and most other countries under the open field system family holdings became hereditary, each partner cultivating the same collection of scattered strips year after year, in central Russia it became usual (apparently pari passu with the development of the open field system since about 1500) for the Mir to redistribute the communal lands periodically. The practice began in the more thickly populated central provinces round Moscow and spread outwards from there. In the nineteenth century general redistributions had become rare everywhere, but partial redistributions were common, until forbidden by law in 1893.

There was something paradoxical about the existence of a democratic organ like the Mir in the completely autocratic body of Russia, and it is not surprising that the 'discovery' of it by the German traveller Baron von Haxthausen in 1843 aroused the liveliest interest. In his description of it (published in German in 1847, the very year of the Communist Manifesto) he said: 'The Communes present an organic coherence and compact social strength which can be found nowhere else, and yield the incalculable advantage that no proletariate can be formed so long as they exist with their present constitution.' Maynard puts the position very clearly as follows: 'The Mir was the darling of the Slavophils for its specifically Slavonic character. The Populist-Socialist loved it because he saw in it the germ of a peculiarly Russian Socialism, which would give the go-by to the proletarianism of towns and the capitalism which oppressed Western Europe. The conservative politician saw in it the hope of keeping the peasant (presumably loyal and religious) apart from corrupting influences. But, all the time, life—or death—was too strong for all three, and the object of their affections was decaying before their eyes. The vitality of the Mir depended upon a virtual economic equality among its members, which made a reality of village democracy. The cash-nexus which established itself with the introduction of cash obligations, put an end to the equality, by giving scope to the talents of the more astute for self-aggrandisement: and the end of the equality meant the domination of the village meeting by the more prosperous, and the beginning of a class-struggle in the village. After it had lost its equalising function, the Mir retained that power of obstructing agricultural innovations which made it odious to the agricultural reformer, and its tendency to hold back the more active and enterprising of its members. But we shall err if we suppose that it was un-popular with the mass of its members. Most peasants did not expect to benefit by the withdrawal of restrictions and had neither energy nor cattle nor implements to do so. To the poor there seemed always the possibility of benefitting by a redistribution; and, even when landless, they retained their rights of common pasture, and feeding, though it were only for goats or poultry. The Mir remained in idea what it had long ceased to be in fact, an agent of equalisation; and equality made a stronger appeal than freedom: a fact which explains some things which would otherwise be unintelligible in the more recent history of Russia.'[1]

To supplement Chekhov's picture of the state of the peasantry, let us see how three particularly well-informed and fair-minded observers out of the large number who have discussed the question analyse the causes of peasant poverty and unrest after 1861. Mackenzie Wallace,[2] writing in 1905, with a close first-hand knowledge of Russia extending back to 1870, discusses first some of the reasons suggested by contemporaries. They are:

1. The demoralisation of the common people—laziness and drunkenness. This explains a little, but not much.

2. The system of peasant self-government in the Mir, adminis-trative and judicial abuses, and the open field system with redistribution, hampering agricultural progress. These he finds

[1] *Russia in Flux*, 32.
[2] Russia II, 208 ff.

also of secondary importance. Much more fundamental reasons are:

3. Inordinate taxation and redemption payments. That these were of great importance is indicated by the fact that the government found it necessary to reduce them progressively, by the abolition of the salt-tax and poll-tax (1880, 1882) and various reductions of redemption payments, leading up to the abolition of joint liability (1903) and cancellation of redemption payments (1905).

4. The dislocation of economic life through the emancipation. The peasant had in practice the choice either of farming his allotted land and spending a great part of the year in idleness, or of leaving the cultivation to his wife and children and seeking employment elsewhere, often at a great distance. In either case time and energy were wasted.

5. The breaking up of the joint family. 'Many large families . . . rich according to peasant conceptions dissolved into three or four small ones, all on the brink of pauperism.'

6. Most important of all, the natural increase of population without a corresponding increase in the means of subsistence.

G. Pavlovsky,[1] formerly of the Russian ministry of agriculture, writing in 1930, considers the problem in relation to the economic development of the country as a whole. New points in his analysis are:

1. A subsistence economy was not made into a capitalistic one by providing free labour alone (at the emancipation), without capital. Without abundant capital and great industrial development, the rapid progress of agriculture was impossible.

2. The main trouble was not, as the peasants themselves thought, lack of land. They had not a bad share of it, and even if they had had it all, it would not have been sufficiently productive without radical changes in technique. These in their turn depended on (1), being hindered by lack of capital investment in agricultural industry, and by the lack of a varied demand from the towns such as made intensive cultivation economic in western Europe.

3. (A combination of Mackenzie Wallace's 2 and 3.) There was an inherent contradiction between a subsistence technique and the necessity to raise cash.

4. (A restatement of Mackenzie Wallace's 4 and 6.) The rapid growth of the rural population, without a sufficient overflow

[1] *Agric. Russia on the eve of the Revolution.*

into industry or undeveloped land, or a sufficiency of domestic industries, etc., for slack periods, or an increased yield of the soil. The growth of the population he ascribes in part to the Mir, because it relieved the individual peasant from responsibility for the excessive increase of his family. This is one answer to Haxthausen's claim above.

Sir John Maynard[1] lastly, while appreciating all these arguments, stresses 'the outrage upon human dignity which the legal and illegal status of the peasantry continued to tolerate. The law for the peasant was the will of the official and of the landlord'.

To return to the vivid concreteness of Chekhov after this long excursus, we may note some answers which he suggests to the question so often discussed by the peasants, whether they were better off after the emancipation than before. They had at any rate talked more interestingly in their discontent in the old days, he says in *Peasants*. Every old man then looked as if he was guarding some secret, as if he knew something and was expecting something. Now they had no secrets from each other, and could only talk about their misery and about food. In the evening the old grandfather would often tell them tales of the good old days, when there was a time for work, a time for eating and a time for sleep, when they had had their shchi and kasha (cabbage-soup and buckwheat porridge) regularly for dinner, and shchi and kasha for supper too, not skilly or tea and bread, as so often now. They had had as many cucumbers and cabbages as they liked too, and could always eat their fill. People were better behaved then. The bad ones might be beaten with rods or sent to another estate far away, but the good received rewards. There was more variety in their life through the gentry, a share in their hunting, and vodka for all when they were acting as beaters. Children and grandchildren never tired of listening to the old man's tales, and the group of little girls looked down wide-eyed from the top of the stove like a host of cherubim in the clouds. But even poor timid Marya, the mother of six, was heard next morning, when she had slept on it all, murmuring to herself as she lit the fire: 'No, freedom is better.' They were wretched, but they were not dependent now on the whims of a 'barin' who, as granny had told them, was a drunken and dissipated spendthrift, whose own family had all come to a bad end.

The 87-year-old lackey Firs, in *The cherry orchard*, speaks of the emancipation as 'the misfortune'. He had elected to stay on with

[1] *Russia in Flux.*

his master, like many domestic serfs. Serfs under a good master had certainly been better off than most free peasants later, though under a bad master the position of domestic serfs was worst of all. We have a picture of the ideal relationship in the household of Ivan Ivanovitch in *The wife*. Everything in his enormous old house was in the patriarchal mould, the furniture, made for eternity by local craftsmen, the gargantuan repast served for dinner, after which all participants were obliged to lie down for a long rest, like the old Oblomovs in Goncharov's novel, and the excessive number of devoted servants. Two women took off the guest's coat in the vestibule, a muzhik in a red shirt hung it up, and various bare-footed little girls and other figures flitted about the house. They turned out to be serfs, orphans with nowhere to go to, faithful servants who would not be driven away, or old retainers living out their days in their old home, like the old people in the servants' quarters in *The cherry orchard*. But these were survivals of a dead past, and this play itself, as we shall see in the next chapter, celebrates the passing of the agrarian age of Russian history, with all its associations, its beauty and its injustice, and the arrival of a commercial and industrial age which, crude as it is, holds out the promise of a better world than the old if men will think and work with a will.

CHAPTER IV

THE LANDOWNER

Russian society was still divided at the end of the nineteenth century, like France before the Revolution, into orders or estates with unequal legal rights. 81.6% were classified as peasants, but they would include a considerable number of urban proletariate of peasant origin at one extreme, and of prosperous farmers at the other. 9.3% were merchants and lesser townsfolk, 6.1% military, 0.9% clergy, and 1.3% gentry. Apart from the military, these were at least in theory hereditary classes, so that sons of village priests who did not enter the church or merchants' sons who did not trade had to be classified for passport purposes as miscellaneous 'raznochintsy' ('of no particular class'). They were no longer water-tight compartments in fact, and if one became a civil servant, there was by now a regular hierarchy, a ladder of fourteen rungs which could be climbed, though until 1906 not beyond a certain point by peasants. The 'estates' ('sostoyaniya', imitated from the German 'Stände') had developed since the time of Peter the Great out of the primary distinction, which still left clear traces, especially on peasant thought, between 'masters' (gospoda) and 'people' (narod), the ·bearded and the clean-shaven—the gentry had of course been compelled by Peter to shave their chins.

Among the smooth-faced there were wide variations. We may note first the distinction, something like that made in Germany between high and lesser nobility, between the old aristocracy, claiming descent from Rurik, or Lithuanian or Tartar rulers, and the 'pomeshchiki' or country squires. The former, to whose number only fourteen families had been added by the Emperor since 1700, bore the title 'knyaz'. There were also about 70 counts and ten barons (these mostly foreign bankers) dating from Peter's time, and the Baltic aristocracy of German origin. The 'pomeshchiki' were descended from 'men of service' who had received grants of land from the Emperor for military or other state service, particularly in the period following the great expansion and tightening-up of the central power in the reign of Ivan the Great (just before 1500). When trade and a money economy were little developed this was the only convenient means of payment a ruler had. It was in exactly the same way that 'ministeriales' in Germany had been rewarded three or four centuries earlier, and as with them, the estates granted at first temporarily, during the tenure of office, became hereditary, and gave rise to a landed class similar in many ways to the old aristocracy.

But the gentry of Russia had in other respects a very different history behind them from that of their counterparts in Germany, or in France and England. In all three countries the aristocracy had a much stronger esprit de corps, born of the struggle to defend their privileges against the monarchy and the rising middle class. In Russia they had had to toe the line with the rest of the Czar's subjects from an early date, under a despotism influenced by oriental traditions. They had derived their rights from the monarch alone, and Peter the Great had insisted on service to the state from all in return for these rights, which he readily conferred on others, of whatever origin they might be, who served him well. Thus rank in the official hierarchy came to confer higher social distinction than did hereditary rank. 'We find plenty of Russians who are proud of their wealth, of their culture, or of their official position,' says Mackenzie Wallace, 'but we rarely find a Russian who is proud of his birth.' Even the court nobility had none of the characteristics of a closed caste, he says, found for instance in Germany, and titles in general did not mean as much as in the west. Nor was the Russian nobility rooted in its native soil in the same way as in the West. They did not call themselves after their native seats, there was nothing in their titles corresponding to the French 'de' or the German 'von'. There were in fact no family seats of the baronial type at all. 'Nature herself in Russia,' says Leroy-Beaulieu, 'seems to discourage these domestic fortresses, it refused, so to speak, both site and materials for them, steep rocks on which to build them and stone for their walls. The wooden house, so often burnt down, so quickly decayed, so easy to move and to rebuild, is a true symbol of Russian life. The very type of their homes is an indication of the uncertain fortunes of the aristocracy.' Some authorities contend that there was in consequence less class feeling in Russia than in the West, but whatever the truth may be about that, there was at the least mutual aloofness between gentlemen and peasantry, which rapidly increased after the Emancipation as old ideas of a social hierarchy broke down.[1]

The ideal age of the gentry had been the reign of Catherine II, for she had confirmed their privileges, and also the abolition decreed by her husband Peter III in 1762, just before she usurped the throne, of that obligation to serve which alone justified their privileged position. They had succeeded in following in this the example of the German and French aristocracy, and Catherine, like the petty princes of her native country, did everything she could to make her court brilliant and impressive on the model of Versailles, while attracting the gentry to the public service by social and material rewards, instead of driving them by sheer compulsion. It was the beginning of the westernising movement in Russian culture, built on the foundation of Peter the Great's state as power. As in Germany, the cultivated courtier had to speak French, the language of civilisation, and his country cousin followed his example as best he could, but this was only a necessary step to the creation of that great national literature in the European tradition, of which Pushkin, in the next generation, was the first outstanding figure.

In the century between 1762 and 1861 the land-owning class, enjoying a life of sheltered ease based on serf labour, were the undisputed leaders in Russian literature and thought, and by far the most influential section of the reading public, which was of course small. There was a popular literature, addressed to the lower middle and tradesman class of the towns, but it was quite separate from literature in the European tradition, and consisted at first of chapbook romances and lives of saints. The literature of what Prince Mirsky calls the 'Golden age of Russian poetry' has an eighteenth-century, 'Augustan' flavour, although contemporary with the European Romantic movement, principally because of 'its distinct social colouring. It was a movement inside the gentry, a movement of *gentlemen*. Hence, in its early stages, the prevalence of light, society verse, of convivial and anacreontic subjects; the cult of friendship, of good company, and of wine. Socially the age of Pushkin marks the high-water mark of the literary hegemony of the gentry. Higher literature is completely monopolized by men of that class.'[2] After the Decembrist Revolt (1825) and the repression of liberal opinion among the gentry which followed it, lower class journalists came to the fore, leading

---

[1] Maynard, *Russia in Flux*, 111 ff.
[2] Mirsky, *History of Russian Literature to 1881*, 96.

up to Belinsky, the son of an army doctor, 'the father of the intelligentsia'. 'Socially he marks the end of the rule of the gentry and the advent of the non-class intelligentsia of raznochintsy to cultural leadership' (Mirsky). Yet the great age of the realistic novel which followed would be poor indeed without the names of Aksakov, Goncharov, Turgeniev, Tolstoy and Shchedrin, following Gogol in the preceding period, all sprung from the land-owning class.

Besides the small number of country gentlemen with literary or scientific leanings there were of course a great many who were primarily officials, serving in some town, and leaving the management of their estates entirely to their bailiff, and probably a still larger number who were backwoodsmen of the type described by Aksakov in his charming *Family chronicle*, or Goncharov in Oblomov's dream, or Mackenzie Wallace in his picture of landed proprietors of the old school. The latter's Ivan Ivanovitch, who is extraordinarily like the elder Oblomov, gave the impression of living entirely outside the struggle for existence. He had been educated at home, and never made to work hard lest it should injure his health. Having no natural inclination for any kind of activity he gladly accepted a nominal official post which allowed him to live on his estate and steadily rise in rank. His marriage with the only daughter of a neighbour was arranged by his parents and turned out happily, for his wife found contentment in satisfying his simple material wants, and monotony did not trouble either of them. Every day in summer he would sit by an open window, sometimes questioning a passing servant and giving him an order. After an ample midday meal, the whole household slept for a couple of hours; even the servants could be heard snoring in the corridors. Then came tea, a drive in the fields, some talk with the peasants and long discussions of plans for next day with the steward. Occasionally there was a visitor, but their chief link with the outside world was through their two sons in the army, though to write a letter to one of them was a serious bit of work that was not embarked on lightly. They read little and did not even play cards, the chief resource of bored officials in country retirement. It was enough just to live and meditate.

Chekhov introduces us to a number of country squires who are made in the same mould as Ivan Ivanovitch, but have had the bottom knocked out of their world by the collapse of the serf system. They find themselves no longer in a self-contained little world where with the minimum of effort and thought they find their simple needs supplied. 'For many of them, who could carry on, somehow, in the old traditional ways, but possessed neither the capital nor the knowledge and initiative necessary to re-organize their farming on new lines, the Emancipation spelt ruin. Indeed, the qualifications now required of a large farmer were very different from those of the old-fashioned Russian country squire. In the case of the latter, one of the principal items of costs did not count, since the necessary labour was supplied by the serfs, who were paid for it not in money, but in land—a commodity still plentiful and possessing in itself, apart from the peasants' labour, very little value. The cost of equipment was also reduced to a minimum, the cultivation of the fields and the cartage of produce being done by the peasants with their own stock. . . . The commercial problems of farming were easily solved, even when, in the second quarter of the last century, the excessive concentration on the production of cereals brought their prices down to a very low level. Since the Emancipation everything changed completely, and the problems of labour and of capital assumed an enormous importance, especially in those localities in which the population was relatively sparse, the peasants' holdings more or less sufficient or easily supplemented by leases, or where other sources of earnings diverted the peasants from employment on the land. Moreover, the peasants had still to get used to employment as hired labour, while the land owners had to learn to handle free labour over which they did not possess the disciplinary powers which made the management of serf labour relatively easy. . . . The extreme shortage of capital was another difficulty, only partly mitigated by the issue to the land owners of redemption bonds in payment for the land allocated to their former serfs.'[1]

Small or thriftless land owners were therefore almost always heavily in debt, living from hand to mouth in houses with perhaps signs of former glories but badly in need of repair, surrounded by neglected woods and fields. Their attitude to life was marked by lack of initiative and energy, combined with a certain Micawber-like fatalism, the product of a long tradition of easy living. One of the old school is seen in Vera's grandfather in *At home*, who sat in the same place day in, day out, playing patience or dozing, ate enormous meals in spite of his age, and glared at the servants. In the old days it had been twenty-five strokes of the birch for the slightest offence, but now only the steward occasionally beat

---

[1] Pavlovsky, *op. cit.*, 99 f.

them. Everything on the estate was neglected, 'in fact there was no systematic farming. They ploughed and sowed simply from habit' and little work was done, although the bustle in the house began at five in the morning. In summer the old man would sometimes drive out to look at the oats and hay. When quarter day drew near they began to look depressed, and aunt Dasha asked Vera to help them with the interest on the mortgage, from the money she had inherited from her engineer father. A younger man, equally feckless, is the prince in *A trivial incident*, 'a man of no great gifts, with something oriental about him. He was straightforward and honest, not a bully, a fop or a rake, and therefore in the eyes of the general run of people rather a colourless nonentity'. He was known in the district as 'His Excellency the Dunce', but the narrator liked him and sympathized with him in the endless series of misfortunes and failures that marked his life. In the first place, he was poor. He had somehow contrived to get through the thirty to forty thousand roubles left to him by his father, though he did not play cards, or speculate, or spend money on women. His stewards, agents and even lackeys ran away with a lot, for lack of supervision, and he was carelessly generous in loans and gifts to all comers, not so much from kindness of heart or over-trustfulness as from the desire to appear the perfect gentleman. There was hardly a squire in the district who was not in his debt, and he was now hopelessly insolvent himself. Some days he would go without lunch and carry an empty cigar case, but he was always well-groomed, fashionably dressed and scented with ilang-ilang. Secondly he was terribly lonely. He was unmarried, and had neither relatives nor friends. He did not easily become intimate with people because of his silent reserve and the exaggerated correctness with which he masked his poverty. He saw little of women and could not be bothered with romances. A certain sincerity and delicacy of feeling, or what he called his abnormal timidity, prevented him from marrying a rich neighbour who was in love with him or, even when his estate was about to be sold up, from taking an official post for which he felt he had no qualifications, though he saw many around him drawing salaries for nothing.

In *Ariadne* there is another decayed gentleman, a bankrupt squire, who had pine-apples and wonderful peaches growing on his estate, and a fountain in the middle of the courtyard, but not a penny in his pocket. He did nothing, knew nothing, was as spineless as if made out of a boiled turnip, and occupied himself with homœopathy and spiritualism. His sister, a beautiful clever girl, was utterly reckless with the family property. If she needed a riding-horse and had no money, she would have a portion of the iron roof torn off and sold for scrap, or sell farm horses for a song in the middle of the harvest. The story of her love affair with an idealistic young neighbour is a study in cold sensuality and love of power.

There is hardly a single land owner in the stories and plays who is not in debt. In *Neighbours* the proprietor of the neighbouring estate, who has such an inexplicable attraction for Ivashin's sister, is paying 12% on a second mortgage, and to raise the interest is reduced to asking all his friends for loans. He is so improvident that when short of fuel he will burn a length of trellis or a cold frame from the garden, after selling all his winter store of fire-wood for five roubles. In politics he is a woolly-minded liberal, who makes any idea that he talks about sound dull and commonplace. He married à la Dostoyevsky, from pity, a girl seduced by a fellow-officer, only to find that he had caught a Tartar, and even at forty-one he is still on the look-out for prodigies of moral valour to perform. He is the kind of fool whose eyes are in the ends of the earth, who will never be able to lay to heart, though he needs it more than most, Goethe's advice to regard as his duty 'what the day requires of him'.

The fullest study of this ineffective quixotism, which Chekhov considered to be so common in his time, is in his first serious play, *Ivanov*. When it was about to be produced in St. Petersburg the company misunderstood it so badly that Chekhov wrote a long letter explaining the characters. 'Ivanov is a gentleman, a university man, and not remarkable in any way. He is excitable, hot-headed, easily carried away, honest and straightforward like most people of his class. He has lived on his estate and served on the zemstvo. What he has been doing and how he has behaved, what he has been interested in and enthusiastic over, can be seen from the following words of his, addressed to the doctor (Act I, scene 5): "Don't marry Jewesses or neurotic women or blue-stockings . . . don't fight with thousands single-handed, don't wage war on windmills, don't batter your head against the wall. . . . God preserve you from scientific farming, wonderful schools, enthusiastic speeches . . ." This is what he has in his past. . . . His past is beautiful, as is generally the case with educated Russians. There is not, or there hardly is, a single Russian gentle-man or university man who does not boast of his past. Why?

Because Russian excitability has one specific characteristic: it is quickly followed by exhaustion. A man has scarcely left the class-room before he rushes to take up a burden beyond his strength; he tackles at once the schools, the peasants, scientific farming, and the *Vyestnik Evropi*, he makes speeches, writes to the minister, combats evil, applauds good, falls in love, not in an ordinary, simple way, but selects either a blue-stocking or a neurotic or a Jewess, or even a prostitute whom he tries to save, and so on, and so on. But by the time he is thirty he begins to feel tired and bored. . . . He is ready to reject the zemstvo and scientific farming, and science and love. . . . He looks for the causes outside himself and fails to find them; he begins to look for them inside and finds only an indefinite feeling of guilt. It is a Russian feeling. . . . To exhaustion, boredom, and the feeling of guilt add one more enemy: loneliness. Were Ivanov an official, an actor, a priest, a professor, he would have grown used to his position. But he lives on his estate. He is in the country. His neighbours are either drunkards or fond of cards, or are of the same type as the doctor. . . . But life makes its legitimate demands on him, he must settle problems. . . . Men like Ivanov do not solve difficulties but collapse under their weight.'[1] It is interesting to note that Leroy-Beaulieu in the early 'eighties made a very similar observation about the Russian character, in discussing the rapid cooling-off of the ideals of the 'sixties: 'Dans l'âme russe le découragement semble toujours sur les pas de l'enthousiasme, l'abattement suit de près l'exaltation.'

In his last and finest play, *The cherry orchard*, Chekhov returns to the theme of the land-owning class and its problems, but he presents their failure now not so much as a matter of personal or national character as of changing conditions of life. The play symbolises, poetically, yet without ever losing touch with reality, the transition from a purely agrarian to a more and more industrial Russia. It brings home to us the perplexity of the older generation of the aristocracy as the ground slips from under their feet, their attachment to the home and the way of life of their youth, with the sentiments of carefree ease and beauty associated with them in their minds, and their inability to master either their economic or their personal problems by resolutely facing facts. The central characters are the mondaine Liubov Andreyevna, the owner, with her brother Gaev, of an estate with a fine old cherry orchard, and Lopakhin, the merchant son of

[1] *Letters*, tr. Garnett, 111 ff.

the village shopkeeper. We have come across him already as a representative of the peasant who has risen out of his class, in the new age of money, through his energy and business ability. Though he stands for another world, he is not hostile to Liubov. On the contrary, he remembers with gratitude her kindness to him as a boy. But the aristocrats, almost in spite of themselves, tend to look down on him, and his proposal for saving their estate, by letting the ground where the cherry orchard stands for building sites, fills them with horror. It is simply unthinkable, yet they see no other way out of their predicament. They watch their doom approaching with paralysed will, still vaguely hoping that somehow they will escape, and bringing their ruin nearer all the time by the reckless extravagance to which they are accustomed.

Gaev, the brother, and his friend Simeonov-Pishchik, are merely background figures, not drawn in the round, but they suggest two types of decadent squire, the one seeking refuge from reality in fine words and sentiments, or solacing himself with billiards and lollypops, and the other, cruder, living on his friends, until minerals are found on his land by English prospectors. The Chekhov who wrote to Suvorin in 1891: 'Alas, I shall never be a Tolstoyan. In women I love beauty above all things; and in the history of mankind, culture, expressed in carpets, carriages with springs, and keenness of wit'—was drawn emotionally, one feels, to his aristocrats, as Goethe had been to his poet Tasso. But just as Goethe's wisdom had seen something right too in the prosaic Antonio, because even poets must have some regard for the society around them, so Chekhov would have the Russians realise that Lopakhin is a good fellow, and that what he represents is something to which Russia has to reconcile herself. For post-revolutionary critics he is even too kind to this bourgeois. He tries to marry him off with Varya, Liubov's adopted daughter, but there is always a hitch, perhaps because their classes are not quite ripe for fusion. And he holds out hope for the future in his picture of Liubov's young daughter, Anya, and the former tutor, Trofimov. Trofimov, the 'eternal student', the raisonneur of the piece, is given lines which express Chekhov's own thought as we know it from his letters, that men have little till now to be proud of; they should cease to be so pleased with themselves and simply work, as at present few do in Russia. Anya, under his influence, is ready to part from her dear cherry orchard. There will be still better places in the world that is yet to be. 'All Russia is our garden', Trofimov tells her, and the garden they are leaving is spoilt for them by the odour of serfdom which still clings to it. But this young man himself, who has not succeeded at thirty in taking a degree, is not a very promising leader towards the better world. As a representative of revolutionary youth he is not really convincing, and that not merely because of the caution imposed on any author by the censorship, say post-revolutionary critics.[1] It may be, as they assume, because Chekhov was here drawing a type he did not know sufficiently well. Or it may be that he saw a good deal of the Ivanov even in Trofimov, and could not help treating him with a certain irony.

We are shown a few exceptions to the general rule of feckless-ness and impoverishment among the landowners. A man could still make a living on a small estate, but only if he was prepared for hard physical work himself, like Alekhin in *Gooseberries* and *About love*, who looked more like an artist or professor than a pomeshchik, and was found by unexpected visitors in a dirty shirt and bathing pants, his face black with dust, working at the winnowing machine. He lived in two dark little rooms in the servants' quarters of his house. He had tried at first to live like a gentleman after the day's work, but now he hardly ever entered his big drawing room hung with old family portraits, though he still kept on his old staff of servants, who had nowhere to go to. If he went to a meeting of the justices in town, for a sight of civilised people, he found he could hardly keep awake. In *The black monk* there is another landowner, who makes a success of arboriculture on a large scale, but only by a fanatical concentra-tion of effort. There were no doubt many like Nicolai Ivanovitch in *Gooseberries*, who were prepared for any sacrifice if they could live in the country in freedom, and if forced by circumstances to live in town would long for the day when they could grow their own gooseberries again, for 'whoever as a boy has fished for perch, or seen migrating thrushes passing over the village in swarms on clear cool autumn days, is spoilt for life as a town dweller, and to his dying day he will feel himself drawn back towards freedom'. Yet as Chekhov makes the narrator say, there was something selfish in this Tolstoyan self-sufficiency and withdrawal from the world, 'a monkishness without heroic self-denial'. 'Clearly, the happy man is easy in mind only because the unhappy bear their burden in silence, and but for this silence his happiness would be impossible. There ought to stand at the door of every self-

[1] E.g. S. Balukhaty, in *Klassiki russkoi dramy*, Leningrad and Moscow, 1940.

satisfied happy man someone with a hammer, to remind him continually by his knocking that there are unhappy people in the world' and that suffering is integral in life. It is Lavrov's cry of conscience we hear in this passage (see page 32).

These and many other pictures bring home to us the variety of human nature represented among the country gentlemen of Russia, who had perhaps more than any similar class elsewhere free room for the indulgence of eccentricities. There is the charming handsome bachelor Khanov in *The schoolmistress*, a man of education and refinement, who is content to spend his days pacing up and down his spacious rooms whistling, or playing chess with his lackeys, and gradually drinking himself to death, or at the other extreme the retired Cossack officer, hardly a gentleman, and not a peasant either, 'philosophising' and boring stray visitors on his lonely farm in the steppes, while his two sons run wild, without any education, and a wretched wife slaves for a husband who 'does not consider women to be human beings' (*The Pechenyeg*). In general, though they are often in difficulties, their whole way of life and that of the masses are poles asunder. The contrast is well expressed in *On official duty*, in the dream of the young examining magistrate called out in winter for a postmortem in a small village on an insurance agent, an impoverished gentleman who had not been able to accept another way of life. After some hours on a heap of hay in an izba he is taken by his companion, the zemstvo doctor, to a friend's country house, where all is brightness and gaiety. It seems incredible that, in an hour, one can be transported from one world to another, only three versts away. At night he dreams of the dead man and the old village policeman to whose life story he had been listening in the izba. They seem to be singing in chorus: 'We tramp, we tramp, we tramp. . . . You are in warm rooms, in brightness and comfort, while we tramp through the frost, the snow-storm, the deep drifts. . . . We know no rest, no gladness. . . . We bear on our shoulders all the burden of this life, both ours and yours. . . . We tramp, we tramp, we tramp. . . .' . . . 'And he felt that this suicide and the misery of the peasants were a weight on his conscience; to be reconciled to the fact that these people, resigned to their lot, should take upon themselves everything in life that is dark and grievous to bear—how monstrous that was!'

But not many amongst the fortunate few were so sensitive. The chief desire of a minority of the gentry at one extreme, balancing the 'conscience-stricken' at the other, was to abate nothing of their claims to privilege and to exclude others rigidly from their class. Such is for instance the *Last of the Mohicans*, a dragon of a woman, who is hauling her meek husband before the Marshal of the Gentry (the gentry like the other estates had their corporate organisation, with a marshal at its head in each district), to complain of his letting down his family name and honour by mixing with merchants and going shooting with his clerk. This is in Chekhov's early vein and rather a caricature, but *At a country house* (1894), from his middle period, conveys, with more personal feeling, a similar idea of aristocratic exclusiveness. The old bore Rashevitch, living on a lonely estate with his two marriageable daughters, in conversation with the only eligible young man who ever calls on him, the examining magistrate Meier, gets on to his hobby-horse, the virtues of *blue blood*, and is making the most extravagant assertions about alleged middle-class intruders, when to his consternation, and the despair of his daughters, Meier tells him that he is himself from the lower middle class, the son of a working man. One of the old man's remarks makes us wonder whether Chekhov had not some time suffered from this kind of talk himself: 'In fact as soon as your proletarian gets above himself, he begins to sicken, to waste away, to go off his head and degenerate, and you will not find so many neurasthenics, mental cripples, consumptives and weaklings of every kind anywhere, as among these fine birds. They die off like flies in autumn.'

If it was important to keep outsiders in their place, it was equally so to maintain traditional ideas of decent behaviour within the class. It was a scandal not only if a son was openly dishonest (as in *A problem*), but also if he engaged for instance in 'black' manual work. In *My life* an architect of good family disinherits his son because the boy, with Tolstoyan ideas in his head, refuses office work and becomes a house-painter. At one point he is even summoned before the governor of the province, because of his father's complaint to the provincial marshal of nobility, and politely threatened with extreme measures if he does not either return to work befitting his station, or leave for a district where he is not known. For girls there was of course the usual taboo on marriage out of their class, and a still stricter one on irregular unions. Even the Azhogin family in *My life*, who had spent so much of their life making light of prejudices, such as reading by the light of three candles (considered unlucky), beginning important tasks on the 13th, and so on, found the

4

prejudice against unmarried mothers too much for them. The ordinary nice girl of this class had thoroughly Victorian ideas about marriage; to be left an old maid was a great misfortune. *The trousseau* is a study of gentlefolk bound by the traditions of their class, and the pathetic or even tragic effect of the passage of time. We see the little house of a colonel's family in a quiet Moscow street, a white house overshadowed by trees. In the drawing-room the atmosphere is stuffy, with a smell of mothballs; the portrait of a bishop hangs on the wall. It is the setting for one of those stories of a respectable army family which could be paralleled in many literatures, the shy daughter with whole chests full of her home-made trousseau, who waits in vain, the father's death, and the uncle, the skeleton in the family cupboard, who sells the precious trousseau for drink and has to be reported to the marshal of the nobility. In some respects it is a first attempt at the tragic atmosphere of the much more subtle and moving *Three sisters*. It is obvious that this conception of marriage has nothing whatever in common with that of the peasantry, described above, and that the difference corresponds to that between the social and economic conditions in the two classes.

Lack of respect for men as men is perhaps the worst of reproaches in the eyes of Chekhov, the grandson of a serf, and it is one that is implied not infrequently in his depiction of the aristocracy of his day. Gorky felt it behind the description of a 'well-fed squire's mockery of a person lonely and strange to her surroundings' in *A daughter of Albion*, though it may be doubted whether he correctly interpreted Chekhov's intention in this early humorous story. Here and in *In a strange land* most Russian readers would probably be more conscious of the criticism of the foreigners. Perhaps, as in *The darling*, according to Tolstoy's interpretation, Chekhov's heart unconsciously triumphed over his intellect—'Like Balaam, he intended to curse, but the god of poetry forbade him, and commanded him to bless'. In *An upheaval*, anyhow, · describing the trials of a governess in an aristocratic family, where the vulgar domineering mistress of the house, a type rather like the Count's wife mentioned in a letter to Suvorin (16/8/1892), towards whom Chekhov had 'the stupid schoolboy feeling of wanting to be rude', has every room searched because a brooch is missing, the intention is perfectly clear. In reality it is the hen-pecked husband who has taken it, or rather taken it back. His wife will not trust a 'pauper', a teacher's daughter, however well educated, and as the maid says: 'You're living with strangers, miss, and though you're a lady—you're a sort of servant here.' Vera finds the same inhumanity in her grandfather and aunt in *At home*. She must not speak to common workmen; her aunt even dismisses one because he is illegitimate, and her grandfather is constantly lifting his stick from old habit.

The story *The princess*, finally, is a regular indictment of some characteristics of the nobility displayed by a vain, empty-headed princess who imagines herself to be conferring a great favour on a monastery by using it from time to time as a quiet hotel. The criticism is put into the mouth of a doctor, formerly in her service, whom she meets again there, and incautiously invites to be perfectly frank with her. First among her faults he puts her lack of human sympathy. That is why she needs so many lackeys to keep out strangers, soft carpets to deaden human footfalls, hushed voices to spare her nerves. She treats all who live on her estates as material for her sole use. The common people are not thought of by her as human; even her distinguished visitors are for her a decoration, not living men. With a fortune of over a million she has done nothing for the common good, for her so-called benevolence, her home for old men, her village school, her crèche, is a farce, in which she plays the part of good fairy, but without deceiving anyone, for all avoid her benefits like the plague, feeling that there is no love behind them. To her her protégés are like so many more lap-dogs, living dolls. If she only treated her servants humanely, and not like outcasts! Her visits to the monastery are another game of hers, in which her rôle is that of pious benefactress. The monks waste their time on her without even material compensation; it takes three days to prepare for her visits, and she has given them a hundred roubles in all. In her heart she has her own god, to whom she thinks she comes near in spiritualistic séances. The Church really means nothing to her whatever. But far more than words are needed to disturb the princess's complacency. She feels herself misunderstood for the moment, but after praying for her enemies, supping in luxury and sleeping long, she leaves next day serene and perfectly happy, re-established in her own esteem as the angel of the house.

One is reminded of Turgeniev's earlier sketch of a Lady Bountiful (in *Death—A Sportsman's Sketches*), who had 'founded a hospital'. She had had a board with the inscription 'Krasnogorye Hospital' nailed up over the door of a lodge on her estate, and handed the Feldscher in charge a red album in which to record the names of patients. On its first page a friend and admirer of hers had written:

> Dans ces beaux lieux, où regne l'allégresse
> Ce temple fut ouvert par la Beauté;
> De vos seigneurs admirez la tendresse
> Bons habitants de Krasnogorié!

Thankful for small mercies, the Feldscher had bought six beds at his own expense, and with the help of a semi-lunatic and a one-armed peasant woman set about healing 'God's people'.

We are brought back to the question of the 'conscience-stricken gentry' touched upon in the last chapter. Again we see what wide circles had been moved by the desire to 'serve the people', yet how mixed were the motives of many such benefactors. How complex the system of conflicting ideas and emotions could be in their mind is well seen in *The wife*, a study of the uneasy conscience of the landowner Asorin. When once brought to his notice, the poverty of the neighbouring village gave him no peace of mind, Chekhov suggests, for a great variety of reasons. He was in the first place a fundamentally decent man, with some feeling for his fellows, but into his sympathy there entered also the egoistic motive of getting rid of a disturbing influence which prevented him from settling to his literary work, as well as the uneasiness of a misanthrope who instinctively disliked and distrusted people and was therefore suspicious of the organizers of relief for this village, and the vanity of an ex-official, which made him think that nothing could be organized properly without his help. More and more it is borne in upon him in the course of the story that the source of his spiritual malaise lies very deep, in his habit of treating others not as personalities but as tools, and that this is also the cause of the estrangement from his wife which still further complicates his attitude towards the relief work, for he discovers that she has been planning it for months. The contrast figure to Asorin in the story is the old-fashioned Ivan Ivanovitch already mentioned, with his house full of former serfs, a model of humanity in his little island of existence, yet a flabby survival of a good type of gentleman, living precariously on inherited capital, completely out of touch with the new life springing up around him. The tangle of social and individual motives underlying the behaviour of Asorin, the nobleman, ex-official, intellectual and human being, is a salutary reminder, such as we are constantly encountering in Chekhov's pages, of the artificiality of any attempt to consider one social class in isolation, or any individual merely as a representative of his class. It is the poet's truth, which tells us

'Wer will was Lebendigs erkennen und beschreiben
Sucht erst den Geist herauszutreiben'

or 'We murder to dissect'.

CHAPTER V

THE OFFICIAL CLASS. ADMINISTRATION, JUSTICE, POLICE

It was not until the year after Chekhov's death that the first timid steps were taken in Russia towards a constitutional government. In his lifetime Russia was a complete autocracy, ruled by a bureaucracy subject to no popular control, except in matters of local government, highly centralised, but so vast as to be quite beyond the effective control of the Monarch at its head. Yet this bureaucracy had for generations attempted to keep its finger on Russian life in all its most important aspects, and in fact to civilize the country by decree. A stream of papers had passed out from the Ministries in St. Petersburg to every corner of the great empire, first to the head towns of the provinces or 'governments', from these to the head towns of the districts into which each province was subdivided, and from these again to the smaller towns and villages. Their scope was amazing. Until the 1860's, not a country school or church could be built which was not planned in St. Petersburg, a fact which explains their striking uniformity, and the same machine-made regularity characterised the whole network of Russian institutions.

The government officials who worked the system were 'chinovniks', that is, each had a clearly defined *chin* or rank in the service. It was Peter the Great who had introduced the 'table of ranks' with its fourteen degrees. The whole of Russian society became a sort of army in which everyone had his rank, and this rank determined his status in society and settled all questions of precedence. 'The system of grades,' H. W. Williams wrote in 1915, 'is one of the forces that hold the bureaucracy together. It secures a certain uniformity of temper, tendency and aim. Russians are the most democratic people in the world, but this carefully adjusted system of grades, decorations, money premiums and, to close with, pensions, corresponding to the *chin* attained, appeals to an ineradicable human instinct for outward symbols of position, security and distinction, and makes of the bureaucracy a world apart, a world in which the interests of all the members are interwoven.' Just as there are equivalent ranks, with different names, in our own army, navy and air force, so in the Russian army, navy and civil service as well there were fourteen grades of officers, and of course a great mass of privates with no *chin* at all. At the bottom in the civil service, corresponding to the 'ensign' in the army, was the 'college registrar'; at the top, on the level of the field marshal, was the chancellor, and in between came the other twelve grades with all their outlandish denominations, each with its particular range of pay, its appropriate uniform and epaulettes, and its prescribed forms of address, from Well born, High well born, High born, up to Excellency and High Excellency. Everyone who obtained *chin*, and became a *chinovnik* or official, entered the privileged classes and became exempt from military service, from corporal punishment and so on, besides acquiring certain positive rights, previously reserved for the nobility. A *chin* of the fourth grade (Real State Councillor) and higher, carried with it hereditary nobility, as well as the rank of general in the civil service and the title of Excellency. Most senior professors, for instance, would attain this grade.

The forms of address and most of the civilian titles were borrowed from Europe, particularly from Germany, with its Hochwohlgeborene, its Hofräte, Staatsräte, Geheime Räte and Wirkliche Geheime Räte, but in Russia they had even less meaning as a description of the bearer's function. One of the weaknesses of the system was in fact that it discouraged specialisation of function. A *chinovnik* of a particular grade was deemed capable of a certain range of functions in any one of a number of services, promotion was by seniority and men were constantly being switched over from one service to another. Before the judicial reforms of 1864 even judges had no specialised training. That administrative experience gained in one service can well be utilised in another is of course recognised everywhere, but the sort of versatility demanded of a Russian official would have done credit to a British cabinet minister.

Though the system had its value in the early days as a method of bringing the nobility to heel, recruiting them for the urgently needed bureaucracy and army and providing men unaccustomed to hard work with a new incentive, it resulted in the end in the encouragement of mediocrity, the weakness of all services where promotion is by seniority. In Russia this defect was particularly marked, because everyone had to begin at, or very near, the bottom and work his way up through all the grades, though anyone who had passed a kind of School Leaving Examination was eligible for the lowest grade immediately, and higher education made promotion through the lower grades rapid.   But what was needed was something like our administrative grade of civil servant for the more responsible posts, instead of their being filled only by promotion from the lower grades.

There were at all times good and bad chinovniks, but comparing the Russian variety of bureaucracy with more efficient systems, such as that of Prussia, in a country almost equally despotically ruled, one easily believes that it deserved, on the whole, the criticisms so frequently levelled against its ignorance, idleness, slavery to routine and venality.   The system was not only inefficient, as was proved by Russia's slow advance in civilisation, and particularly revealed in every great crisis, from the Crimean War onwards, but it had an unfortunate effect on many sides of Russian life.   It encouraged place-hunting and the pursuit of external signs of distinction even in learning and the arts, and discouraged disinterested creative work and individual initiative everywhere.   It falsified current values, till many came to think that only those kinds of efforts were worth while which were recognised by the bureaucratic slaves of the autocracy, and that the supreme art in life was to advance in *chin* and earn a safe pension, no matter how immoral the means involved.

Chekhov brings before us officials of all ranks and shows us examples of how the system worked.   Because of the strict censorship he could not have criticised the system, and still less the autocratic form of government which it buttressed, even if he had wanted to do so, but what he brought home to every reader, often by means of irony and ridicule, was the fundamental inhumanity of it all as revealed even in trifling details, and what he suggested to everyone was: 'We cannot go on living like this'. It is always from the human angle that he views his officials, in their relationships with each other and with the public, but it is obvious that he understood that their responsibility was not mainly individual, but shared by Russian society in general.   The whole Russian world was out of joint.

To begin with the lower grades of the hierarchy, we find in an early story, *The civil service examination,** the mingled comedy and pathos in the situation of a middle-aged post-office assistant, who after twenty-one years of service is presenting himself for an oral examination.   If he passes he will be admitted to the lowest, the fourteenth grade, that of 'college registrar' (meaning originally something like 'ministry filing-clerk'). He is particularly nervous about geography, because he has offended the geography master at the local 'gymnasium', who will be one of his examiners, by refusing to serve him in the post-office out of his turn. However, in spite of some slips in dictation and bad lapses in geography and arithmetic he is allowed to pass, for the examination in his case is clearly a matter of form. Celebrating his success afterwards with the teachers in the restaurant, his one regret is that he spent a month on stereometry, only to find that it was not on the syllabus.

Even if once admitted, it was very hard for clerks who had not had a good school education to gain promotion. In some ministries four-fifths of the officials employed in the 'seventies, we are told, had had no education at all, and one-eighth only a primary education. In *Small fry* we see into the mind of such a petty official, sitting in his shabby uniform at his desk on night duty, while outside the Easter bells are calling all to the early mass, from which they will return home to the great feast of the year. He is trying to write his dutiful Easter congratulations to the hated superior, who for ten years has prevented him from being promoted from a post at sixteen roubles a month to one at eighteen. The dingy office with its dark-brown peeling walls, the smelly lamp, the cockroach crawling over the desk, all seem to reflect his hopelessness at the thought of his future. He will never rise beyond 'titular councillor', he tells the sympathetic hall-porter, because he is not educated. His appearance, his very name, stand in the way of promotion. Yet he cannot help brooding over possibilities of advancement. Shall he steal (as their chief, the general, is said to have done), or play the informer, like someone else he knows? No, it is all too difficult. The arrogance of the seniors and the abject toadying of the juniors are seen again in *A conqueror's triumph,** a description of a party at the Chief's, where after an excellent meal (pancakes with sour cream and caviar, sturgeon soup, roast partridge, and wine and vodka in abundance), the guests smoked cigars and listened to the Chief's stories of how he was once an under-dog himself, laughing at all his jokes, even when they were highly personal remarks about themselves, and even running round the table and crowing like cocks if he told them to.

How much store might be laid on the lowest of ranks, even by people of independent means, is illustrated in *It has been abolished.** When a retired army officer of the lowest rank, an ensign, is led to believe that the rank he holds has been abolished, he feels that

4*

the bottom had been knocked out of his existence, that people can treat him now as of no account, and he frets and fumes over it for weeks. *The captain's uniform** give us a tailor's view of the quality, and shows us both what the ensign in the last story thought he was losing with his rank, and the kind of servility that became second nature with some of the common people, especially no doubt those who gave personal service to people of rank. An old hen-pecked tailor in a small town, who in St. Petersburg had been employed by a firm patronized by the first four grades of *chin*, reminisces in his cups about the great days when he was an artist in his craft, and about his exalted clients. He never sees a gentleman now. One day he receives an unexpected order from a captain for a uniform. He makes it with great care, and it seems to him quite normal that he is not immediately paid for it. He calls day after day, is told roughly each time to get out, and finally he is knocked down and half killed by the drunken captain, but the rougher the treatment, the better it seems to please him. 'You can tell a real gentleman right away,' he says, 'that's just how they all were in St. Petersburg.' The reverse relationship is shown in *An inquiry*, where we see how the public might be treated by even the meanest of those in authority. The story relates with comic exaggeration how a subordinate official completely disregarded the presence of a landowner who wished to make an inquiry, until first one, then two and then three rouble notes had been laid on his desk. When his price had been paid he was obsequiousness itself, conducting the inquirer to the door on leaving, and pocketing a final rouble with all the skill of a conjuror.

As to the question of bribery, the impression we receive from this and other stories is that in the old Russia very few lower grade officials would refuse a tip, and that most of them expected one according to a more or less recognised tariff, to supplement their very poor salaries. The public was just as much accustomed to these gratuities as it is here with waiters and porters, and Thomas Mann tells us that Russians were wont to complain of the lack of 'freedom' in Germany, because they could not obtain favoured treatment in a post office, for instance, by trying to tip the officials. Among higher officials what can only be described as corruption had been almost universal before the age of the great reforms in the 'sixties, and according to Chekhov was still very common in the 'eighties and 'nineties, or a story like *The orator* would not have been accepted as true to life, as Chekhov's stories undoubtedly were. The Orator is called upon at short notice for a funeral oration in a churchyard, and by ill luck mistakes the name of the deceased official. He sings the praises of another official, who happens to be amongst those present, and the victim's chief quarrel with him when it is all over is that he said of him: 'He had no thought of private gain, he was not to be bought, he would never take a bribe.' It is all very well to say such things about the dead, but to say them about the living can only be regarded as mockery, he complains.

Some more examples of bribery of people in public positions may be mentioned here to save returning to the point. In *The cattledealers* it is railwaymen and officials. A dealer taking cattle a long way to market by train has first to bribe the guard and driver, to induce them to make a start again after a two hours' halt at a small station. He hands over a ten rouble note 'without any explanations, without moving a muscle, with that assurance and straightforwardness with which bribes are given and taken, probably, only in Russia'. Next time it is a station-master, then drinks to a guard, and so on throughout the long journey, which cost him fifteen roubles for each beast in freight charges, and six roubles for each in extras of this kind. *A happy ending* introduces a respectable middle-aged railway-guard who considers tips from passengers who have no tickets (called in Russia 'hares') a normal source of income, to be reckoned along with his pay and what he makes on the candles. Mr. Maurice Baring tells us the same kind of thing in *What I saw in Russia*. In *In the coachhouse* it is doctors and police officials who are bribed to issue a false death certificate for a lady's son, who has committed suicide, in order that he may receive normal burial. In *My life* railway engineers, for lack of a sufficient bribe, place the station well outside the town. 'In the whole town,' says the hero of the story, 'I never came across a single honest man. My father (an architect) took bribes and imagined that they were given to him out of respect for his intellectual qualities; the pupils at the *gymnasium*, to make sure of promotion, went as boarders to their teachers, who made a fine thing out of them. The wife of the Military Commissioner took money when recruits were being selected; so did the doctors, and the town medical officer and veterinary surgeon took a regular toll from butchers and restaurateurs. In the District School they did a trade in certificates giving exemption in the Third Category' (from military service); the church superintendents (Blagochinny) took money from the parish clergy and elders under their charge. If anyone went on business to the Municipal Board, the Department of Public Health, Trade or whatever it might be, the clerks would call after him, "Don't forget your manners!" and the caller would turn back to give them thirty or forty kopecks'. Even at the club, a paper-hanger was told by a gentleman in gold spectacles, one of the committee, to charge twelve kopecks a piece on the bill, if he did not want a beating, although he actually received only seven.

In consequence of this wide-spread corruption, the first reaction of anyone whose request was turned down by an official was to conclude that he wanted a bribe, or a bigger one than he had received. So in *Darkness* a young peasant simply cannot get it into his head that the zemstvo doctor is unable to release his brother, who has been unjustly sentenced to three years imprisonment, from the prisoners' ward of the hospital, and thinks he only refuses because a peasant cannot pay him enough. And in *Out of the frying pan into the fire** an irascible choirmaster, when refused what he thinks justice by both the Justice of the Peace and the Monthly Sessions, suggests to each in turn that they have been bribed. 'Of course you can't live on your salaries alone, I understand that perfectly,' he says, 'but just wait, we shall still find a court that cannot be bought.' He is committed for contempt of court before he can appeal to the Senate.

Of the other faults most frequently criticised in the bureaucracy, idleness and slavery to routine, there are many indications. Laevsky in *The duel*, a twenty-eight year old official of the Ministry of Finance in a Caucasian sea-side town, a rather degenerate intellectual of good family, parades his idleness but seems quite secure in his post. Papers are brought to his house for him and he signs them on the window-sill unread. Two of Orlov's three intimates in *An anonymous story* are idle officials, one a careerist to the marrow who has reached the fourth grade and holds a lucrative sinecure, and the other, the spoilt child of a great scholar, a musician manqué whose attitude to his work, as to everything else, is unusually careless and flippant. When Chekhov shows us the inside of an office, the people are usually killing time, as in *Small fry*, or *Vint,** where clerks supposed to be working overtime are found playing cards—and their chief joins them. Dilatory routine is castigated in *A lot of paper,** which purports to be a selection from three dozen letters exchanged between various authorities about an epidemic in a village school. Incidentally it is an amusing revelation of the intricacies of 'chancellory' style. The first report is sent by the village elder on 19th November, and orders to shut the school are finally dispatched by the school inspector to the village schoolmaster on 22nd February! Meanwhile the zemstvo doctor has reported that the epidemic has long been over and asked the executive bureau to spare him the unnecessary excogitations of their clerks, a phrase about which they complain, without result, to the district chief of police. An appendix reproduces a cutting from a newspaper about the gorgeous wedding of a paper-manufacturer's daughter, whose dowry was a million roubles.

Intrigue and influence naturally played a big part in so lax a system. *Ladies* is a case in point. A provincial director of education finds himself compelled to pass over a really deserving candidate for a clerkship because a young man of means, an amateur actor and friend of the ladies, has interested the wives of all sorts of important people and even obtained a testimonial from the governor. Like so many of his class, he only wishes to 'serve' in an office conveniently near home because a gentleman liked to have some official connection, and the director is sure that he will be useless and soon resign. '*Anna on the neck*' shows how much a pretty wife could do for the advancement of a most commonplace official. Because of the impression she makes at a ball she is taken up by society, and the favour of the governor helps the husband to promotion and the Order of St Anne. The tables are amusingly turned on the pompous bureaucrat who thought he was doing the daughter of a seedy secondary school master a great honour in marrying her without a dowry. From *Fat and thin* we see that in spite of the seniority rule, two men who entered the service at the same time might advance at very different rates, for of the two former schoolfellows who meet after many years at a railway station, the thin man is quite pleased with himself at having reached the 13th grade (college assessor), and gained the Order of St. Stanislas, while the fat man is already a privy councillor (3rd grade, 'reserved for very old or very distinguished members of the Civil Service, for ministers and ambassadors, and the like'—H. W. Williams). Chekhov has perhaps exaggerated the gap between them a little for comic effect. The contrast of the two types, and the electrifying effect of the fat man's revelation of his rank, is exquisitely comic, and at the same time full of understanding, especially of the less successful of the two. The description of the embarrassed fidgetting of his son, a gawky schoolboy, is a gem in itself. The thin man is the complete petit bourgeois. His pay is poor, but his German wife gives music lessons, and he earns a little pocket money by making cigar holders. He smells of ham and coffee-grounds, and is encumbered with much hand-luggage. The fat man has obviously dined well at the buffet, and smells of sherry and fleur d'orange. We are told that he had been something of a fop already at school, perhaps to suggest that he is well-connected. When the thin man learns of the other's rank, to the fat man's disgust his official servility overcomes all natural feeling. He seems to shrivel up, he laughs nervously, bows and scrapes, uses 'you' instead of 'thou' and addresses his friend no longer as 'Misha' but as 'Your Excellency'. It was by stories such as these studies of mainly minor chinovniks that Chekhov first made his reputation in Russia, which was primarily of course that of a humorist with a satirical turn.

Of the two detailed studies of high officials in St. Petersburg one dates from this early period, and it is the more amiable one, *The privy councillor*. When the narrator was a small boy, in 1870, his uncle, a privy councillor and general, having no money to go abroad, visited his sister on her country estate. The frantic preparations for such a distinguished guest, the deep impression made by his luggage and his manservant, the ceremonious behaviour of the tutor in his presence, and the disappointment of the small boy who tells the story to find that the 'general' is a sprightly little man in a white silk suit, instead of a warrior with gold epaulettes and a collar up to his ears, are splendid material for comedy. The scented dyspeptic old bachelor, who, though he finds everything charmingly fresh and naive at first in the country, spends all the day working in his room, proves such a trial in the end to his sister, with his dinner at seven and his visit from the governor, that she gives him the money for his usual holiday abroad. One can well believe that there were such high officials among the older generation, survivals of the age of the great reforms. Though he too is 'weak, like all men' and a little ridiculous, there is something that makes the boy rather sorry for him, when he leaves them, perhaps just the thought that he is lonely and old, or perhaps a dim feeling that for all his efforts to provide himself with every comfort, there is something that he has missed in life.

The other St. Petersburg official, Orlov, in *An anonymous story*, is also a completely self-centred bachelor, but he has none of the old-world charm of the privy councillor. An atmosphere of disgust and hopelessness hangs over the whole story, which was written seven years after the other one, in 1893. We have the impression that Orlov is intended as a symbol of official St. Petersburg in the 'eighties and 'nineties, the disillusioned age. The original aim of the retired naval lieutenant who tells the story in becoming Orlov's lackey was to acquire information, which he needed apparently for political, revolutionary purposes, about Orlov's father, a leading personality in government circles, but he loses sight of this aim as he becomes more and more interested and at the same time repelled by Orlov and his world, which is his own world too.

We learn first the routine of a St. Petersburg gentleman's life. He wakens about eleven, rings for his lackey to help him to dress, and comes out, washed and perfumed, into the dining-room of his flat to drink coffee, while his lackey and parlourmaid stand by the door, ready to perform any small service. At one o'clock he drives to his office, returning at about eight, after dinner, to read for an hour or two in his study. A stream of miscellaneous new books, French, German and English, as well as Russian, comes into the house, which he reads very quickly and throws away. After ten he begins to prepare for his evening pleasures, often putting on evening dress, but very rarely the uniform of a court chamberlain (Kammerjunker). He returns some time in the small hours.

Orlov was a man about thirty-five years of age, with 'the St. Petersburg look' about him, narrow shoulders, long waist, sunken temples, eyes of an indeterminate colour, and a thin, dingy coloured growth on head, chin and upper lip. The most striking feature about him was the ironical smile that was habitual with him, by a sort of reflex action, whenever he took up a book, or talked to people—except to his lackey, who did not count for him as human. It was at his parties on Thursdays that his lackey got to know him best. He had to stand then for four or five hours by the door, to pick up a fallen card, pass the ash-trays, fill the glasses and so on, harder work, he found, than a spell on watch in the navy. The guests, always the same three men, came at ten, played cards till two or three, and then took supper and talked.

The description of this talk reveals the negative, ironical view of life current in these circles. 'The irony of Orlov and his friends knew no bounds and spared neither persons nor things. They spoke about religion—irony, they spoke about philosophy—irony, and if anyone spoke about the state of the people—irony again.

In St. Petersburg there is a special breed of people who insist on making jokes about everything in life; they cannot even pass a starving man or a suicide without some silly remark. But Orlov and his friends did not make jokes, they spoke with irony. They said that there is no God and that personality vanishes completely at death; the only immortals are those in the French Academy. There is no supreme good and there cannot be, because its existence would presuppose human perfection, which is a logical absurdity. Russia is just as boring and wretched a country as Persia. The intelligentsia is hopeless; in Pekarski's opinion, it consists mainly of stupid people who are fit for nothing. The common people are drunken, lazy, dishonest and degenerate. We have no science and learning, our literature is crude, our commerce exists only on a basis of swindling, its maxim is "Cheat or you will not sell".'

As the wine went round they passed to more cheerful, smoking-room topics. They ragged each other on their conquests, and began to talk about women in general. Their view of woman was naturally anything but romantic. The world never had been moral, it certainly was not now, and it never would be—and why should it? Orlov's friends were vastly amused when one day his mistress took it into her head to leave her husband and move into Orlov's flat. This did not suit his book at all. Nothing was less to his liking than domesticities. For a woman to be pregnant, to have children or to talk about them was for him bourgeois and bad form. His view of love, as he explained to his friends, was purely physical; all that concerned him was how to make the conditions as pleasurable as possible, but Zinaida wanted to make him love saucepans and curling-pins, and to link his private life inseparably with hers. In his view she was incurably romantic, convinced that she had done a very brave thing in leaving her husband, like a Turgeniev heroine.

The working-out of this affair, complicated by the gentleman-lackey's protective devotion to the lady, does not change our view of Orlov, but the letter which the lackey writes to him on leaving makes explicit Chekhov's moral criticism of 'the St. Petersburg chinovnik, the counterfeit man'. Orlov, the lackey says, is in reality afraid of life. He wears the frock-coat of European civilisation, but like any hookah-smoking Asiatic sitting idly on his feather cushions, he thinks only of avoiding hunger and cold, pain and mental distress, of escaping from the struggle with life and nature. How soft, effortless and comfortable his life is—but how boring! That is why he must spend so much of it in playing cards. And that is the secret of his irony. Bold, free thought would disturb his quiet, so, like thousands of his contemporaries, he has surrounded thought with a palisade of irony. As to his views on women, it is true that lewdness is in men's blood and is fostered by their education, but we do not deserve to be called men if we do not strive to overcome the animal in ourselves. Orlov knows this, but he deceives his conscience by shifting all the blame on to women. The resemblance in many points here to the doctor's indictment of the high nobility in *The Princess* is clear, and the last section of the letter is a return to the theme of Ivanov, the question why Russians in their thirties lose heart and give up the struggle.

It will be seen that we can obtain from Chekhov's stories many impressions of the chinovnik in general. *Vint** is an amusing reminder of the mechanical uniformity everywhere in Russia of this hierarchy that we have been studying, and of the range of government departments represented in the chief town of a province. 'Vint' is a card game employing the ordinary French cards, and in this story some government clerks have had the idea of using fifty-two cards with portraits of their colleagues on them instead of the ordinary pack. They are arranged by suits, officials of the palais de justice being hearts, those of the provincial administration clubs, those of the ministry of education diamonds and those of the state bank spades. In each suit the ace is an official of the fourth class (real state councillor, the highest likely to occur in the provinces), the king one of the fifth class (state councillor), the queen the wife of an official of either of these two classes, the jack a college councillor (sixth class), and so on down the scale. Besides making mild fun of the 'ranks', Chekhov often satirises in his early stories the scramble for the orders which were conferred for good service, and the resulting snobbery, as in *The order**, about two teachers of a gymnasium, dining out and wearing one the 'Anna' and the other the 'Stanislaus' order, luckily *both* of them borrowed for the occasion, or in *The lion and the sun*, about the efforts of a mayor beyond the Urals to gain a Persian order by his attentions to a chance visitor.

Before discussing some of the separate branches of the government service, it is necessary to say a little about its organization. The central organs of government in St. Petersburg were the *Council of State*, the *Committee of Ministers* and the *Senate*, representing the legislative, the administrative and the judicial power respectively. The *Council of State*, mainly composed of high officials or retired officials, framed bills, discussed the annual budget, and received reports from the ministers on all the principal affairs of state, but it had merely a consultative character. The views of both the majority and the minority were presented to the Emperor, and he decided freely on the action to be taken. The *Committee of Ministers* was not really a cabinet, for it had no common responsibility, each separate minister being individually responsible to the Emperor, and there was not even a prime minister, the Emperor acting as his own. The ten ministries were those of the Court or Household, Foreign Affairs, the Interior, Finance, Justice, Education, Communications, State Domains, War, and the Navy. The *Senate*, once of considerable importance, had been practically reduced to a court of appeal.

For administrative purposes, European Russia was divided into forty-nine provinces (gubernii), and each province into a number of districts (uyezdy). The average province was about as big as Portugal, but they varied greatly in size, as did also the districts, according to their situation and population, those of the north and east being very large but very thinly populated. There was a governor at the head of each province. By the second half of the nineteenth century the powers of the governors had been so severely pruned that they could do very little without consulting the central government, though they naturally had much personal influence and were great social figures in their various provinces. The governor represented the Ministry of the Interior. The other ministries were represented in each province by resident officials, each supported by a considerable staff. In each of the districts of which the province was made up—there might be as few as eight, or as many as fifteen—the only representative of the central government was the District Chief of Police (*ispravnik*), who was a landowner appointed by the governor. He had under him in each of the principal towns of the district a City Chief of Police (*stanovoi pristav*). In smaller towns a police superintendent (*nadziratel*) was in charge, assisted by one or two policemen (*gorodovoi*).

The fact that a police official performed in effect the duties of a sub-governor, a post that in most western countries would have been occupied by an administrative official, is some indication of the multiplicity of the functions demanded of the police in addition to the maintenance of order. This is in accordance with the wide meaning attached to the word 'police' in Germany, for instance, at the time when Peter established the Russian system. We have seen above that the police were still responsible until 1899 for the collection of taxes from the peasantry. The police were in fact *the* representatives of the government to the ordinary man. In particular they made him aware of the innumerable things which one was forbidden to do. In the large towns even the concierges of the big blocks of flats which were usual there were compelled by the government, at the owners' expense, to help the police in keeping an eye on everyone who went in or out, by night or day (cf *The clever concierge**).

As they had so many things to do, and shared in an intensified degree all the usual faults of the bureaucracy through being less easily controlled from above in all their varied tasks in widely scattered places, the police were remarkably inefficient in the maintenance of order and the prevention of crime, especially in the country districts after the Emancipation, when the 'counting-houses' of the landowners, with their disciplinary powers over the peasants, were greatly missed. The elected village and cantonal authorities proved incapable of keeping vagabonds, incendiaries, thieves and drunkards in check and a special rural police force of armed and mounted *uryadniki* was created in 1878. They operated singly, each in a specified area, and though welcomed at first soon proved as tyrannical and inefficient as the bulk of the police force. According to the squires, the demoralizing effects of the Emancipation were more in evidence than ever, so a further step was taken in 1889 for the tightening up of discipline in the villages through the establishment of Land Captains (*zemski nachalniki*) all over the country, usually ex-officers from the landed gentry, who exercised a general control over rural institutions, and in particular settled partitions and other disputes about land, and acted as judges in all small cases. The effect was to remove some of the democratic features introduced in the reforms of the 'sixties, in the village communes, the zemstvos, and the courts of the justices of the peace. These new 'official squires' were thoroughly detested by the villagers, but they survived until 1917.

In addition to the regular police there existed from 1826 to 1880 a political police force of so-called 'gendarmes', with a high-ranking Chief of Gendarmes at its head. The Third Section of the Imperial Chancellory over which he presided was as good as a separate ministry, its special task being to maintain the security of the state. The gendarmes were also supposed to keep the corruption and arbitrariness of the regular bureaucracy itself within bounds, but they found their counter-revolutionary activity a more congenial task. In spite of the unlimited powers conferred upon them they proved no better than the ordinary police against the nihilists. In 1880 the Third Section was nominally abolished, but the gendarmes continued in their functions much as before, though now under the Ministry of the Interior with the regular police. Russia has in fact never yet been able to dispense with her secret police, and they have continually reappeared under different names.

It goes without saying that this constant surveillance, a necessary feature of an uneasy absolutism in an increasingly democratic age, left a profound mark on the Russian character. Leroy-Beaulieu describes it as 'l'esprit de défiance et par suite l'esprit de frivolité'. For fear of compromising themselves people were reduced to saying nothing serious, and this was one source of the inertia and indolence which were so much in evidence among the educated classes. All but the most vigorous tended to be reduced to the state of mind of Chekhov's *The man in a case*, which is far from being merely an amusing anecdote. This Greek master at a gymnasium, who tried to surround himself as it were with a shell into which he could retire like a snail, wearing galoshes and carrying an umbrella in the finest weather, hiding himself behind dark spectacles and a turned-up collar, plugging his ears with cotton-wool, was in his shrinking attitude to life the very type of the servile citizen. He kept his mind too as it were in a case. Whatever was forbidden he was quite clear about, but there was always something annoyingly indefinite about other things, so if anything new was suggested, a dramatic circle for instance, he was always very nervous about what might come of it. Any kind of departure from the regulations, even if it had nothing to do with him, made him acutely miserable, and he infected others with his feeling, so that 'people began to be afraid of everything. They were afraid of talking aloud, of sending letters, of making new acquaintances, of reading books, afraid of helping the poor or teaching others to read and write'. We appreciate the significance of this list of fears if we remember what Chekhov wrote about the talk on the Amur steamer (p. 9), or in Vienna (p. 10), or if we think, in more recent times, of Nazi Germany.

Chekhov tells us nothing directly about the higher authorities, because he had no direct contacts with them and in any case could not have spoken freely, but in many of his stories, especially the early ones, he gives us vivid vignettes of the police in action. In *Minds in ferment* we see the haste with which they try to disperse anything that resembles a crowd, and the resentment felt by the educated at their free use of force for this purpose. 'Don't wave your arms about! Even if you are the chief, you have no right to be so free with your fists', the better-class people cry, or 'Push the peasants about, but don't you dare to touch gentlemen! Keep off!' The policemen cannot make any impression on the crowd that has gathered in the market square, through two men staring at some starlings, and summon their chief, who orders the firemen to turn the hose on them. Fortunately there is no water, and anyhow a counter-attraction soon draws them away, but a number of names are taken and some men are lodged in gaol—not however one who is to give a party next day! In the evening the chief of police reports the affair to his superior. It was only by God's mercy, he declares, that no blood was shed, and he concludes with the revealing remark: 'In the absence of evidence, those responsible are for the present in custody, but I propose to release them in a week or so.' His view of the law is evidently very like that of the *Man in a case* or of *Corporal Prishibeev*,* namely that nothing must be considered to be permitted unless the law says so. 'Does the law say that the common people may go about in droves?' the corporal asks the Justice of the Peace, when he is brought up for assaulting various police officers. He is a former non-commissioned officer who is more zealous than the police themselves in ferreting out what he imagines to be offences. In town he used to report everything to a gendarme, and even in the country, when he sees a few people in a group, he cannot help shouting to them 'Disperse!', and using his fists if they do not.

The remark 'Push the peasants about, but don't dare to touch gentlemen!' reminds us that equality before the law was an ideal that had by no means been attained in Russia, though in the judicial reforms some attempt had been made to approach it. *A chameleon* re-inforces this impression, by showing how a police superintendent in a small town changes his tune when he is told that a dog that has bitten a shopkeeper belongs to the general who lives in the town. Before this, thinking its owner to be a mere tradesman, he was threatening to make an example of him for letting it run wild. Then somebody says it is not the general's dog, and he veers this way and that until it is finally established that the dog belongs to the general's brother who is visiting him, and the policeman turns on the man who claims to have been bitten.

As to the other multifarious activities of the police, we have seen the city chief of police (*stanovoi pristav*) interviewing peasants for non-payment of their dues (p. 54). In *Appropriate measures** we see the police superintendent (*nadziratel*) in a small town leading the 'sanitary committee' on one of their rare tours of inspection of the shops. He is accompanied by the medical officer, two members of the town council, and a representative of the trades, with a policeman or two bringing up the rear. They are talking with many gesticulations about taking appropriate measures against lack of cleanliness, bad smells and so forth, and make for a grocer's shop. After a few perfunctory questions their attention is diverted by the grocer's invitation to them to have a drink, and vodka and smoked sturgeon put them in a very good humour. After a morning's arduous labours of this kind they end by retiring to the 'Rhine cellar of wines and vodka' to fortify themselves, and here the police superintendent discovers that the trayful of apples they have confiscated as rotten are not so bad after all, and go very well with the vodka. Similarly in *A chameleon* the policeman accompanying the superintendent is found to be carrying a sieve full of confiscated gooseberries, which will no doubt not be wasted.

In the chief village of each canton the policeman was a peasant, the *sotski*, appointed by the cantonal committee. He helped to maintain order, though that was more the business of the mounted policeman (*uryadnik*), he conducted vagabonds and other offenders to the town (as in *Dreams*), but he was chiefly occupied, as we see in *On official duty*, in taking official forms and documents from one authority to another, and to landowners and peasants all over the countryside. He had been constantly on his feet for thirty years, so that they ached if he was not walking. 'To the treasury office, to the post, to the house of the city chief of police (*stanovoi pristav*), to the land captain, to the assessor, to the zemstvo bureau, to gentlemen and peasants, to all orthodox christians. I take parcels, summonses, tax sheets, letters, forms and notices, and nowadays, your honour, they send out all sorts of forms, yellow ones, white ones, red ones, to be filled in with figures, and every landowner, or priest, or rich peasant has to write down ten times a year how much has been sown and harvested, how many quarters or poods of rye, how many sheep, how much hay he has, what the weather has been like and what insects he's seen. Of course, you can write what you like, it's just a regulation, but I've got to deliver them and then call again to collect them. . . . It's all right in summer, when it's warm and dry, but it is no fun in the autumn and winter.' All this he does for 84 roubles a year, with very few tips, because the gentlemen are very hard nowadays, and easily offended. He is more likely to get a bite and a drink at a peasant's than at a gentleman's house. Here then we see the 'papers' from the St. Petersburg ministries and the zemstvos of the district and province arriving at their ultimate destination, and we realise how close was the net-work they wove over the life of even the poorest peasant. No wonder that for years a certain eccentric barin has always greeted the *sotski* with derisive laughter and called him a name that he doesn't understand—'Administration'.

The *sotski* carried papers not only from the central government, but from local government organs, the zemstvos and the cantonal committees. The latter (see above, p. 55) were set up at the time of the Emancipation, when a considerable measure of self-government was granted to the village communes and to the organized groups of neighbouring communes called cantons (*volosti*). These bodies were competent however to deal only with peasant affairs. There existed still in each district and province the elective assemblies of the gentry set up by Catherine, which had been given control of local affairs but in their lethargy had made little use of it. They did not even appoint the district chief of police (*ispravnik*) any longer, as formerly. He was nominated now, as we have seen, by the governor. Their triennial meetings were social occasions, and at them the gentry elected their marshal of the gentry, kept the equivalent of Debrett up to date, did something to look after minors, and that was about all.

A larger administrative unit was needed, which would deal with district matters affecting all classes, and after much deliberation by learned commissions the Zemstvo was created in 1864. It is described by Mackenzie Wallace as follows:—'The Zemstvo is a kind of local administration which supplements the action of the rural communes, and takes cognisance of those higher public wants which individual communes cannot possibly satisfy. Its principal duties are to keep the roads and bridges in proper repair, to provide means of conveyance for the rural police and other officials, to look after primary education and sanitary affairs, to watch the state of the crops and take measures against approaching famine, and, in short, to undertake, within clearly defined limits, whatever seems likely to increase the material and moral well-being of the population. In form the institution is Parliamentary—that is to say, it consists of an assembly of deputies which meets regularly once a year (for a fortnight), and of a permanent executive bureau (*zemskaya uprava*), elected by the Assembly from among its members. If the Assembly be regarded as a local Parliament, the bureau corresponds to the Cabinet. Once every three years the deputies are elected in certain fixed proportions by the landed proprietors, the rural communes, and the municipal corporations.' Eventually thirty-four of the forty-nine provinces of European Russia, made up of 360 districts, received local self-government under this law.

In the district assemblies then landowners, former serfs and representatives of the towns debated their affairs in common, though through their superior education the nobility would naturally have played the chief part, even if the system of representation had not favoured them from the beginning. The President was the Marshal of Gentry of the district. Members were not elected in the manner familiar to us but, like members of the Lower House in Prussia under the 1850 constitution, by groups of electors, corresponding roughly to the three 'estates', peasants, nobility and townspeople. A number of members roughly proportionate to the total property interests of the group in the district was allotted to each. The peasant elections were indirect. The electors were themselves elected by the cantonal committees. The landowners' electoral group consisted of all owners of a fixed amount of land, varying in different districts but never very large by Russian standards. The townspeople's group was also on a property basis. The representation of the various groups was weighted in a way which made the gentry predominant, and this predominance was greatly increased by the Zemstvo Law of 1890. There were further provincial zemstvos, the assemblies of which were composed of representatives chosen by the district assemblies from their own number, to deal with affairs concerning more than one district. Here the gentry were still more markedly in the ascendant because peasants could not well afford to attend.

The Zemstvos were in an anomalous position from the beginning, as no organic link was established between them and the central administrative system, the officials of which retained most of their old functions. The best work of the zemstvos was done in fields which the central government had scarcely touched, especially education and health services. They were most seriously handicapped by shortage of funds. Russia was a poor country, and though landowners and peasants alike, in progressive districts, assumed a considerable burden of local taxation to further their ideals, they had to meet a heavy compulsory expenditure on such things as the cost of local administration, of the courts of the justices of the peace, the posting service, recruiting offices, barracks and police stations. They were moreover watched by a jealous and suspicious central government at every step. They were only allowed for instance to build and equip schools, not to have any control over the teaching. In the establishment of hospitals, zemstvo doctors and medical outposts they made a good beginning, but they only touched the fringe of the problem. How much there was to be done is indicated by the fact that in the mid 'eighties, about half the number of children born died before reaching the age of five. The supply of doctors was quite inadequate, 300 graduates or so a year in the 'eighties, and most of them were snapped up by the towns. We have seen how much Chekhov could always find to do as a doctor wherever he went in the country. The zemstvos had to make extensive use of half-trained 'feldshers' at 200 to 300 roubles a year. They had a large number of devoted women helpers however, who studied medicine and found an admirable outlet for their idealism in work among the peasant women and children. They are much in evidence in the stories. On the whole then, though the zemstvos did not work the miracles that were expected of every new institution in Russia, they proved how fruitful the principle of representative government, conceded here for the first time in Russia, could be in local affairs, and they paved the way for its extension to national affairs. They became the focus for all the practical idealists in the country and played an important part in the 1905 revolution.

In discussing the police system, we noted already the establishment in 1889 of Land Captains to exercise a general control over rural institutions. During the fifteen years preceding that time, after the abolition in 1874 of the Arbiters of the Peace, who had been appointed to wind up the serf system and organise the beginnings of peasant self-government, there were district committees to exercise supervision over the self-governing cantons and communes. They were called 'District Committees for Peasant Affairs' and were composed of some local authorities, notably the district chief of police, an honorary justice of the peace (see below) and the 'permanent member', under the presidency of the marshal of the nobility. The really important person was the 'permanent member', a salaried official appointed by the government on the nomination of the zemstvo. He had only to shake off his committee to become a land captain. The permanent member often plays a part in Chekhov's tales. The official mentioned above for instance (p. 64), who is so unfavourably impressed by the young parish priest in *A nightmare*, is a permanent member.

The activities of the zemstvos are often mentioned incidentally in Chekhov's work, and we know that in Melikhovo and earlier he gave them all the help he could in their medical and educational activities, but he does not deal with the institution at any length. He evidently thought the zemstvo an excellent institution which was not sufficiently appreciated and supported. At the beginning of *In the court* for instance he draws a picture of the drab surroundings in which the zemstvo committees have to meet. At the chief town of the district, he says, there is a stone house, painted brown, out of harmony with its surroundings, where the zemstvo bureau, the monthly sessions, the peasant affairs, licensing, military committees and various others meet in turn. 'It is a depressing sight with its cheerless barrack-like exterior, its dilapidation and the complete absence of any kind of comfort, either outside or in. Even on the brightest spring days it seems to be covered by a dark shadow. . . . Inside it is like a barn and extremely unattractive. It is strange to see how easily all these elegant public prosecutors, permanent members, presidents, who at home would make a scene about a smell of cooking or a spot on the floor, grow accustomed here to the drone of the ventilators, the repulsive smell of fumigators and the dirty walls, always covered with a film of moisture!' The description suggests that a society which houses its institutions in this way does not rate them very highly. It is characteristic of Chekhov's liberal landowners, like *Ivanov* in the play, to take an active part in zemstvo work when fresh from the university, and to lose heart and perhaps turn against it later. In *The party* too there is a young man of this type, who already uses expressions like 'we zemstvo workers', though it is not a year since he came down from the university. 'Before another year is out', Olga says of him, 'he, like so many others, will get bored, go off to St. Petersburg and, to justify his desertion, will say everywhere that the zemstvo is no good and that he is disappointed in it.' When asked by

Pleshcheyev, in reference to this passage, whether he was not afraid of being regarded as a liberal, Chekhov wrote that he had never concealed his sympathies, and that he certainly loved the zemstvo and trial by jury.

The third great reform of the reign of Alexander II was the complete re-modelling of the system of justice, and we obtain frequent glimpses of the new courts in Chekhov's tales. The older judicial system had been based on western continental models in the time of Peter the Great's father, when procedure in the German states, for instance, was secret and written. The courts were notoriously corrupt and dilatory, even when Russian law, for long a chaos, had been in some measure codified at the beginning of the nineteenth century. The commission appointed by Alexander II studied the administration of justice in the west, particularly in England and France, and they recommended a system based on the leading principles which they found there, notably the separation of justice and administration, equality before the law, public oral procedure and the jury system. A double set of new courts was established, the one, where the judges were the elected Justices of the Peace, imitated chiefly from England, and the other, for more serious cases, with pro-fessional trained judges, imitated from France. But below both, the court of the canton (volost) was retained, as established by the Emancipation laws, which meant that for much the largest class, the principle of equality before the law was abandoned, as they were not tried according to the same law as other classes. In these courts peasants were tried by their fellows according to peasant notions of right, based on age-old customs and ways of thinking peculiar to their class. Their competence was restricted to minor civil cases, involving sums up to a hundred roubles, minor dis-orders—drunkenness, petty thefts, minor assaults—and disputes about land and the like, involving the law of the 'mir'. Elected peasant judges, who could not be village or cantonal elders, sat every fortnight, on a Sunday, and decided cases with the help of the cantonal clerk, on common-sense principles. They were often accused of selling justice for vodka, but on the whole seem to have worked well.

There is an early sketch by Chekhov which, though not con-cerned with an official cantonal court, gives us a good notion of village ideas of justice. It was published in a weekly in 1881 under the title *Village pictures, (a) The Court.*[1] Behind a table in an izba

[1] Reprinted in *Complete Works* (1944), I, 121 ff.

humming with gnats and flies sit seven people, the master of the house Yegorov, a shopkeeper, supported by the village elder (who does not say a word, but respectfully lights the pipe of the gendarme), the feldscher, the parish clerk, the bass singer, a gendarme on a visit to the village, and the culprit's godfather. At a respectful distance stands the shopkeeper's son, a barber's boy home for a holiday, accused by his father of stealing twenty-five roubles from a chest of drawers. As the cottage is being used as a medical 'point' there is a peasant woman lying groaning in the porch, while a curious crowd is looking in at the window. After a prolonged talking match, in which the boy scores off several of his judges, for he has not lived in a provincial capital for nothing, it is decided that as he will not confess, he must be flogged, and flogged he is by his father, while the rest look on approvingly. When he has had twenty-one strokes with the belt his mother comes in with the money, which she has just found in the forgotten pocket where her husband had put it. The boy takes his unjust beating most philosophically, and it is relished as an entertainment by all the rest, even by the peasant woman waiting for the feldscher to attend to her broken rib. For some time afterwards the gendarme is to be heard walking up and down outside and calling out 'Another one, another one; That's the stuff for him'!

There are several scenes from higher courts. There were first the courts of the justices of the peace, who in Russia were elected by the district zemstvos, though the governor had to approve of them. The regular justices of the peace were paid a salary of round about 2000 roubles, but out of this they had to provide a court-room, usually in their own house (see, e.g., *An unpleasant affair**), and even pay their clerk. They were landowners, usually not very well off, untrained in law but possessing the equivalent of a secondary-school education. Their function was to try petty cases, involving no difficult law, and to settle everyday disputes, if possible by conciliation, as in the cantonal courts, of which the new courts were in many ways a glorified version. *An unpleasant affair** gives an example of a case settled out of court, against the will of the offending party, a doctor who lost his temper with a drunken feldscher assistant and struck him. People of his own class, like the president of the zemstvo bureau and the J.P., cannot understand his passion for abstract justice, but that some advance had been made is shown both here and in *As intelligent as a log**. In this story a retired military gentleman cannot get it into his head that times have changed since the reforms, and that the friend whom he has helped to elect J.P. has to listen seriously to the valet who has brought a charge of assault against the retired cornet, his master. It is not the valet who is punished for his impudence, as his master wishes, but he himself who must pay ten roubles damages for striking his valet with a comb. Domestic service from the lackey's point of view is forcibly characterised in the valet's evidence. A similar conflict of old and new ideas about justice and social privilege occurs in *Out of the fryingpan into the fire**, in which a choirmaster is brought up before a J.P. for insulting people in a restaurant. He is sentenced to two months' imprisonment (the maximum sentence that a J.P. could impose was three months). Being quite unable to understand the verdict, as he thinks it is the other man who has insulted him, he says to the justice: 'Your late mother Varvara Sergeyevna—God grant her the Kingdom of Heaven—would have had people like Osip (his opponent) whipped, but you connive at his offence', which reminds us again that the J.P. was a local landowner, and that proceedings were not very formal. On appeal, the case came before the monthly sessions, made up of all the J.P.'s of the district, excluding in each case the one whose decision was in dispute. From this court the only appeal was to the Senate, acting as Cour de Cassation.

From *Perpetuum mobile** we get the impression that not every president of monthly sessions took his duties very seriously. Private affairs came first in this story, and a delay of a day or two in opening the proceedings was neither here nor there. In *The party* it is vanity and love of authority in a president of monthly sessions that is emphasised, and in a letter to Pleshcheyev Chekhov expressed the fear that this passage would not pass the censor, adding: 'All the presidents in our courts are like that'. 'In the president's chair, in his uniform, with his gold chain of office on his breast, he was quite another man. Self-important gestures, a loud voice, "What is that you say?" humming and hawing, an off-hand air. The consciousness that he was a person in authority prevented him from sitting quietly in his seat. He had to be constantly ringing his bell, looking sternly at the public, and raising his voice.'

In addition to the regular, salaried justices of the peace, a large number of honorary ones were elected, who included most of the men of any distinction, in the district, even if they only had a summer villa there. The intention in the early days was to give higher status in this way to the regular justices. As the idealism of the 'sixties ebbed away, the courts of the justices of the peace gradually lost their popularity. We have noticed that it is only in Chekhov's early stories that they play a part. 'Their history resembled that of the zemstvo and many other institutions in Russia—at first enthusiasm and inordinate expectations; then consciousness of defects and practical inconveniences; and lastly, in an influential section of the public, the pessimism of shattered illusions, accompanied by the adoption of a reactionary policy on the part of the government' (Mackenzie Wallace). In 1889 the functions of these courts were divided in the country districts of central Russia between the new Land Captains and the regular courts. Where they survived, the justices of the peace were appointed by the government, no longer elected by the zemstvos.

The regular courts too consisted of a lower and a higher court. Both were closely imitated from the French system and given similar names, the lower one being called *okruzhny sud* (tribunal d'arrondissement), and the higher *sudebnaya palata* (palais de justice). The lower court served several Districts (*uyezdy*), and the higher several provinces. At these courts procedure was much more formal. The sittings were public, there were three judges present, one of them presiding, and speeches were made by officially recognised advocates. They were at first, at any rate, not always trained lawyers, as there were not enough to go round. The bar as a profession in Russia dates only from these reforms in 1864.

When dealing with criminal cases, the lower courts made use of a jury on the English model, and there was no appeal to the higher court. For civil cases there was no jury, and there was a right of appeal. In both civil and criminal suits, the Senate acted as a 'cour de cassation', with power to revise cases on the ground of technical informality. While the jury was borrowed from England, the method of preparing and conducting the prosecution in criminal cases was borrowed from France. There were special examining magistrates or 'juges d'instruction' (*sudebnye sledovateli*), whose business it was to conduct all criminal inquiries, instead of the police, as hitherto, and there were 'procureurs' (*prokurory*), something like our public prosecutors, to conduct the prosecution in court. The examining magistrates were made irremovable, unless convicted of some crime, but it was found, in Russian conditions, that many became very idle, like the one visited by the prince in *A trivial incident*. 'The man receives 250 roubles a month and has practically nothing to do, though he thinks he is honestly doing his duty.' It became normal therefore to make appointments that were nominally temporary, though they might be continued for many years. The lawyer in *On official duty* is a young acting examining magistrate of this kind.

One of the duties of an examining magistrate was to accompany the doctor who conducted a post-mortem examination. As Chekhov had sometimes been the doctor on these occasions, we have several stories about such a pair, *Perpetuum mobile**, *The examining magistrate*, and *On official duty*, for instance. In other stories we see this official making a preliminary examination of an arrested person, as in *A malefactor*, when a peasant accused of having removed bolts from the railway lines to act as sinkers is quite fairly interrogated, and then sent to prison to await his trial. Then in *The Swedish match*, which calls itself a detective story, we see the officers of the law come into action one after the other. The mysterious disappearance and presumed murder of a retired officer is reported first to the city chief of police (*stanovoi pristav*) of that part of the District, who after visiting the scene of the supposed crime sends word to his superior, the district chief of police (*ispravnik*), summons the mounted policeman (*uryadnik*), and writes a note to the examining magistrate (*sledovatel*). The latter arrives in an hour or two with his assistant and begins his detective work. He is followed by the district chief of police and the doctor. Some arrests are made after a day or two, and the suspected persons are questioned day after day by the examining magistrate, until it is discovered through the zeal of his young assistant that the man who had disappeared is very much alive, the prisoner of love of the young wife of the old city chief of police himself!

The next stage, the trial of a criminal case in the arrondissement court, is seen in *In the court*. The work of the examining magistrate is finished and he does not appear in court—though the public prosecutor at one point complains privately to the presiding judge that the inquiry has been badly conducted. The presiding judge has, as always, two colleagues to support him. While the clerk to the court is reading the charge, a long document, in an expressionless droning voice, the president asks one of his colleagues some private question about where he is staying. The public prosecutor meanwhile is reading Byron's 'Cain'. The defending counsel is playing with a pencil. 'His young face was devoid of expression, except for that mask of cold boredom which is usual

on the faces of schoolboys, and of officials compelled to sit day
after day in the same place, with the same faces, the same walls
in front of them. The speech he was about to make did not worry
him in the least. And what sort of a speech would it be? He
would reel it off before the jury, without fire or feeling, on the
instructions of the authorities, following a well worn pattern,
conscious that it was colourless and boring, and then he would
go—hurry off through the rain and mud to the station to catch
the train to town for his new orders, to go to some other town in
the District, and make another speech—What a dull life!' No
wonder that the accused felt he was being judged not by living
men, but by a sort of machine, for he did not understand that they
were just as accustomed here to the dramas and tragedies of life
as the staff of hospitals are to death, and looked on them with
the same detached gaze. In the early story *Drowsy thoughts** it is
the same deadly dullness that is stressed. There too the clerk
reads monotonously, taking no notice of commas and full stops,
so that it sounds like the buzzing of bees, and the defending
counsel is lost in a day-dream about his home, until he finally
dozes off.

The danger that threatened the new courts, Chekhov seems to
say, was a soulless routine, resulting in inhumanity and injustice
through the lethargy and lack of imagination of the lawyers. The
point is put more directly in *Ward No. 6*, a story about the mental
ward in a hospital. In explaining how Ivan Dmitrich, one of its
occupants, came to have persecution mania, Chekhov tells us
the kind of thoughts by which he was obsessed just before his
illness. He had been in close touch with the courts through his
occupation, and came to imagine that the police were about to
arrest him, though he was innocent of any offence. 'A mis-
carriage of justice is perfectly possible with the present legal
procedure,' he told himself, 'and there is nothing surprising in it.
People who stand in an official, professional relationship to the
sufferings of others, judges, police officers, doctors, for example,
grow hardened in the course of time, by force of habit, to such an
extent that even if they wish, they cannot take up any other than
an impersonal attitude towards their clients. In this respect
they are exactly like a peasant slaughtering sheep and calves in
his farm-yard and not noticing the blood.' This is not the author
himself speaking, of course, but it is plain from the tone of the
stories just quoted that Ivan Dmitrich puts Chekhov's own views
here in an extreme form.

These views are all of a piece with those which sent Chekhov on his journey to Sakhalin. Through his brother Michael's legal studies he came to know a good deal, as we have seen, about prison conditions. In the letter to Suvorin already partially quoted (9/3/90) he wrote: 'From the books I have read and am reading, it is evident that we have sent *millions* of men to rot in prison, have destroyed them—casually, without thinking, barbarously; we have driven men in fetters through the cold ten thousand versts, have infected them with syphilis, have depraved them, have multiplied criminals, and the blame for all this we have thrown upon the gaolers and red-nosed superintendents. Now all educated Europe knows that it is not the superintendents that are to blame, but all of us; yet that is not our business, we say, it is not interesting.' In the same letter he writes at length about the large-scale disturbances among university students in Moscow, who demanded greater freedom in every respect. A fortnight later he wrote: 'The cabmen approve of the students' disturbances. "They are making a riot for the poor to be admitted to the universities," they explain, "learning is not only for the rich." It is said that when a crowd of students were being taken by night to the prison the mob attacked the gendarmes to try to rescue the students. They are said to have shouted: "You have taken to flogging us, but they stand up for us".' And earlier, 'They are flogging people in our police-stations; a rate has been fixed; from a peasant they take ten kopecks for a beating, from a workman twenty—that's for the rods and the trouble. Peasant women are flogged too. Not long ago, in their enthusiasm for beating in a police station they thrashed a couple of budding lawyers, an incident upon which the *Russkiya Vyedomosti* has a vague paragraph to-day; an investigation has begun.' It is quite clear from the letters then that Chekhov's interest in courts and prisons was the inevitable result of his liberal outlook, his indignation at injustice and cruelty.

The often inhuman harshness of Russian justice even after the reforms manifested itself even more clearly in the final stage, the punishment meted out by the courts. The whole of *Sakhalin island* was, as we have seen, devoted to this topic (p. 8*f*). In Chekhov's imaginative work there are several references to life in Siberia, particularly in *In exile* and *Dreams*. *In exile* is a study of three types of exile in Siberia. Old Simon, a village priest's son, after many years there has so completely renounced all thoughts of a normal free life that he does not desire anything better than the

5

life he is leading, as ferryman on a broad Siberian river. A young Tartar, smarting under the injustice of his sentence, for he claims to be quite innocent, the victim of corruption, and longing for his clever young wife, is the picture of misery. Simon's assurance that he will get used to it is no comfort to him. He wants none of his philosophy; life is joy and pain, and to renounce both for peace of mind is a kind of death in life (compare the professor's view in *A dreary story*, that equanimity is a paralysis of the soul, a premature death). So the two of them take opposite views of the third type, a gentleman, who also has never renounced. Soon after his arrival he had persuaded his wife to join him, but after three years she could stand it no longer in spite of all he lavished on her, and ran off with another man. Now he lives only for his daughter, who is pining away in this desolate place. The background, the dreary slimy banks of the river in late spring, with ice still floating on the water and snow showers in the air, is sketched from Chekhov's memories of the Irtysh. We see how, in Siberian banishment, a gentleman not condemned to penal servitude can still buy an estate and lead a gentleman's life, while a penniless Tartar cannot earn more than ten kopecks a day by incessant toil and must beg from door to door in the villages. We are reminded how the more fortunate provide for indigent newcomers as a matter of course, just as in *The steppe* we hear that in Russia proper the public took gifts of food to prisoners in gaol at Easter, for after centuries of oppression prisoners, so many of whom were known to be merely political offenders, had come to be looked upon by the Russian people as brothers in distress. We are told by Leroy-Beaulieu that in the north-east of Russia there were villages where peasants were still in the habit of leaving a loaf and a jug of water on the window-sill or in the doorway of their izba, for any fugitive from Siberia who might pass in the night.

Such a one is the vagabond in *Dreams*, the gently nurtured illegitimate son of a nurse in a gentleman's household, who as a mere boy had innocently become the accomplice of his mother when she poisoned her master through jealousy. He had been condemned to six years' penal servitude, but like so many others had escaped and made his way back on foot across Siberia. At last he has been arrested for having no passport and is being taken to town by two village policemen. He hopes, by pretending to have lost his memory, to escape the fate of being sent back to the torture of penal servitude. If he is merely exiled, for vagabondage, to eastern Siberia he will be content, for of this virgin country in the far east beyond Lake Baikal he has the same happy memories as Chekhov himself. Of the horrors of penal servitude on Sakhalin Island we have a glimpse at the end of *The murder*, a night picture of convicts called out to coal a steamer in stormy weather. The fate of three of the people implicated in the murder illustrates in a small sample various aspects of life on Sakhalin as Chekhov had seen it. There was in the ordinary way no death penalty in Russia for non-political crimes. It had been abolished as early as 1753, though the knout continued to kill many men until it too went in 1845. The man who had murdered his half-brother in the story was therefore sentenced to twenty years' penal servitude. This had been increased to a life sentence and he had received forty strokes of the lash for attempting to escape, besides being flogged on two other occasions for allowing others to steal his prison clothes. Cruel physical punishment lingered longest in prisons and in the army, though as we see by the letter quoted above it was still in use, illegally, against the common people. Count Witte himself corroborates this, in the memorandum which he wrote to Nicolas II in 1898, where he mentions arbitrary punishment, generally corporal, as one of the grievances still suffered by the peasantry. But the other two sent to Sakhalin were more fortunate. The waiter, sentenced to ten years as an accomplice, had by this time been allowed to take a post as lackey to an official, while another so-called accomplice, a girl of eighteen, sentenced to six years, had been given permission to live with an ex-convict and had already three children by him. A typical feature of Russian criminal justice at this time is the long period that the prisoners had to wait for trial, eleven months. A prisoner in *In the ravine* waits well over six months and in *Dreams* the trial is not over for two years. The same feature is very prominent in Tolstoy's *Resurrection*.

We have made the acquaintance of all the principal types of official to be encountered throughout Russia in the later nineteenth century. The story *The marshal's widow* will serve to pass some of them in review again, by introducing to us the principal people gathered together at the house of the widow of a marshal of the nobility in a certain District, at the annual service in memory of her husband. One would find there of course his successor, who would be ex-officio president of the zemstvo assembly, and in addition the chairman of its executive committee, the 'permanent member', the two regular justices of the peace, the district chief of police, the two city chiefs of police serving under him in different sectors of the District, and the zemstvo doctor. There were also present, besides the priest, deacon and parish-clerk conducting the service, a teacher or two and all the landowners, making in all about fifty people, the cream of District society, who surreptitiously turn a strictly teetotal gathering (the late lamented having met his death while under the influence of strong liquor) into a well-furnished bottle party, not a very edifying spectacle.

The instruments of autocracy with which we have been dealing would of course have been useless if the government had not also had at its disposal a sufficiently strong armed force to suppress any dangerous opposition or rebellion. The army may therefore fittingly be considered now, as the ultimate guarantee of that stability of the central state structure, nervousness about which so frequently stifled promising reforms. Chekhov's mature life fell in the period of peace between the war with Turkey and the war with Japan. He did not himself serve in the army, and it was only in the last year of his life that he had much cause to think about the military efficiency of his country. He wrote no war stories, and he left stories about army life to men like his friend Shcheglov (Leontiev), who had served in the Turkish campaign, but he was naturally not blind to the incalculable influence of the army on the private lives of his contemporaries. Characteristically, he was interested in soldiers as men, and in their contacts with other men.

The Russian army too had been affected by the wave of reform in the 'sixties, under the leadership of Dmitry Milyutin as Minister of War. Serious efforts were made both to humanise army life, by the abolition of cruel punishments, the reduction of the period of service from twenty-five to sixteen years, and later (1874) the introduction of compulsory military service for all classes, to distribute the burden more fairly—and to increase its efficiency, by the reform of the military schools and the stress laid on education both for officers and men. Under the new law service was for six years. Though it was in principle compulsory for all able-bodied males, exemption could be granted on account of home circumstances, to only sons and the like, and the higher the standard of education a man attained, the shorter became his period of service, a fact which explains in part the enthusiasm shown for education by some of the peasantry. The country was divided into military districts, and the quota of recruits required (for not all available were required) was chosen by lot.

Chekhov's most interesting references to the life of the common soldier are to be found in the story *Gusev*, begun during his return voyage from Sakhalin. It shows us discharged soldiers returning by sea from service in the Far East, many of them seriously ill with consumption and paralysis, smuggled on board along with the healthy. There are many deaths and burials take place at sea like those Chekhov had seen on the way to Singapore. Some home truths about the army are put into the mouth of a village priest's son, who is typical of the revolutionary intellectuals and agitators of the time. Gusev, a private, in the opposite bunk, has himself no grumbles, except the enforced absence from his home, where he is needed. As an officer's servant he has had an easy enough life, and only been beaten once, and that was his own fault. But his neighbour has no patience with peasant ignorance and submissiveness. 'Your doctors put you on the boat,' he tells him, 'just to get rid of you. They were sick of you, cattle as they call you. You could not pay them anything, you were a lot of trouble, and you put their accounts out by your deaths—you were of course just cattle. And it wasn't hard for them to get you off their hands. All that was necessary was first, to have no conscience or human feeling, and secondly, to take in the steamship company.' . . 'They tell you that the wind has broken from its chain (a phrase used by Gusev about the storm) or that you are cattle, Hottentots (Pechenyegs) and you believe them; they hit you in the jaw, and you kiss their hand; some animal or other in a racoon fur coat insults you, then throws you a tip, and you say: Let me kiss your little hand, sir!' He himself is the incarnation of protest, claims to see through all the shady tricks of the masters, and refuses to be silenced.

The other army stories are about officers in civilian society. In *The kiss* it is a reserve artillery brigade passing through a village on the way to camp, and invited to join a party at the house of the local squire, a retired general. It is a charming picture of polite society, tea, dancing, billiards, the scent of poplar leaves, roses and lilac through the open windows, an atmosphere of ease and luxury. The officers are welcomed by the general and his family, but more as a social duty than from genuine pleasure, for officers are no rarity in these circles. *The husband* on the other hand depicts the wild excitement in a little District capital when a cavalry regiment on manoeuvres spends a night there, for here this is an event. The shopkeepers and innkeepers have hopes of good business and the ladies are all agog for a dance, which is duly arranged in the club. The officers dance with the ladies, who are in the seventh heaven, while fathers and husbands hang about in the vestibule or at the buffet, and one husband at least is mean enough to hurry his wife away from the bright scene, because he cannot bear to see her enjoy herself. The officers seem to symbolise romance, youth, escape from the everyday world of surly husbands and household cares; to judge by the effects, you might think that the music of the regiment marching in 'came not from soldiers' buglers, but from heaven itself'.

The same symbolism is an important element in the play *Three sisters*. There life in the chief town of a Province is represented as deadly dull but for the presence of a brigade of artillery, and there are few things more moving in drama than the fading of its gay music as it marches away, contrasting so vividly with the mood of the sisters whom happiness has passed by. Masha, the teacher's wife, attracted by a battery commander, finds the officers much more cultivated and gentlemanly than the civil servants like her husband, but to an unprejudiced eye there is not a great deal to choose between them. The officers are of many types, ranging from the harmless young clowns Fedotik and Rode, with not a thought in their heads, through the besotted newspaper addict, Dr. Chebutykin, to Masha's Colonel Vershinin, and the rivals for Irina's hand, the philosophising Baron Tusenbach and the would-be Lermontov, Solyony, who finally kills Tusenbach in a duel. The representatives of the civil service are Masha's husband, a master at the 'gymnasium', a spiritless pedantic toady, and Andrei, a general's son, and the brother of the three sisters, a new version of Ivanov, a promising young scholar who turns into a shifty henpecked gambler, holding down a safe official job. The atmosphere of the play, 'gloomier than gloom' as Chekhov called it, results not only or chiefly from private disappointments and entanglements which might happen anywhere—two ill-assorted marriages, and the remorseless passage of the years over sisters without parents, or husbands, or a clear aim in life. It is peculiarly Russian and of Chekhov's time. There is the nostalgia for Moscow, the sisters' home in youth, though that kind of feeling could no doubt be parallelled in other lands, and is in any case rather a longing for the past, perhaps, than for Moscow itself. Above all, there is the influence of a lifeless and perverted society. It is the world of officers and officials, children of the former serf-owning class, for whom life had been made economically so easy and politically so free from responsibility, that they had never known what real work meant, nor any aim in life but the satisfaction of their private impulses. 'I have never done a stroke of work in my life,' says Tusenbach. 'I was born in St. Petersburg, that cold and idle city, in a family that had never known work or material cares. I remember that when I came home from the cadet school, a lackey would pull off my boots, while I played the naughty child, and my mother looked at me with worship in her eyes, and could not understand why others did not do so too. They shielded me from work.'

A second characteristic of this world is their feeling of the aimlessness of their life. There are several of them who preach the gospel of work with fervour, and two of the sisters at least practise what they preach, but the commonest phrase in the play, after 'We must work', is 'I am tired'. It is not only work that is needed, but an aim to work for, some understanding of their world, and of that they despair. The wisest of them can only hope that if men will only work, without any thought of their own happiness, the future will bring both happiness and understanding. Russians, Chekhov often tells us, were much given to wistful thoughts of the future, and here one of the 'philosophers', Vershinin, himself is made to say: 'We do not know what happiness is, we only long for it.' Yet though there was a large 'escapist' element in these thoughts of the future, one passage at least of Tusenbach's is strangely prophetic, written as it was in 1900: 'The time has come, an avalanche is moving down on us, a mighty, wholesome storm is brewing, which is approaching, is already near and soon will sweep away from our society its idleness, indifference, prejudice against work, and foul ennui. I shall work, and in some twenty-five or thirty years everyone, everyone will work too.'

A quotation from a letter to Suvorin (9/12/1890) summing up Chekhov's impressions of the Sakhalin journey, when he probably saw more of official Russia than at any time before or afterwards, will show how much there is of the author himself in these speeches of his characters, and serve to sum up the impressions that we have derived from his work: 'God's world is a good place. We are the one thing not good in it. How little justice and humility there is in us! How little we understand true patriotism! A drunken, broken-down debauchee of a husband loves his wife and children, but of what use is that love? We, so we are told in our own newspapers, love our great motherland, but how does

that love express itself? Instead of knowledge—insolence and im-
measurable conceit; instead of work—sloth and swinishness;
there is no justice, the conception of honour does not go beyond
"the honour of the uniform"—the uniform which is so commonly
seen adorning the prisoner's dock in our courts. Work is what is
wanted, and the rest can go to the devil. First of all we must be
just, and all the rest will be added unto us.'

CHAPTER VI

THE CHURCH

It is fitting to consider the Russian Church immediately after the state services, because for two centuries it had in a sense been one of them. When the Great Russian nation was being shaped in the Muscovite period (fifteenth to seventeenth centuries), 'the dominant elements in the church, in extolling the grand princes of Moscow as the Tsars of All Russia, magnified and extolled them as successors to the divinely instituted Byzantine autocracy, as requiring all honour and obedience and as wielding authority not only in all temporal matters but, with reservations, in religious matters'.[1] The Muscovite monarchy was a theocratic monarchy, regarded as deriving its authority directly from God. It was 'the political expression of the class of privileged landowning clergy',[2] and nothing could have been closer than the alliance between church and monarch. Though religious reasons continued to be put forward by the Orthodox as the prime justification of the monarch's authority, the inevitable struggle between church and state resulted in Russia in the total subordination of the national church. The monasteries were deprived of most of their land—they had at one time owned about a third of the realm—and of any power of political interference. Even the church's own affairs were controlled from 1721 by the Holy Synod, a board modelled on similar bodies in the German protestant states. The members, though all but one were ecclesiastics, were appointed by the Tsar and given no choice but to further the purposes of the state. The all-important lay member, the Chief Procurator, was in the nineteenth century a sort of minister for the state religion, which was consciously used as an instrument of power from the accession of Nicholas I (1825). 'Karl Marx regarded the organised Churches as enemies to social revolution. By ascribing divine origin or divine sanction to human institutions, they placed them out of bounds except to the impious or the unbelieving. In Imperial Russia the state of the Orthodox Church confirmed, for

---

[1] Sumner, *Survey*, 89.
[2] Mirsky, *Russia*, 135.

the revolutionary parties, the inferences which Marx had drawn. Not only this or that Church, but religion in general, assumed the aspect of a defender of oppression.'[1]

These high matters of church and state are not directly discussed by Chekhov, but the all-pervasive influence of the church on Russian life is evident in everything that he wrote. We have seen in the chapter on the peasant his estimate of the extent to which orthodoxy still controlled the life and thought of the village, and the part played by the parish priest. The present chapter will describe the impression gained from his work of the attitude to religion among other classes, of the rites, observances and sacraments of the church, of the rôle of the white or parish clergy generally and that of the black clergy or monks, and finally of the innumerable expressions of religious feeling to be encountered in his day in Russia outside the Orthodox Church.

Chekhov's own attitude to religion is quite clear from his letters. He had been brought up in the strictest orthodoxy by his father, whose susceptibilities he would not have liked to offend even when his scientific training had shaken his beliefs. At Melikhovo, his brother tells us, when the family went to bed at 10, all was quiet in the house, except for a subdued sound of singing and monotonous reading. This was their father celebrating evensong in his room. A simple peasant faith like this was no longer possible for Chekhov, and he told Suvorin that he had no religion, but that does not mean that his attitude was purely negative, like that of so many of 'the drowsy, apathetic, lazily philosophising cold intelligentsia, who blithely deny everything, as it is easier for a lazy brain to deny than to assert'. His works and letters without exception express the traditional Christian ethics. What he hated above all things was insincerity, violence and inhumanity, the treatment of men as mere instruments and not as personalities, and his own life was full of acts of Christian charity. Moreover the solemn rites of the church, the sound of the Moscow bells, a good choir, the savour of Church Slavonic, the mystery of old monastic buildings never lost their hold on him, and made it easy for him, like the great majority of the educated, to conform, and even to join with enthusiasm in the traditional Easter celebrations. He never spent an Easter night in bed, his brother tells us. In Moscow he would listen to the Easter bells on the Kammeny Bridge and then go from church to church, not returning home till Easter night was over. At

[1] Maynard, *Russ. peasant*, 357.

home the brothers would join their father in the chorale 'Christ is risen', Anton singing bass, before sitting down to break their fast.

Chekhov would have called himself an agnostic. He could not accept the Christian story as more than a beautiful myth, and detested pretentious crusades against materialism like Bourget's *Disciple*. Scientists 'seek for truth in matter, because there is nowhere else to seek for it; it is only matter that they can see, hear and feel. . . . I think that when dissecting a corpse, even the most inveterate spiritualist will inevitably ask himself, "Where is the soul here?" And if one knows how great is the similarity between bodily and mental diseases, and that both are treated by the same remedies, one cannot help refusing to separate the soul from the body'. But he was not satisfied with materialism, and sometimes had his intimations of immortality. Here for instance are some ideas that he once expressed in conversation to Suvorin: 'Death is a cruel thing, a disgusting punishment. If after death the individuality perishes, then there is no life. I cannot console myself with the thought that in the universal life I shall have finished with pain and suffering. The universal life has a goal. I don't know the goal. Death arouses something bigger than horror. But when one is alive one thinks little of death. At any rate, I do. And when I am dying I shall see what it is like. It is terrible to become nothing. People take you away to the cemetery, and then return home, have tea, and make hypocritical speeches. It is disgusting to think of it.'[1]

It was with Chekhov as with all Russians. 'The Church is an element in the national consciousness,' says H. W. Williams. 'It enters into the details of life, moulds custom, maintains a traditional atmosphere to the influence of which a Russian, from the very fact that he is a Russian, involuntarily submits. A Russian may, and most Russian intelligents do, deny the Church in theory, but in taking his share in the collective life of the nation he, at many points, recognises the Church as a fact. More than that. In those borderlands of emotion that until life's end evade the control of toilsomely acquired personal conviction, the Church retains a foothold, yielding only slowly and in the course of generations to modern influences.' All Russians, for example, dated their letters in the Old Style, thirteen days later (in the present century) than the rest of the world, simply because of the conservatism of the Church. Chekhov still, perhaps unconsciously,

[1] A. Tchekhov, *Life and theatrical reminiscences*, Lon., 1927, p. 38.

used pious phrases like 'May the Saviour preserve you' repeatedly in his intimate letters to his wife. To quote Williams again: 'The average Russian intelligent does not dream of going to church on Sundays, and of priests on the whole he has an exceedingly poor opinion. But at certain important moments of his life he invokes the Church's aid. He goes to church to be married, and before marriage, confession and communion are necessary. The priest christens his children, and every Orthodox Russian bears the name of a saint, Greek, Jewish, Roman or Russian. And when he dies priest and deacon again come into his home and sing a mass for the repose of his soul, and afterwards, with solemn and touching ceremony commit his body to the ground. There is one great festival of the year in which all Russians, whatever be their standing or opinions, joyfully take part. Nowhere is Easter celebrated with such tremulous intensity of feeling as in Russia.'

The established religion had clearly left a deep imprint on Russian manners and customs, but it was only amongst the peasantry and uneducated that its rites were practised with conviction by large numbers. Even in the village, as we have seen, the great majority were inclined to look on religious observances as a kind of magic, a magic in which, unlike most of the educated, they still believed. The cultured part of the public, as Chekhov wrote to Dyagilev (30/12/1902) had moved away from religion, and was moving further and further away from it, whatever people might say and however many philosophical and religious societies might be formed, and this because of the whole trend of modern culture. A typical example is the medical professor in *A dreary story*, who says of himself that though he knows he soon must die and should be occupying himself with the question of what happens after death, his mind is indifferent to such questions, much as he appreciates their importance. It is only science that really interests him still. It is only by science, he is convinced, that man will conquer nature and himself. Yet he knows that he would have been happier, and not so tragically incapable of guiding others, like his ward Katya, if his thoughts and feelings had been bound together by 'a common idea, or the God of a living man', and that lacking this he has nothing. Similarly with almost all Chekhov's professional men and officials. They had little or no personal religion, but they were married in church, their children were christened, and they usually attended communion at Easter, for this was compulsory for all the Orthodox by law, though the law was not easy to enforce, and in any case certificates of attendance could be bought (see above, p. 66). When they died there were elaborate funeral services and perhaps memorial services for years after, as in *The marshal's widow*. A friend of Orlov in *An anonymous story*, the St. Petersburg barrister and man of affairs Pekarsky, expresses the view of the governing class in the sentence: 'It is not intelligent to believe in God, but religion must be preserved, for the common people need some restraining principle, or they will not work.'

The importance of the Church in the national consciousness, in the routine of daily life, is brought home to the reader in innumerable ways. Churches with their cupolas and far-shining cross enter into the description of every village of any size; in towns they are innumerable. In the town in *The bishop*, for instance, the capital of a province, there are forty-two churches and six monasteries. In every peasant's house and even in the entrance-halls of hospitals there is an icon; a visitor who does not cross himself and bow to it is distrusted by simple folk (cf. *A troublesome visitor*). The phrase 'to cross oneself' occurs on every other page. Peasants cross themselves when entering a house, before and after a meal, at the mention of a dead friend (with the phrase 'The kingdom of God to him!'); in *The darling* people passing under the window of a woman who has just lost her husband cross themselves when they hear her weeping, and a husband tells his wife to cross herself when she wakens up with a cry in the night. Passers-by cross themselves when they hear a monastery bell ringing for a service, or during the service when the choir sings fortissimo. The gesture was of course a silent prayer, and played a great part in prayers of any kind, in private or in public. It was a characteristic of Russian prayer that it was expressed in action more than in words. 'The peasant prays with all his limbs. During the service he spends his time crossing himself, raising at the same time his head and his right hand, then bending in two between every sign of the cross, and raising himself to begin all over again, without a pause,' says Leroy-Beaulieu. He uses the expression 'une espèce de gymnastique sacrée' of these restless gestures, which are directed towards the altar and the icons. The most devout would kneel at intervals, and prostrate themselves, as they had done in the old days of serfdom to their masters.

The small boy of nine in *The steppe*, who, having nothing else to do, went into the church in a strange village on a Sunday morning, behaved no doubt as he had seen his elders do. On entering he first stood with his head against someone's back, for everyone was standing, as usual, and when he got bored with the singing made his way up to the kind of rood-screen that separated the altar from the nave and was called the iconostasis, because on it the most precious icons were displayed. In the front row of the congregation he saw a lady and gentleman, who must have been the squire and his wife, standing on a rug, with chairs behind them which they had brought themselves, for there are no pews in a Russian church. The boy went up and kissed each of the icons, kneeling and prostrating himself before each in turn till he touched the cold floor with his forehead, because he liked the feeling. Even an adult congregation in a big church, in stories like *The bishop* or *Easter Eve*, is shown in restless movement, and at a wedding the officiating bishop has to quieten the congregation with the words: 'Do not walk about in the church or make a noise, but stand quietly and pray. You must show respect in God's house' (*The teacher of literature*).

The congregation, it will be seen, played the same passive rôle in church as in political life, and there was indeed an evident similarity between the Russian idea of religion as primarily praise and worship of an all-powerful Father and the subjects' attitude towards their Tsar. A bearded, long-haired priest in a robe of cloth of gold, 'swinging a censer in the smoke of which the sacred pictures in their glittering frames take fantastic forms, and the shadows within the altar become full of mystery, . . . the sad sweet slowly rising and falling tones of the choir, the familiar but solemn Slavonic words of the prayers and the sonorous responses of the deacon' (Williams) held the rapt attention of the congregation for two hours or more on end in a kind of sacred play, impressive as great art is, even when its symbolism is obscure. Priest and deacon 'were fully conscious of the solemnity of their rôle and played it with the dignity of masters of the divine ceremonies' (Leroy-Beaulieu), while the unaccompanied singing of the great Russian choirs was amongst the best in the world.

Chekhov's most detailed picture of a great religious festival is the story *Easter eve*.[1] Waiting for the ferry across a river in spring flood, on a night brilliant with stars (an admirable setting!), the writer sees bright red lights appear on the other side, then a deep-

---

[1] Written in 1886, and therefore not inspired, as Mrs. Garnett, following Michael Chekhov, says, by the visit to the Holy Mountains in 1887. *Uprooted* alone was the outcome of that visit.

voiced bell and a cannon shot are heard, and the peasant beside him calls 'Christ is risen'—it is midnight on Easter Eve. Two more cannon are fired, more red lights are seen, and when he is on the ferry tar barrels blaze up at the water's edge, throwing long reflections towards him, and rockets shoot into the sky. How beautiful it is! But the lay brother working the ferry is sad, and he tells of the death of his friend Nicolai, the gentle hierodeacon, whose songs of praise had so often moved him to tears. It is rare creative spirits like Nicolai, one feels, unknown outside their monastery, who have in the course of the ages built up the temple of religious art. He is clearly for Chekhov the type of the poet, and when Merezhkovsky in a review called him 'a failure', Chekhov rejected the term. 'How is he a failure? God grant us all a life like his: he believed in God, he had enough to eat and he had the gift of composing poetry. . . . One would need to be a God to distinguish successes from failures infallibly.'

Reaching the other bank, the writer finds outside the monastery gate a chaos of vehicles, horses and people, fitfully illuminated by the blood-red lights, and inside the gate amongst the tombstones men and women from the country all around, with bags of Easter cakes to be blessed by the priest. In the church itself it is a scene of joyful excitement. 'At the entrance there is a ceaseless struggle where opposite currents meet. Some are still coming in, others going out and quickly coming back again, to stand still awhile and then again move on. People flit from place to place, stroll about and seem to be looking for something. A wave starts from the entrance and runs through the whole church, stirring even the front rows, where the sedate and slow-moving stand. There can be no question of concentrated prayer. No one is praying, and there is a sense of unaccountable gladness everywhere, like the joy of a child, seeking a pretext to break out and express itself in movement, even if it is only a heedless swaying and jostling.

The same extraordinary liveliness is immediately apparent in the Easter service itself. The holy door in every chapel is wide open, thick clouds of incense float in the air around the candelabra; wherever you look, you see lights, the gleam and crackle of candles. It is useless for the priest to read; the busy joyful singing of the choir goes on without pause to the end; after each hymn of the canon the clergy change their vestments and come out with the censer, and this is repeated almost every ten minutes.'

Easter Day is for strict Orthodox Russians the culmination of a seven weeks' period of preparation, made up of Shrovetide, or Butter Week, as the Russians call it, when milk products and eggs may be eaten, but no meat, and the six weeks of Lent, when all this is 'skoromnoe' or forbidden food. In *Shrove Tuesday* (literally 'On the eve of the fast') we see a middle-class family conscientiously stuffing themselves with 'skoromnoe' before it is too late, to the detriment of their digestion and their temper. At ten o'clock there was a very Russian incident: 'The cook Anna came into the dining-room, and—plumped herself down at the master's feet. "Forgive me, Pavel Vasseilich, for Christ's sake," she said, getting up, all red in the face. "And you forgive me for Christ's sake!" answered Pavel Vassilich nonchalantly. Anna went up to all the family in the same way, fell down at their feet and asked forgiveness.' To all, except an old midwife, who was of her own class. It was the custom to ask forgiveness of everyone in this way, particularly when on the way to confession. In Holy Week everyone must confess and communicate. The story *In Passion Week* shows us confession and communion through the eyes of a boy not yet nine—children take communion from the age of seven, so there is nothing corresponding to confirmation in the Orthodox Church. 'The bells are ringing, it's time to go,' they tell him, 'and see you behave yourself in church, or God will punish you.' He hastily swallows a last piece of white bread and takes a drink of water, knowing that after confession he will not be allowed to eat or drink until after communion next morning. Then off he goes through the streets, where this evening there is every sign of spring. He refrains from jumping up behind a cab with two other boys, and shyly enters the church. We see him, in contrite mood, in the queue, watching people go one by one behind the screen where the priest stands, separated but not hidden from those waiting their turn. The old Adam comes out in a brief scuffle with his enemy Mitka, who is in front of him, and then his turn comes. With burning cheeks he answers the priest's questions—confession cannot be a very searching affair when so many must be heard in a short time, and questions and answers are in very general terms. The priest gives him absolution, laying the end of his stole on his head, and he passes on to the deacon to have his name entered in the register. How hungry he is when he reaches home! He feels ready to suffer any kind of torture, to live in the wilderness without his mother or to feed bears out of his own hand, if he may first eat just a single cabbage pie! Early next morning, Maundy Thursday, dressed in his best clothes, he goes to communion, and everyone seems to share his feeling of gladness and freedom, but his well-meant approaches cannot bridge the social gulf between him and Mitka, the washerwoman's son.

Mention has been made in an earlier chapter (p. 63) of the principal events of the church calendar, and of a summer procession of clergy bearing icons from village to village. Two or three other outdoor ceremonies, each invoking in its particular season the blessing of God on some activity of man, in a beautiful traditional rite, may be illustrated from the stories. There is in winter at Twelfth Night the blessing of the waters, whose teeming fish meant so much to a population that fasted for a third of the year, in *Art*. Two men are seen at work on a frozen river, a stolid old church watchman and a stocky little peasant, very down at heels but full of the confidence of the expert, and earning the co-operation and admiration of the village for this one thing in which he is a real artist. They cut a round hole in the ice, set a red wooden frame round it, build beside it of wood a lectern and a high cross, glaze it all over with ice and adorn it with a dove resting on the cross and other things, carved in ice and dyed in bright colours. When it is unveiled next day to the delight of thousands, this 'Jordan' sparkles in the sun as if it were inlaid with diamonds and rubies, and the clergy come down a path strewn with fir and juniper branches from the church on the bank, with banners and icons. The waters are blessed and the cross is plunged into them, to the accompaniment of shouts and rifle shots and pealing bells, while the crowd scramble for certain pegs from the wooden frame, which bring one luck for a whole year. In summer there are processions with the cross, to bless the cattle and to pray for rain, like the one seen in a day-dream by the deacon in *A duel*. 'In front peasants bear the church banners, and women and girls the icons, then come choirboys and the parish clerk, with a bandage round his cheek and a straw in his hair, then the deacon, the priest in his velvet cap carrying the cross, and behind them a crowd of peasants, men, women and children, kicking up the dust; the priest's and the deacon's wives are amongst them, wearing kerchiefs. The choir chant, the children cry, quails call, a lark carols above. . . . Now they have stopped and sprinkled the cattle with holy water. . . . They go on further and going down on their knees pray for rain. Then refreshments, and talk.'

Chekhov's agnosticism did not prevent him from entering with sympathy into the spirit of these popular religious rites, nor does his work show any trace of antipathy towards the clergy. Indeed his picture of them as men is on the whole decidedly more favourable than, for instance, that of the official class. His village priest in *A nightmare* earns our pity and admiration, and in several other stories he introduces representatives both of the 'white' (parochial) and 'black' (monastic) clergy of various grades, who with one exception are all men of character, inspiring respect. There is father Christopher in *The Steppe*, a rosy-cheeked old priest of eighty, who still looks out on God's world with surprised delight in his eyes and a smile on his lips. Whatever his influence on his town parish may have been, and it is hard to believe that it has been other than good, he has himself found peace of soul, and desires nothing better of life than what he has been granted. Talking to a boy just leaving home for a 'gymnasium', he looks back with pleasure on his own schooldays. At fifteen, he says, he had spoken Latin and composed Latin verses just as well as Russian. As a young man he had read Greek and French too, and studied mathematics, philosophy, history and 'every kind of learning', rather a big claim, to be sure, but it seems clear that he had had the makings of a scholar in him and would have pursued his studies further at Kiev, if his father, a deacon himself, had not insisted on his taking a post. He had obeyed, for 'obedience is better than fasting and prayer', he had married and brought up a family, and now they are happily off his hands, the daughters married and the sons in professions. At eighty he is going off to market to sell wool for his inexperienced son-in-law.

Very different is the black sheep mentioned already in Chapter III, Father Anastasius in *The letter*. We have seen the kind of reputation that had led to his suspension (p. 65). Native weakness of character was at the root of it all, but like the deacon in the same story, he had not enjoyed the same kind of education as Father Christopher or the 'Blagochinny'. The deacon and he did not know either Latin or Greek, for they had begun as parish clerks (dyachok), who are always represented as men of very moderate education and culture. The deacon, a good simple-hearted man, comes to ask advice about his son to the priest whom he assists. The priest has a large town parish and is 'Blagochinny' or superintendent over a number of smaller parishes round about. He is a handsome, rather humourless man of fifty, whose features habitually wear the expression of dignity. He has the reputation of great learning and intelligence—he would have been a bishop, Father Anastasius says, if he had not married. What is particularly well brought out in the story is the great strain imposed on a priest by the Easter services, following weeks of fasting and the confessing of his parishioners one by one, and secondly the importance of the sons of the clergy as possible recruits for the intelligentsia. Here the deacon's son is only seen through the eyes of his father and the priest, for both of whom he is a renegade from the true faith, though his father cannot find it in his heart to be very severe with him. The priest however had never cared for him even as a boy because he talked too much, did not cross himself when entering a room and was offended if addressed as 'thou', all signs of insubordination. As a student he had ceased to go to church, and acquired the habit of raising ticklish, insoluble (? political) questions with a conceited air. Now his father has heard that he has been known to give a visitor roast turkey to eat in Lent, and is living in sin with a certain Madame. Despairing of influencing him himself he persuades the Blagochinny in his greater wisdom to dictate a reproof, which he does with some gusto. The delicate art of the story lies in the play of character between the three churchmen, the priest, the deacon and the old reprobate, Father Anastasius, who listens full of 'Schadenfreude' to the news of another sinner.

The higher clergy, bishops, archbishops and metropolitans, were celibate, and it was one of the chief functions of the monasteries to train them. They were recruited from archimandrites and abbots and continued to live in monastic houses, like the hero of Chekhov's story *The bishop*. This masterpiece, one of the most moving and concentrated of all Chekhov's works, in describing the last days of a bishop, evokes the whole atmosphere in which he moved and gives us in outline the story of his life. The order in which impressions are presented to us, the cutting of the film, so to speak, is arranged with consummate skill. Chekhov's typical bishop (the title itself suggests that the picture was meant to be taken as typical) was one of nine children of a poor country deacon, himself descended from a line of deacons and priests going back for countless generations. 'His love of the ritual of the church, the priesthood, the sound of church bells was inborn, deep, ineradicable.' In his earliest memories he saw himself as a little barefoot boy, following the icon in summer processions with the naive smile of unquestioning faith and unalloyed happiness. At the church school his intellectual development was slow, at

fifteen they even thought of putting him in a shop, but at the
seminary and the academy he grew into a scholar, and afterwards
returned to the seminary for three years as a teacher of Greek,
before becoming a monk. Promotion after that was rapid. He
became inspector (sub-rector), then after writing a thesis rector
of the seminary and an archimandrite at the age of thirty-two,
but serious illness soon compelled him to go abroad to a warmer
climate. On his return eight years later he was made a vicarial
bishop.

In depicting what it felt like to be a Russian bishop, Chekhov
puts first the loneliness that this office imposes on its occupant as
a man. 'He could never grow accustomed to the fear which he
involuntarily inspired in people, in spite of his quiet and modest
disposition. Everyone in this province, when he looked at them,
seemed to him little, frightened, guilty. In his presence they were
all overcome by timidity, even old head priests, they all fell at
his feet, and not long ago one suppliant, an old village pope's wife,
could not utter a single word for fright.' Even his own mother
could not behave naturally towards him now. She used 'you'
instead of 'thou', and in his presence seemed to think of herself
as the deacon's wife, seeking protection for her grandchildren,
rather than as his mother. It was only his last illness which broke
down the barrier and made him simply her child again. There
is an indescribable pathos in Chekhov's handling of this relationship. The second feature he stresses is the minute bureaucratic
control exercised throughout the church. 'And the papers,
coming in and going out, numbered tens of thousands, and what
papers! Every *blagochinny* in the whole diocese gave marks for
conduct to priests, young or old, and even their wives and
children, fives and fours, sometimes even threes, and about such
matters serious "papers" had to be read and written. He had
never a free minute.' Such features in Russian life assumed a
disagreeable prominence for the bishop on his return from abroad.
He seemed to meet with coarseness and ignorance everywhere,
and listening to the petty personal complaints which were brought
to him when he was acting as substitute for his superior, the
eparchial bishop, he understood why the latter, who as a young
man had written a treatise on 'The freedom of the will', now
found his spiritual life choked in trivialities, and seemed no longer
to think about God.

The bishop's only confidant, a seventy year old monk, who
had been steward to the eparchial bishop and worked with

eleven bishops in his time, had long since forgotten why he ever became a monk, and never thought about it. Listening to him it was hard to know whether he liked anyone or anything now, his phrase about everything he saw was 'I don't like it'; it was even doubtful whether he believed in God. Yet with all his eccentricities he was kind-hearted to simple people like the bishop's mother and niece, and they were not in the least afraid of him.

Monks and monasteries figure in several other stories besides *The bishop*, but they are always presented as seen by a visitor, and there is no hint of the slackness and drunkenness which Williams for instance mentions as common in some monasteries. In *Uprooted* there is a full description of the Holy Mountains monastery on a great feast day, its striking situation on the Donets, the motley crowd of ten thousand visitors, including hundreds of pilgrims from near and far, filling to overflowing all the huge guest-houses and every available corner elsewhere, the patient kindness of the lay brethren with this trying throng, the endless round of long services and the picturesque procession in boats to the hermitage. *Easter Eve* is principally concerned with the drama of the Easter celebrations, but in the conversation with the lay brother about Nicolai the veil is lifted a little on life within the monastery walls. The view of the monks suggested is that they are good men, but often rather rough and uncultured. 'In our monastery the people are all good, kind, devout,' says the lay brother, 'but—there is no gentleness and delicacy in them, they are all from simple poor homes. They speak too loud, they shuffle with their feet when they walk, they are noisy and they cough, but Nicolai spoke gently and sweetly, and if he saw that anyone was asleep or saying his prayers, he went past like a mouse or a little gnat.' In *The Princess* we notice the same readiness in the monks, no doubt for reasons of monastery finance, to give themselves special trouble with the rich and powerful as is suggested several times in *The bishop*, and even the archimandrite is shy and awkward. In *The two Volodyas* a visit to a convent and the motives that led a lively young woman to take the veil are touched upon.

'There is in the Russian people,' says H. W. Williams, 'a capacity for religious emotion which the official church with all its wealth of tradition and complexity of ritual fails wholly to satisfy, and which seeks an outlet in all kinds of irregular ways.' These irregular expressions of religious feeling too find their reflection in Chekhov. We see mass pilgrimages to famous shrines, as in *Uprooted*, and individual pilgrims, devoted to a life of wandering from shrine to shrine, in *A dead body* and *A woman's kingdom*. In the former a young 'strannik' or wanderer comes out of the night, chanting a psalm, to the fire, beside which the two peasants are watching the body. He is making the round of the monasteries, but his religion does not save him from mortal fright at the sight of a corpse. In the latter it is a woman pilgrim who is guided by the spirit at Christmas time, as often before, to the kitchen of a hospitable house. She is a little sharp-featured woman of fifty, with a sly and spiteful look in her eyes. She says long prayers before the icon on entering, but the advice she offers to the mistress of the house about marriage is hardly in keeping with her religious professions. 'For thirty years,' she says, 'I have thought only of my sins, and been afraid, but now I see what I have let slip through my fingers. O it's a fool, a fool I am, she sighed. A woman's time is a short time, and you should treasure every day of it. . . . Don't listen to anyone, have your fling till forty, and you'll have time enough left to pray for forgiveness.'

There are occasional references to the numerous Russian sects, and in *The murder* we find a detailed study of the sectarian temperament in two cousins, whose family for generations had been deeply religious and inclined to heresy. One of them had gone on pilgrimage with his mother every summer from the age of twelve. As he grew up he performed great feats of self-imposed fasting and asceticism, and fell a victim to spiritual pride. Because no priest came up to his high ideals he began to hold services for himself in a small hired room, services following a very severe rite and lasting sometimes ten or twelve hours through the night. He was looked upon by some as a saint, and gained a following of peasant women and old maids. In their gatherings strange things happened, very much as among the Khlysty, with their ritual dancing. 'Suddenly their legs begin to tremble as if they had the fever in them, then someone calls out, then another—I too am all of a tremble, like a Jew in a frying pan, I don't know why, and our legs begin to jump. It is a miracle indeed; against your will you begin to jump and wave your arms, and there are cries and shrieks, and we are all dancing and running after one another until we fall down.'

Fortunately he was convinced by his employer before long of the error of his ways, and when he had to return to his native village at forty-five as the result of an accident, he tried to persuade his cousin, who also had his own chapel in his lonely

country inn, and conducted services there with his sister, that
anything that went beyond the normal was of the devil, but his
interference, combined with disagreements about their common
inheritance, so got on their nerves that one day, after a quarrel
about fasting, they killed him.   It is a grim story, showing the
extraordinary forms into which religion could blossom in un-
tutored peasant minds, and how completely such a religion might
be divorced in most respects from ordinary morality.   It is only
after years on Sakhalin Island that the murderer at last attains
to the simple faith of the ordinary peasant.

It was not only among the peasantry that religious emotion
overflowed into unusual channels. *On the road* narrates the spiritual
adventures of a man of birth and education, who holds that
faith is a kind of talent, with which the Russian is particularly
richly endowed.   'Russian life is an unbroken series of new beliefs
and enthusiasms, and unbelief or negation is a state it has not
even approached.   If a Russian does not believe in God, it means
that he believes in something else.'

He himself in the course of forty years had exercised an infinite
capacity for belief on a great variety of objects.   In his boyhood
it was what his mother or his nurse told him, then what he read
in books or learned at the gymnasium.   But his first real enthusiasms dated from his university years.   At first it was for
knowledge, pure science, then, when like a second Faust he discovered that final truth was unattainable, it was for nihilism, and
the service of the people.   This led to slavophilism, a passion for
everything Russian, religion, language, art.   His last creed had
been the Tolstoyan non-resistance to evil.   And all these beliefs
in turn had been held not in the manner of a German doctor of
philosophy, but to the exclusion of everything else in life, at the
cost of suffering and impoverishment for himself and his family,
frequent imprisonment, ceaseless wanderings.   The belief that
sustained him at the moment was in the boundless capacity of
women to sacrifice themselves for men, and his chance companion
for the night in an inn parlour was so moved by the intensity of
his conviction that she was ready herself to exemplify its truth.
This devotion to an idea, to the exclusion of common sense, was
of course the mark of the Russian intelligentsia, of whom the hero
of *On the road* was only a more than usually plastic representative.

CHAPTER VII

THE INTELLIGENTSIA, EDUCATION AND THE LIBERAL PROFESSIONS

'Intelligentsia' is a Russian word, first used apparently in the 'sixties by a novelist (P. D. Boborykin, born 1836) as a substitute for Pisarev's 'proletariate of thought'. By Chekhov's time it had developed at least three different but connected meanings. In the first two of these it denoted a social class, conceived either very broadly, as anybody with a certain education, in Maurice Baring's picturesque phrase, anyone 'who tucks in his shirt, which is equivalent in English to wearing a collar', or more narrowly, as anyone who has received a higher education, and entered a liberal profession, but not the government service. In its third sense it meant anyone, whatever class he might belong to, who shared the advanced political and social views which had come to be regarded as typical of the educated middle class, who naturally felt the lack of political liberty more than the privileged nobility or officials, or the unawakened peasantry and commercial classes. As the revolutionary movement started among them, the educated came to be particularly suspect in the eyes of the government; 'intelligentsia' therefore often meant the same as 'revolutionaries', 'an inner circle, a sect, almost an order of knighthood. The Russian intelligentsia assumed this form in the 'sixties and it subsisted till the Bolshevic revolution',[1] though many professional people took neither a direct nor an indirect part in the movement. In the West, on the other hand, the intellectuʑl élite have by no means always been of the extreme left. A comparison between Russia and the West shows that in any country education is only one element in the formation of the intelligentsia's point of view. Another important factor is the relationship of its members to the older social classes in that country, and this is bound up with the history and structure of society there.[2]

The characteristic feature about English developments was the early growth of a strong middle class and its approach to the legal

---

[1] Mirsky, *Contemporary Russian Literature*, 43.
[2] See K. Mannheim, *Ideology and Utopia*, 138 ff; *Man and Society in an Age of Reconstruction*, 98 ff.

status of the nobility. 'The forms of English parliamentary life abolished the distinctions of feudalism,' says Professor G. M. Trevelyan. Younger sons of noble families early took to commerce and intermarried with burghers. The intellectual leaders of the nation sprang for centuries largely from a middle class that had close links with the aristocracy, so that 'the English of Burke's time could not understand what the French Revolution was about'.[1] In France the bourgeoisie had to assert by force the claims of their estate against aristocratic privilege. The claims were formulated and the struggle was inspired chiefly by a middle class élite, living by the work of their brains, not their hands. In Germany too the distinctions of feudalism lived on into modern times. Owing to her economic and political backwardness, her middle class was smaller and less conscious of itself than the French bourgeoisie, and the effect on them of Rousseau and western liberalism was not to stimulate political action, but to drive them in upon themselves, in the pursuit of personal freedom of mind. This tendency was strengthened by the secularisation of religious emotion which was taking place in that age, a factor which had tended all over Europe, from as early as Petrarch's day, to turn clerics into intellectuals, detached from national and class interests. It is characteristic that Germans use the term 'an educated man', to express social approval, very much as we use 'a gentleman'.

It is no accident then that the word 'intelligentsia' came from Russia, for the social position of the educated there was a quite peculiar one. Before the Emancipation the only educated people were, with few exceptions, either sons of the gentry or of the white clergy. The gentry had been forcibly educated by Peter the Great, as we have seen, to provide officials. Later many of them, especially the poorer ones who went into the army or occupied low civil posts, were attracted by the advanced political thought of the West even more than by its literature, science and art. The Decembrist rising of 1825 was the result. The Church's need of educated men for the priesthood had been met, through special institutions, long before lay education for the needs of the state had been begun, though its influence on the education of other classes had been slight. As the sons of the clergy, for whom these schools were provided, were too numerous to be absorbed by the Church, many had to turn to secular callings. These men must often have had a good deal in common with the detached

---

[1] G. M. Trevelyan, *History of England*, 195.

intellectuals of the West, but coming as they usually did from poor country homes, they could not easily forget the sufferings of the peasantry, and responded readily to the ideas of the early socialists. Neither gentry nor popes' sons had anything in common with the still uneducated and little developed merchant class. But they were soon reinforced by the large numbers of 'raznochintsy' who were given the opportunity of educating themselves after the Emancipation, and who also proved receptive to new ideas. The revolutionaries of the 'sixties, we are not surprised to learn, were for the most part students, teachers and educated men of all kinds. It does not follow, of course, that most intellectuals were revolutionaries. Many would be sympathetic to revolutionary ideas, but passive, and many would simply conform, without conviction, with the fashions of opinion current in their class. It was in any case inevitable that in this class discontent with the form of government and the social system of Russia should be widespread, for reasons which are plain to anyone who looks into the history of education in Russia and the place of the educated in society.

There were good reasons for the emphasis laid by Chekhov in his letters and other writings on the ignorance of his countrymen. 'Distrust of the natural sciences, even in their technical applications, and of Western ideas of free government; desire to make university education, and even secondary education, a privilege of the wealthier classes; neglect of primary education, coupled with the suppression by the ministry of public instruction of all initiative, private and public, in the matter of disseminating education among the illiterate classes—these were the distinctive features of the educational policy of the last twenty years of the nineteenth century.'[1] But the reactionary government had to deal with forces which proved in the end to be beyond its control. Like Mephistopheles stamping out the innumerable growing points of life, it had to admit that however many it buried, fresh blood was constantly circulating everywhere.

As we have seen, the church had long possessed a number of schools and seminaries of its own for the free primary and secondary education of the sons of the clergy. It had also four theological academies comparable with universities. There was a long history behind these ecclesiastical educational institutions, because of course in Russia, as in the West, the first schools of any kind had been provided by the church, which for centuries had a monopoly

[1] Encycl. Brit. 11th ed., article *Russia*.

of learning, handed down from generation to generation through church schools and through the monasteries. The Kiev Academy, founded in 1631, to counter the efforts of the Jesuits in that region, was in effect the first Russian university, and it was soon rivalled by the Moscow Slavo-Greco-Latin Academy (1685), which for a time had control of all tutors to the sons of the gentry. Two further ecclesiastical academies were founded later, at St. Petersburg (1797) and Kazan (1842). The church schools and seminaries for the sons of the clergy were systematically developed from the early eighteenth century onwards by the Holy Synod, and in the 'forties of the nineteenth century secondary schools were set up for their daughters. We gather from what the deacon says in *A duel*, for instance, that the ecclesiastical schools were not luxury establishments. Most of the boys came from poor homes, with little more refinement than those of peasants, but the priests' sons were more fortunate than any other section of the population in having education so readily available if they were able and willing to use their advantages, a fact which had important social consequences. Large numbers could not find posts in the church or did not desire them, and they were unfitted for manual work. Their only hope was an occupation for which some degree of education was essential. The abler among them studied at a university or technical institute, if by one means or another they could maintain themselves there, and became doctors, lawyers, civil servants, teachers, journalists, technicians. Those who for lack of money or ability could not continue their studies, or could not complete them, became minor officials, primary school teachers, clerks. A considerable number found difficulty in fitting into any niche, and from the middle of the nineteenth century they became the chief component of the growing intellectual proletariate.

For the sons of the gentry, officials and professional men the path to higher education was not so well blazed, unless they were destined for the services. Then they might be fortunate enough to be admitted to the Corps of Pages, or one of the twenty-five Corps of Cadets, which prepared boys of 10 to 17 for a dozen military or naval academies. Schools of vocational training of this kind, for future servants of the state, had been amongst the earliest of Peter the Great's foundations, and had been carefully fostered since his time. For future high officials there was the Alexander Lyceum, where Pushkin had been a pupil, a very exclusive boarding school and academy of legal studies, and the

Imperial School of Law, a similar institution founded later, but these were quite small. The great majority of the sons of the gentry were educated either by private tutors or at the state-inspected private schools, which after dubious beginnings and a period of almost total suppression were again allowed free scope after the middle of the century, by which time the state secondary schools were firmly established. As we have gathered, the spoilt darlings, the Oblomovs, were common among those whom their easy circumstances deprived of the most obvious motive for diligence, but laziness and indifference were overcome in some by the desire for an official rank, in others by the ambition to hold their own in polite society, where the interest in literature and the arts, though diminished since the great days of the 'forties, was still strong, while after the military service law of 1874 higher education was further encouraged because of the concessions made to the educated.

When Chekhov went to the university in 1879, 70% of the nine thousand students in Russia's nine universities came from the families of the gentry, officials and clergy, but that figure does not tell us much about their circumstances, because a large proportion of the lesser gentry, as well as most of the clergy and the minor officials, were poor men, though they belonged to the privileged classes. The sons of the clergy would have come from their seminaries, and the poorer gentry's and officials' sons, as well as the 30% of the 'raznochintsy' and commercial classes, from the state gymnasia. In 1905 there were 220 of these in Russia, and 26 incomplete gymnasia or 'progymnasia', with some 100,000 pupils in all. There were also 147 'real' or modern schools, with about 50,000 pupils, preparing not for the universities but for the technical schools, or for commerce. The gymnasia, established for the first time under Alexander I at the beginning of the nineteenth century, to feed the new universities planned at that time, had had many ups and downs, but they had steadily grown in numbers and efficiency under strong central direction. One great difficulty of the universities and higher schools had been the building up of a staff of competent Russian teachers. Students had had to be sent abroad for training, chiefly in the German universities, in order gradually to replace the Germans, teaching in Latin, who had been almost the only teachers available in the Russian universities in the early nineteenth century. They in their turn produced teachers for the gymnasia from their own pupils.

A second difficulty had been the varying attitude of the government towards higher education. Taking the nineteenth century only, it had been liberal and constructive under Alexander I until 1812, then reactionary with a clerical bias in his mystical later years. Nicholas I, frightened by the Decembrist rising (1825), and inimical to any social or political change, had tried to reserve higher education for the sons of the gentry and higher officials, to maintain the caste principle, but the intellectual movement of the 'thirties and 'forties, largely centred in the University of Moscow, now the equal of any in Europe, was not to be dammed back, and it made of the opinion of educated society a social force independent of the autocracy, a most important influence in bringing about the great reforms under Alexander II in the 'sixties. The reforms themselves, aiming as they did at a modernisation of economic and social life, made greater calls than ever on higher education and technical training, opening up new careers in law, local administration and industry. A general improvement and extension of the whole educational system, including elementary education, was demanded by the spirit of the age. The government removed the restrictions on admission to the universities, reformed them in 1863 in a liberal spirit and encouraged poorer students by numerous scholarships. Alexander's grant of 500,000 roubles for scholarships was followed by large numbers from private benefactors and groups, and students flocked to the higher schools and universities. In the thirty years following the accession of Alexander II, the number of university students was nearly quadrupled, and that of pupils in gymnasia and real schools quintupled, in spite of the brake that was applied by the government after the student Karakozov's attempted assassination of the Czar in 1866, through the raising of fees, the reduction of scholarships, and the revision of school curricula. Finally after years of discussion the Universities Statute of 1884 abolished the liberal regulations of 1863, under which the universities had enjoyed a large measure of autonomy, and placed staff and students under the strictest possible bureaucratic control, both in teaching and discipline. In matters of discipline the ministry's inspectors, sub-inspectors and agents were all-powerful, and at any sign of apparent disorder called in the police and cossacks. Students had come to be considered a dubious and dangerous body of young men who could not even be allowed to meet in small groups in each others' rooms, still less to have any kind of societies or clubs. Even in 1914 H. W. Williams wrote of them: 'The students are held to their book-learning, their minds are fed on abstractions, they are artificially held aloof from the normal process of life that creates its own forms and builds strong characters. It is no wonder that students in this position become absorbed in abstract politics, or when bitter experience has shown the futility of politics, are oppressed by the sheer emptiness of life, grow reckless, live morally and materially from hand to mouth, and in large numbers find refuge in suicide.'

There are many students in Chekhov's stories and plays, and though they are all individuals, there is a generic resemblance between them because of the basic conditions of their life. They do indeed seem to us to live, both morally and materially, from hand to mouth. The third year medical student in *Anyuta*, for instance, lives in a squalid untidy room, the cheapest of a block of furnished rooms, with his twenty-five year old mistress Anyuta, who ekes out the twelve roubles a month he receives from home by embroidering men's shirts. He is her sixth. His predecessors have all graduated and gone down, and one of them is a professor by now. She stands patiently with her blouse off in the cold room while he marks in her ribs with charcoal, to help him in getting up his anatomy for the examination. She even lets him lend her sans cérémonie to an artist friend as a model. There is certainly some truth in the remark of the art student: 'Excuse my saying so, Klochkov, but you do live like a filthy pig, don't you?'—and that not only with regard to the unmade bed and the wash-basin where cigarette ends are floating in dirty water. If their attitude to women is any indication, the personal culture of many of the students is low. 'These students don't count us as human beings,' says the draper's assistant to the little dressmaker *Polinka* in that marvellous tête à tête in a draper's shop, as he sells her trimmings and buttons under the eyes of his colleagues. 'They only make friends with shopkeepers and dressmakers because our ignorant ways amuse them and because they can get drunk with us.' Her student admirer will never marry her, however much she may love him. 'When he is a doctor or a lawyer he will think of the past sometimes and say to himself: "Yes, I had a little blonde girl friend once upon a time! I wonder where she is now?" ' Again, in *A nervous breakdown*, a study of prostitution in Moscow, it is students who are the principal clients of the street of tolerated houses. They are good fellows, and their gaiety is infectious as they go out on the spree singing snatches from opera, but on some points they are morally insensitive to a degree, or so it seems to

Vasiliev, with his 'talent for human feeling'. The evidence quoted by Izgoev, in his essay in *Landmarks* (1909), based on enquiries made among Moscow students, strongly supports this view.

In view of the entire absence of sport and organised student activities, the impossibility of early marriage and the traditional tone of Russian good society in sexual matters, it was natural that young men should behave in Moscow or St. Petersburg as they did in similar circumstances in Paris or Berlin. Chekhov, like his old professor in *A dreary story*, probably did not consider them degenerate on that account. They smoked and drank too much for the professor's liking, and 'married too late'. They were careless and indifferent about the large number of their fellow-students who were poor and even starving. But he looked upon these things and their weakness in modern languages and even in Russian, as faults that would pass, due to the conditions in which they lived, and the pain they caused him was nothing to the delight and stimulus he derived from each succeeding generation. He was attracted no doubt by their youthful freshness and naiveté, as the other scholar was by *Ivan Matvyeich*, his eighteen year old copyist, in spite of his unpunctuality and his ignorance of Turgeniev and Gogol. It was so refreshing to hear him talk about his native Don country, and how they caught tarantulas there, with a lump of resin on a string.

There are signs enough in Chekhov of the poverty that was so wide-spread among Russian students, but he seldom refers openly, no doubt from fear of the censorship, to the great part they played in the revolutionary movement, which was almost entirely kept going by successive waves of devoted young enthusiasts. After twenty-five or so, many writers tell us, they tended to lose heart, like Chekhov's liberal gentry. The one clear example of the type, Trofimov in the *Cherry Orchard*, is indeed an 'eternal student' of nearly thirty, though he expresses some of the ideas of the younger generation. Even if he is hungry, sick and as poor as a beggar, his soul, he says, is filled day and night with a vague presentiment of happiness. It is faith in man's power to control his own destiny through reason and science that buoys him up. The errors of the past, great as they have been in Russia, can be redeemed, he believes, but only at the cost of suffering, and intense, unceasing labour.

As to the staffs of the universities, *A dreary story* shows us many aspects of university life through the eyes of an elderly professor of medicine of international reputation, a privy councillor and 'general'. He is himself entirely devoted to science, without any thought of popular fame or political influence, but his wife and daughter are conscious of their social position and make him live beyond his means, so that though their table is no longer Russian but French, not a cheerful family affair but tediously solemn, served by a man-servant in white gloves, the servants have to be kept waiting for their wages, and the professor feels a resentment, for which he despises himself, against his officer son and his daughter, a student of music, who add to his burdens. The insight with which Chekhov interprets the complex mind of a distinguished scholar is admirable. The portrait is completely convincing, not least in that we feel ourselves to be in the presence of a man of real eminence. One may perhaps attempt to distinguish between the traits characteristic of the professor, of the Russian professor and of the 'old' man. Parenthetically it may be remarked that his age is 62, and that Chekhov's middle-aged and elderly people strike us now as about ten years older than their age. Much that we hear about a day in his life might be true of many scholars of similar standing elsewhere, his daily routine, his attitude towards his work and his pupils, his lecturing and his feelings about it (though his skill in this art is exceptional), his interviews with a cheerful ignoramus and with a would-be researcher with no ideas of his own about a subject. The university head porter, with his encyclopaedic knowledge about staff and students, past and present, his innumerable stories and legends, is a character, but he too is not exclusively Russian, any more than the professor's industrious but uninspired demonstrator, with his reverence for everything German and ignorance of all but his speciality. An English reader will note that nothing is of course quite the same as here. The lecture lasts nearly two hours, the young medical graduate wears a white tie, the porter knows all the rumours about coming appointments, and the minister's conversations with the curator about them—a detail which conjures up the whole bureaucratic background. It strikes us as odd too that this medical professor's day does not seem to include laboratory or hospital work.

Thoroughly Russian features are the old and neglected university buildings, whose dark corridors, sooty walls and general decrepitude have played a big part, the professor thinks, in the history of Russian pessimism. One is reminded of the picture of the zemstvo building in an earlier chapter. Russian too and of the period is the behaviour of two colleagues, when one calls on the other on business, the polite gestures about the comfortable chair: 'We gently stroke each other's waists, touch each other's buttons, and it looks as if we were feeling each other over and were afraid of burning our fingers'; the official phrases that creep into their conversation: 'as I have already had the honour of telling you' and so forth; the slightly forced cheerfulness and mutual deference. Still more characteristic of the time is the conversation of a philological colleague, gently and smilingly ridiculing everyone and everything, 'in a half philosophical, half jesting tone that reminds one of a Shakespearian grave-digger'. 'Science,' he says, 'has now, thank God, outlived its day. . . . And indeed, what has it given us? Why, between educated Europeans and Chinamen, who have no science, the difference is negligible, purely external. The Chinese have never known any science, but what have they lost through that? . . . There is a prejudice among the masses that science and art are higher than farming, trade or industry. Our sect lives on that prejudice, and it is not for you and me to destroy it. God preserve it!' It is the fin de siècle irony of Orlov, the St. Petersburg chinovnik, over again, and it is characteristic that the speaker is like Orlov a nobleman, the bearer of a name famous in Russian letters.

The professor himself is not of that stamp. His happiest memory is of his day-dreams at the seminary (he is evidently a priest's son) of going to the university and becoming a doctor, and he has lost none of his passionate interest in science and faith in its beneficent power. A tireless worker and a man of talent, he has contributed to that great advance of scientific medicine in the later nineteenth century which Chekhov so much admired. With the privat-docent Dr. Dymov in *The grasshopper*, a gifted martyr of medical science, he represents the innumerable Russian scholars who, in spite of all obstacles, were steadily repaying Russia's initial debt to the West. In his work he is happy and great, but he does not escape the personal tragedy to which the one-sidedness of the intellectual life so easily leads. The stylistic device that he is made to tell his own story misled many early readers into identifying the author's views with his, an interpretation vigorously rejected by Chekhov in various letters. The professor is a character in a drama, not a mouthpiece, and we must not forget that in regard to his family life we hear only one side of the case. Chekhov seems to have intended to convey the impression that through his very devotion to science, ordinary human feeling has gradually

6

dried up in him. 'It is one of his principal traits,' Chekhov wrote (to Pleshcheyev, 30/9/89), 'that he is too little concerned about the inner life of those around him, and while they are weeping, going astray and lying, he with unruffled calm discusses the theatre and literature If he had been of a different turn of mind, Liza and Katya might not have come to grief.' Just before the end, the professor makes a similar comment on himself when, horrified at the equanimity with which he receives the news of his daughter's marriage to a man he detests, he uses the phrase already quoted about equanimity as a paralysis of the soul, a premature death.

The development of secondary education had run a course parallel with that of university education. There had been secondary schools of a kind in Russia, apart from the special institutions for officers and private schools already discussed, since the reign of Catherine II in the eighteenth century, but the system of state schools was not efficiently organised until the beginning of the next century under Alexander I, when the French scheme of Condorcet was taken as the model. Parish schools with a one-year course led up to District schools with a two-year course, and these again to Provincial schools, or 'Gymnasia', which provided four years of teaching. The schools were open to all classes without fees, text-books were supplied free and maintenance grants were available in considerable numbers. Under Nicholas I this surprisingly democratic policy was reversed. The gymnasia were open now only to the sons of the gentry and higher officials, and of the first gild of merchants. The clergy of course retained their own schools. The aim of education was defined as the maintenance of orthodoxy, autocracy and nationality. In each school an 'inspector' was made responsible for the discipline and morals of the pupils, and as in the universities later he served also as a check on the staff. Seven years of instruction were now provided, at first with a mathematical and classical bias, but after 1849 with less stress on classics. For the sons of the nobility and higher officials attending gymnasia boarding houses were established, which added gentlemanly accomplishments to the curriculum and made these state schools more attractive to the upper classes.

There was a growing demand for secondary education through-out the reign of Nicholas I, but it was not until the 'sixties, when the first wave of reform under Alexander II made the need for educated men greater than ever, that the gymnasia were again thrown open to all classes, with many new scholarships to help the lad of parts. The schooling of Zhelyabov, the principal organiser of the assassination of Alexander II, was typical. The son of a serf, he received his first education from his grandfather, a sectarian, in the country, learning to read church script. Then his father's master took an interest in him, and after teaching him himself for a time, sent him as a boarder to a school in the nearest town. A scholarship of thirty roubles a month enabled him later to proceed to the university. Private tuition was so much in request both in schools and universities that many poor boys maintained themselves, as Chekhov himself did in his last years at school, by coaching others. We have an example in *The coach**, where a seventh form boy is seen teaching the stupid son of a retired official. Not all the boys and girls who crowded into town lodgings during their years at school or university were as fortunate as little Yegorushka in *The steppe*, who lived with a friend of his mother's for ten roubles a month. They were often herded together in slum quarters, obtaining cheap meals at the students' canteen which existed in all universities, in conditions which naturally bred revolutionary ideas.

It was with a view to weeding out potential sources of unrest such as these at the earliest possible stage that the reactionary measures inspired by Karakozov's attempt on the Tsar's life in 1866 were directed in the first place against the schools. By the gymnasial regulations of 1871 the subjects in the curriculum that seemed most likely to stimulate thought and discussion, history, Russian literature and general geography, were severely cut down in the time-table, the gaps being filled with what was now considered the eminently safe subject of classics. Earlier in the century Latin and Greek had been held to be dangerously republican in their literary tendencies, but now they were to be taught with the most rigorous insistence on grammar, primarily as a mental discipline. The example of the Prussian gymnasium, and perhaps the English Public School, may have had something to do with the belief, which events proved to be completely erroneous, that Latin and Greek grammar would serve as a brake on advanced thought and a stimulus to disciplined orthodoxy. As a further precaution, severe restrictions were placed in the 'eighties on the right of admission to secondary schools and universities of Jews (who were not to form more than two per cent of the student population of St. Petersburg and Moscow), and of children of small tradespeople or personal servants and so on, while school fees were doubled. At the same time standards were raised to an unprecedented level with the express object of excluding as many as possible from the university, to which only those were now admitted who had 'completed the course' of a gymnasium. During Chekhov's last seven years at school less than a thousand boys on the average passed each year in the 180 gymnasia and pro-gymnasia of Russia, one-eighth of the original number of entrants.[1] No wonder that parents were in despair and that suicides were frequent even among boys of thirteen. That is the background to a story such as *A classical student*, where we see how poor Varya, in spite of kissing all the icons before leaving home, fails in the Greek examination and is taken away from school by his indignant mother to be sent into business, after she has had him beaten, not without Schadenfreude, by the lodger, an ambitious shop-assistant.

As to the atmosphere prevailing in a gymnasium, which was of course a state institution, served by chinovniki, we have already had an indication in the picture of the abjectly timid *Man in a case*, who was, characteristically, the Greek master, and drawn, according to Michael Chekhov, from Anton's own teacher at Taganarog. *The teacher of literature* shows us a master who does not dare to make the usual speech over the grave of a friend and colleague because the headmaster had not liked him, and in *The three sisters* too the behaviour of Kulygin makes it clear that the 'leadership principle', or something like it, obtained in schools as well as universities, for Masha's pedantic husband loses no opportunity of ingratiating himself with the rector of the gymnasium, even shaving off his moustache in imitation of him when he becomes sub-rector or 'inspector' of the school. 'Do you call yourselves teachers, educators?' says one of Chekhov's teachers to his colleagues. 'You are just slaves of red tape. Yours is not a temple of science, but a public security department, with the same sour smell as a police-box.'

There had been a demand for education in modern subjects of practical utility since the beginning of the century, and Alexander I's state schools had at first a markedly 'realistic' tendency, but this had soon been forced into the background by the classicists, until in 1864 the first 'Real' schools on the German model were set up side by side with the classical gymnasia. Conservative opinion saw in these however one of the sources of materialistic nihilism, and by the 1871 regulations they were put

[1] Stepniak, *Russia under the Tsars*, II, 117.

on a lower footing than the gymnasia, both as to state aid and admission of their pupils to higher institutions. As we have seen, it was only those who had been through a gymnasium who were now admitted to the university; the 'Real' school qualified its pupils only for admission to technical institutes. Many left to enter commerce before completing the course. Like all other higher schools, these schools were badly overcrowded, in spite of the high standards demanded, and the efforts of the Zemstvos to found secondary schools, in addition to the primary schools which were their principal concern.

One surprising feature was the provision already made for the education of girls. Girls of the upper classes were not by any means wholly dependent on governesses for their schooling, for there were a large number of 'Institutes', boarding-schools for girls, as well as cheaper day-schools, the state gymnasia for girls. Again and again we hear in Chekhov of the 'Institutka' or boarding-school miss. The prototype of these Institutes was a girls' school set up on sensible principles in 1764 by Catherine II, at the Smolnÿ Monastery. Others followed, and the schools were carefully fostered by successive Empresses, until the well-endowed scheme was finally put under the control of a special government department (Department of the Institutions of the Empress Maria) in 1825. They were reserved for the daughters of the nobility, and were intended to fit them for marriage or, if they needed it, to earn their living as governesses. Schools for the daughters of the clergy followed in the reign of Nicholas I, and day secondary schools for all classes in the early 'sixties. The secondary education of girls was consequently as well provided for in Russia as anywhere in Europe. University education for women was naturally in demand at an early date, but many difficulties were encountered by its advocates. First individual women students were admitted by some St. Petersburg professors to their classes, but the practice was forbidden after a few years, in 1863. Then, through private initiative, Women's Higher Courses were established in 1870 in St. Petersburg, and soon in one or two other universities, but these unsystematic evening courses were found unsatisfactory, and many women continued to study abroad, especially in Zürich, where they came under the influence of Bakunin and other revolutionaries. Regular women's courses in arts and science were therefore sanctioned in St. Petersburg in 1878, with proper entrance and final examinations, still distinct from those for men. In the same year medical courses were opened to women in the St. Petersburg Military Academy, which prepared for the degree of woman doctor. For political reasons however all these courses were suspended once more in the reactionary later 'eighties. The arts and science courses reopened in 1889, with new restrictions on the number of students, while medical courses for women only became available again in 1897. The demand for all courses far exceeded the supply.

Such were the schools and universities in the 'eighties and 'nineties. A very high proportion of the students who passed through them went straight into the government service. The completion of even a secondary school course gave the right, as we have seen, to a low official rank, and many went no further. A comparatively small number of graduates entered the free professions, and these were on the whole less free than in the west, because as 'chin' was regularly conferred on doctors, surveyors, engineers and so on who were in private practice, as a sign of social recognition, they were to some extent dependent on the favour of the authorities, in addition to being constantly under supervision in this well-policed state.

Most of the graduates of the schools of law took up one or other of the offices under the Ministry of Justice described above, or served in some administrative capacity. Outside the civil service there was for lawyers the new profession of barrister, naturally much sought after in the years following the legal reforms, with the public oral procedure which they introduced. They found lucrative employment in handling the affairs of capitalistic big business in this age of expansion. Chekhov draws one for us in Lysevich (*A woman's kingdom*), the rich gourmet with ingratiating manners, a ready tongue, a carefully cultivated literary sense and a taste for the original. As legal adviser to a big engineering firm he has what is virtually a sinecure, yet for all his charm he never forgets to send in his account (which amounts to 12,000 roubles a year), personally asks for his present at Christmas time, and makes anything he can out of the firm on the sly. Another barrister with a big practice, who has none of the charm of Lysevich and still fewer scruples, is Pekarsky in *An anonymous story*, a director of a railway company and a bank, legal adviser to an important government establishment, and so forth. As we have seen, his St. Petersburg cynicism knows no bounds. He likes to be a power behind the throne, with a low official rank but unbounded influence. Lower down the social scale is the notary in *Old age*, who in his early days had been a 'striapchy', the sort of scrivener of little education and low standing, who had conducted suits before the courts in the old days of written procedure. The architect whose divorce he had arranged meets him again when both are old, and only then learns the full extent of his iniquities. The lawyer had bribed the wife to take the blame on herself—only on that condition could the husband marry again according to the church law which prevailed in these matters—and it transpires that it was only one of his petty villainies that thousands of roubles had stuck to his fingers in the process.

Doctors naturally play a considerable part in Chekhov's work, and they are drawn from a more intimate knowledge than any other class of professional men. We see them in private practice, or attached to some hospital, usually a zemstvo hospital in the country, or engaged as specialists or university teachers in a large town. They are all drawn as individual men, but as is Chekhov's way, they are brought before us with their whole surrounding atmosphere, so that there is something in every story which throws light on their profession and on the world they live in.

In *Enemies*, for instance, the theme is a conflict of temperaments, in rather unusual circumstances, between a doctor and a landowner, the absorption of each in his own private suffering and his consequent selfishness, yet each is typical of his class. The landowner calls on a winter night to ask the doctor to drive fourteen versts to his dying wife. The doctor, utterly exhausted, has been fighting for days and nights for the life of his own son, and the boy has just died. It is inhuman, he feels, that he should be asked to leave his wife at this moment, yet the other's insistence, and his own professional conscience, prevail. When at last they arrive, they find that the 'dying' wife has eloped with her lover. This anecdote is made Russian and of its time particularly through the character of the landowner, a flabby, self-centred creature, proud of his capacity for emotion but incapable of human feeling for the suffering of another, especially of one outside his own class. The doctor's indignant outburst is prompted by the special circumstances, but its similarity to the tirade of the doctor in *The princess* is too close for the reader to take it as purely individual, and not as a reflection in an intensified form of what the author felt about relations between doctors and some of their aristocratic patients. 'It is mean and contemptible,' he says, 'to play with human beings in this way. I am a doctor. You consider doctors, and all other workers who do not smell of fine perfumes and prostitution, as your lackeys, and mere vulgarians. Do so if you wish, but you have no right to make a stage property of a suffering fellow creature.' The landowner characteristically thinks that money will put everything right, but the doctor refuses to be paid in money for insults.

Chekhov's fullest study of a country doctor is to be found in *Uncle Vanya*. Dr. Astrov too sometimes travels thirty versts to find that his patient does not need him. The calls at all hours of the day and night, the long hours on the road and the dullness of provincial life, with the inevitable reaction, drink, have made an eccentric old man of him, he says, at forty, but he is generally regarded as much above the average in intelligence and creative idealism. Even in his hobby of tree-growing he expresses his longing for that order and rationality which he misses in the world around him. Dr. Dorn, on the other hand, in *The sea-gull*, is content to prescribe Valerian drops for all maladies, and holds that a man of sixty has no business to take a cure. He is a cultivated man of the world, spoilt by the ladies, who has spent the savings accumulated during thirty years of practice in the course of a single foreign tour. This is not the only feature in which he resembles the apostle of culture, Dr. Ragin, in *Ward no. 6*.

The zemstvo doctors too are of all types. Most of them are idealists to begin with, but many succumb in the unequal struggle with disease, ignorance and social injustice. *Ionich* sketches the decline of Dr. Startsev from an eager young zemstvo doctor to a fat, irritable, middle-aged man with a big practice in the town, coining money and investing it in house-property, while *The wife* shows us Dr. Sobol working so hard that he has not read a book for ten years. Life in the wilds has played havoc with his family life and made a muzhik of him, he declares, when for once he has the opportunity of lunching in civilised society. He seems to stand this life better than most because, with his robust and uncomplicated nature, he knows how to put first things first. He and his contemporaries, he feels, are as it were in a burning theatre together, and all their courage and determination will be needed if they are to survive. They must coolly face the facts and put personal vanity aside. It is evident that he is approved of by the author, whereas the zemstvo doctor Lvov in *Ivanov*, though honest and idealistic, is a narrow-minded doctrinaire with little understanding of men.

Two or three longer stories deal with hospitals in the early 'nineties and their staffs, showing how far Russia, in spite of the great medical discoveries of the age, had still to go in providing medical services for the mass of the people. The lack of properly equipped hospitals and trained personnel, particularly in the remoter parts, was most acute, according to these stories, and the efficiency of those men available was as usual greatly reduced by personal shortcomings, rooted to some extent in the general conditions of the time.

Ward no. 6 is a study of two contrasted failures or 'superfluous men', as Chekhov's critics called them. It is full of that sense of futility and frustration so common in his work, but it would be short-sighted to take it simply as a picture of border-line types of character, for these are obviously symbolic figures, who would be felt by many contemporaries to express their own problems. Dr. Ragin has many good qualities and we have much sympathy with him. He is a gentle, dreamy, scholarly man, who through his father's insistence has taken up medicine, but belongs to it with only a quarter of his mind. Every afternoon and until late in the night he is to be found reading and pondering over history and philosophy, and when his only friend the postmaster visits him in the evening, their chief topic over their beer is the absence of intelligent society in this little town. 'Intelligence is the sharp dividing-line between animal and man, it is evidence of the God-like quality in man and in some measure takes the place of the immortality that is denied to him.' Dr. Ragin exemplifies the passion for culture, self-perfection, 'Bildung' which possessed the intelligentsia, but which, as in the German intelligents who largely inspired it (we have seen how much Russian education owed to them), tended to provide them with an escape from the world about them, rather than an inspiration to re-shape it. Dr. Ragin loves sweetness and light, but he is constitutionally incapable of giving an order and getting things done. He finds the hospital to which he is appointed, in a town 200 versts from the railway, in indescribable chaos when he arrives, dirty, lacking the most elementary equipment (even a thermometer!), and exceedingly badly staffed, but he soon reconciles himself to the idea that things are past mending, and settles down to seeing half a dozen out-patients every morning and leaving the rest of the work to his feldsher assistant. He rationalizes his conduct by reflections such as that if humanity learns to relieve its sufferings by pills and drops, it will completely give up religion and philosophy, in which till now it has found not only a refuge from all ills, but even happiness. At other times he persuades himself that it is

6*

the age that is responsible for his shortcomings. 'I myself am nothing, only a fraction of an inescapable social evil. All the officials in the district do harm by their work and are paid for nothing. So it is not I who am guilty of dishonesty, but the times. If I had been born a hundred years later, I should have been different.'

But a patient in the mental ward of his hospital, when he at last by chance visits him, a young official suffering from persecution mania, tells him the truth about his philosophising. The ward is simply a prison, where five harmless lunatics are confined by force in revolting conditions, and receive no treatment. When the doctor tries to comfort him with the reflection that contentment is to be found only within oneself, so that there is no difference between a warm study and this ward, Ivan Dmitrich is not impressed by his quotations from Marcus Aurelius and asks what right he has to preach this gospel. Has he himself suffered? 'You despise suffering,' he says, 'and let nothing surprise you for a very simple reason. . . . All this is a philosophy which admirably suits a Russian sluggard. Suppose you see a muzhik beating his wife. "Let him beat her," you say, "they will both die sooner or later all the same, and he is outraging by his blows not his victim, but himself." ' In a word, it is an excuse for standing aside from all the problems of life. He needs to do nothing, his conscience is clear, and he has a feeling of superiority into the bargain. This is not philosophy, but sheer laziness. Chekhov rubs in the lesson by letting the doctor himself end his days in the same ward, and experience the sufferings he has for so long theoretically despised.

Several other hospitals are mentioned in the stories, but none of them is as bad as this one. The zemstvo hospital in *An unpleasant affair**, for instance, seems to be well run by a conscientious, but overworked doctor, assisted by a feldscher addicted to drink and a young midwife. The feldscher gets on his nerves so much that in a fit of temper he strikes him. *The runaway* shows us another hospital, in the charge of a good doctor with a sense of humour and skill in handling children. In all of them we hear of the long queues of out-patients every morning, who cannot receive much individual attention for lack of time. It is plain that all these hospitals were understaffed. The universities, as we have seen, did not turn out nearly the number of doctors required, and far too much use had therefore to be made of half-trained feldschers. Even experienced doctors would have had to be extraordinarily versatile to deal with all the medical problems presented to them. With the limited knowledge of those days and in the absence of specialist help they had to be content with modest results. We see from *Surgery** that they had to be dentists too in the country. Here a parish clerk suffers agonies at the hands of a confident feldscher, in the absence of the doctor. And it seems to have been particularly difficult to find conscientious and reliable feldschers, as it was to find clerks, shop-assistants and similar lower middle-class workers. According to the justice of the peace in *An unpleasant affair**, there were no sober and dependable people in between the peasant and the professional man. The doctor in the story thought it was because such men were a new social class, neither peasant nor gentleman, with no traditions of their own. After a youth of hardship they had reached positions that brought them some twenty-five roubles a month, not enough to keep their families from going hungry, and had no prospects of further advancement. As they had no time to read or to go to church, and were not admitted to cultured society, they lived from hand to mouth with no hopes or ideals to sustain them, and it was not surprising that they should drink and steal.

The shortage of Russian doctors, dentists and other professional men was to some extent made good by using Germany's surplus, a natural development in view of the part that had been played by Germans in the building up of the Russian educational system, and the general difference in cultural level between the two neighbours. German immigrants had preponderated to such an extent over all others for a century or more that the common people spoke of all foreigners as 'Germans'. Accordingly Chekhov chooses German or German-Jewish names for a great many of his doctors, the specialist Schreck in *The grasshopper*, Dr. Dorn in the *Sea-gull*, the doctor who can hardly speak Russian in *Typhus*, von Sterk and Magnus in *Martyrs*, and several in *Intrigues**, where a doctor is preparing his speech for a branch meeting of a kind of Russian medical association. He is going to accuse the President, Dr. Prechtel, of being a Prussian spy, and anticipates trouble from von Bronn and Grummer. Similarly the dentist in *A gentleman friend* is a convert named Finkel, and the zoologist in *The duel* is called von Koren because, as Chekhov explained in a letter: 'The multitude of Wagners, Brandts and so on, in all the scientific world, made a Russian name out of the question for a zoologist—though we have Kovalevsky.'

It is not surprising that writers and actors, in addition to doctors, should be among Chekhov's favourite subjects, for he was in constant touch with them from his first years in Moscow. His picture of both tends to be satirical. We gather from his letters that he had not a high opinion of the Russian authors of his day as a class, though he greatly admired Tolstoy, Garshin, Shcheglov, Korolenko, Gorky and many other individuals. The average Russian literary man seemed to him, according to his letters to Suvorin, more stupid than his readers, and greatly inferior to his French contemporaries. 'A Russian writer lives in the gutter, feeds on woodlice and sleeps with washerwomen; he does not know either the history, or the geography, or the science or the religion of his own country, or its administration and legal procedure either.'[1] In the stories too the minor writers who appear are represented as absurdly self-important nonentities. The journalist in *Hush!* comes home full of self-pity, wakes his wife for tea and beefsteak, and settles down to his all-important creative work at a writing-table where busts of famous authors, a well-thumbed volume of Bielinsky, the father of the intelligentsia, and heaps of manuscripts all speak of the literary man. Not a sound must disturb his labours, or his sleep after them, for this nonentity at the office is a tyrant at home. *Excellent people* introduces a law graduate employed in the head office of a railway, who writes feuilletons and calls literature his real occupation. Even in the way he flings his hair back or flicks the ash from his cigarette one recognises the writer, he is tireless in literary social activities and much given to sayings such as, 'What is life without conflict? Forwards!'—though he never enters into conflict with anyone or takes a single step forward. The intelligentsia of his stamp, it is implied, occupied themselves with all kinds of trifles but never got down to the big problems of the day.

The bitterest criticism of the lesser intelligentsia is to be found in a feuilleton in the Novoe Vremya (1891), a 'caractère' of *A Moscow Hamlet*[*][2] who, wherever he is, declares life to be un-utterably boring. He has forgotten all he ever knew even in literature, but makes up for his ignorance by impudent cheating. When he knows nothing whatever about a work he will say, 'This is old', or 'This is borrowed from Lope da Vega', or 'Im-mortal Molière, where art thou?' He is only half civilised, 'asiatic', in his way of living. His house is richly furnished perhaps, there are pictures, busts, a tiger skin, but the vent in the stove is stuffed

[1] 15–5–89.
[2] Reprinted as a supplement to Vol. 3 of the letters (Russian ed.).

up with a woman's blouse and he spits on the carpet, the kitchen is filthy and the other rooms undusted and cobwebbed. He is not put out by low ceilings, cockroaches, damp, or by drunken friends lying down on his bed in their boots. Yet he is extremely self-satisfied. No play, for instance, ever comes up to his high standards, no picture seems to him to contain an idea, and he is so envious of the success of others that he will stick at nothing to blacken their good name. Trofimov's description of the intelligentsia in *The cherry orchard* (act II) is in an exactly similar tone. The great majority of them, he says, are ignorant, lazy and conceited. They do not treat peasants or their servants as if they were men like themselves, they read nothing, talk about science without knowledge and have little taste in art. Though they may look so serious and dignified, ninety-nine per cent of them live like savages in their own homes. 'All our fine talk is just meant to divert our own and other people's attention. Show me the crèches and reading rooms about which we talk so much. They only exist in novels, there are none in real life. There is only dirt, vulgarity, asiaticism.' Maurice Baring, [1] quoting this speech, says that Chekhov gives us in his work a true picture of the old intelligentsia (before 1905), one similar to that drawn in *Landmarks* (Viekhi), a severe criticism of the intelligentsia published in 1909.

Chekhov's personal opinions as expressed in his letters are equally unflattering, for he suffered much from the petty jealousy and intrigues of his colleagues, and found the literary and artistic set in Moscow, or rather perhaps the hangers-on, intolerably boring. He describes an evening at the Society of Art and Literature when, after a story of his had been read, they danced, ate a poor supper and were cheated by the waiters. 'If actors, artists and authors really make up the better part of the Society, it is pitiful. It must be a fine society which is so colourless and aimless, so lacking in taste, in beautiful women, in initiative. They put up a Japanese scarecrow in the hall, stick a Chinese sunshade in one corner, hang a carpet over the banisters on the stairs and think that artistic. A Chinese sunshade but no newspapers! If an artist in decorating his house does not get beyond a museum scarecrow with a halberd, shields and fans on the walls, if all this is not accidental but deliberate and underlined, then he is not an artist, but a pompous ape.' [2] A letter to Orlov of February 1899 shows that Chekhov did not change his views in

---

[1] *The Russian People*, 1911.
[2] To Suvorin, Nov., 1888.

later life. The whole educated class, he says, are the sons of their age. At the university they are full of idealism and give great hope for the future, but when they go out into the world they are soon as bad as the rest, and you find them as doctors owning villas (like Dr. Startsev above), hungry chinovniki, and thieving engineers (as in *My life*), or even as Katkovs and Pobiedonostsevs. 'I don't believe in our intelligentsia. It is hypocritical, false, hysterical, half-educated, lazy. I don't believe in it even when it is suffering and complaining, for its persecutors come from its own midst. I believe in individual people, I see salvation in individual personalities, scattered here and there all over Russia, whether they are educated men or peasants. Though they are few they are a power that counts.' Their steady unobtrusive work is transforming the country *in spite of* the intelligentsia. It is exactly in this strain that Vershinin speaks to the *Three sisters* of the spread of culture by diffusion from families such as theirs.

Chekhov is inclined in such passages to confuse the whole of the educated class with the intelligentsia in the narrower sense, who thought of themselves as a special group with a mission in life, whether political and social, or artistic, and consciously flouted existing traditions and conventions. It was these sections who were so severely criticised after the 1905 revolution by the writers in *Landmarks*. According to one of these critics (Hershenzon), they were so intent on improving the lot of the people that they had no homes of their own worthy of the name. In spite of their good intentions, there was no discipline or consistency in their lives, and their days passed in idleness, slovenliness and measureless disorder. Another (Izgoev) said that their social idealism simply made them bad at their job, bad teachers, engineers, journalists, for they were scorned by their comrades if they gave their whole minds to it. A third (Frank) spoke of their antipathy to culture, for them a useless and morally harmful relic of gentility. It is a picture of confusion of aims and consequent futility that these writers, like Chekhov, drew. Yet the confusion is understandable. Thousands in every generation from the 'seventies onwards found the appeal made to their conscience by Lavrov and his successors irresistible. They said to themselves, as he urged them to do in his *Historical letters* (1868-9): 'Every comfort in life that is mine, every idea that I have had the leisure to acquire or evolve, has been bought with the blood, the sufferings, and the labour of millions. . . . The evil must be put right as far as possible. . . . Evil must be overcome in the process of my life. I shall not free myself from responsibility for the price of blood paid for my development unless I make use of this development to reduce evil in the present and in the future.' But though this indicated the direction in which they must advance, it gave them no plan of the route, and Populists, Terrorists and all their successors made their way as best they could, after endless discussions at every stage and leaving stragglers by the score, into the unknown.

From the Populists onwards, perhaps the majority of the intelligentsia in the narrower sense practised a certain asceticism, as Frank says in *Landmarks*, with regard to art and bourgeois culture. They took a strictly utilitarian view of culture, one which has left its mark even on present-day Russia, where, as Klaus Mehnert has pointed out, the word culture has no longer the same meaning as in western Europe. 'That which is of use to the Revolution, to class, is good, cultured; that which is harmful is bad, uncultured, philistine.'[1] But non-Marxist Russian historians at least look upon the intelligentsia not simply as protagonists of social reform, but as the growing point, as it were, of the mind of society, the essentially progressive element in every respect. For Ivanov-Razumnik, for instance, in his *History of Russian social thought*, the intelligentsia are the people who consciously aim at creating and propagating new forms and ideals, all directed towards the increased freedom of the personality, in contrast with the petit-bourgeois, the suburban philistines, who have no conception of personality. The cult of personality led to the same kind of extravagances in Russia as in the west. Romantics, bohemians, intelligentsia are recognisably the same breed, inspired by western individualism in its many forms, and in Russia especially by the German philosophers, from Kant to Nietzsche. Chekhov gives us a good picture of the intelligentsia in its bohemian aspects in *The grasshopper*. The idea behind this story is similar to that expressed in the letter to Orlov, detestation of self-important cliques and sets and mere fashions of thought and behaviour, and praise of the honest work of a self-forgetful pathologist. The bright young thing whom he calls the Grasshopper married, to the surprise of her many artistic friends, all, at least in their own opinion, rather above the ordinary, her devoted 'bear' Dymov, a doctor on the staff of two hospitals. She furnished their flat in the 'arty' style which, as we have seen, Chekhov disliked—their bedroom was a 'cave', draped with black

[1] *Youth in Soviet Russia*, 1933.

cloth and lit by a Venetian lantern—and continued to lead the life of a Moscow butterfly, while her husband worked all day and played the butler at her Wednesday evening parties. Pretty, vivacious, flattered by everybody, a successful lion-hunter, she lived solely for sensation, and ended by deceiving Dymov with an artist, on a painting trip on the Volga. Only when her husband, who during the long drawn-out affair with the artist, had 'depressed her with his magnanimity', lost his life in healing another did she realise that he was perhaps the one distinguished man she had ever known.

While *The grasshopper* is full of studio atmosphere, *Talent* is a close-up of a young painter and two of his friends. He is bored and tired after a summer in the country, during which he has not finished a single picture, for he spends most of the day in bed, yet after a glass or two of vodka he still has day-dreams of his future greatness, and when his friends visit him they talk excitedly of plans which they never accomplish. They are victims of the law of nature, Chekhov says, which condemns all but two or three per cent of promising beginners in the arts to end as failures. They dress the part and talk in the true romantic strain of the artist's need of freedom—from the marriage tie, for instance, or from the necessity of paying one's rent, but we feel that they are impelled towards art not so much by genuine talent as by conceit and indolence.

Trofimov's words in the *Cherry Orchard* and the criticisms in *Landmarks* of the slovenly and undisciplined home life of some of the intelligentsia are most fully illustrated in *The Duel*. Laevsky in this story, an arts graduate, has run off to the Caucasus with the wife of another intellectual. They persuade themselves at first that their aim is to escape from the vacuity of their intellectual life in St. Petersburg, and have plans of living on their own vineyard by the sweat of their brow, but Laevsky soon realises that they are really running away from the husband, and that a neurasthenic like himself is not fitted for physical toil. He obtains a post under the Ministry of Finance, does as little work as possible, and amuses himself by drinking, philosophising and playing Vint with the local officials. He likes to think of himself as a victim of the degenerate age, the modern counterpart of Pushkin's Onegin or Byron's Cain, turning his weakness into a source of vanity. After two years he is heartily sick of Nadezhda Fyodorovna, and when he hears of her husband's death his one aim is to get back to St. Petersburg without her, lest she should want him to marry her. But she prefers to be free, she has not 'lived' yet, she tells the respectable Marya Konstantinovna, who is already horrified by her way of life, her dirty and neglected house and the odd dresses which she herself thinks so original. As a contrast to Laevsky Chekhov imagines a zoologist, Von Koren, apparently of German Jewish extraction, an active and masterful nature, with Nietzschean ideas about improving the human breed without pity for the unfit. He considers Laevsky ripe for liquidation, and mutual hatred leads to a duel between them, the upshot of which, combined with the deacon's description of the pair of them as 'spoilt children of life', indicates Chekhov's point of view. Laevsky becomes a new man, because the shock of facing death brings him into touch again with reality, destroying the network of lies in which he was entangled, while at the same time Nadezhda too is brought to realise the cumulative effect of deception. It is not the unconventionality but the insincerity of these intellectuals that Chekhov castigates. The further implications of this complex story, in which representatives of the four faculties illustrate and discuss the problem of modern man, will be considered in the last chapter.

The theatre was a passion with Chekhov even as a Gymnasiast, when he saw everything he could in the local theatre and was already thinking of plays of his own. One of these that has survived in manuscript was completed at the university with the title 'A fatherless generation'. It is already a critical study of contemporary types, contrasted with those of the 'sixties and 'seventies. In Moscow he was constantly in touch with the theatre and writing about it and for it, in his feuilletons, criticisms, 'Moscow notes', short stories and farces. The stage and the spoken drama in these years of reaction were at a low ebb. The imperial theatres in St. Petersburg and Moscow, hampered by the censorship, by bureaucratic control and by lack of competition, served up imitations of Ostrovsky's pictures of manners and all kinds of lighter fare. The provincial theatres in the larger towns were visited by touring companies, whose repertoire corresponded with the low level of provincial culture, for their existence, like that of the odd private theatres tolerated in the two leading cities, was on the most precarious foundations. It was only late in the 'nineties that visits of outstanding foreign companies like the Meininger, and the performance of the plays of Ibsen, Hauptmann, Maeterlinck set new standards, which inspired the foundation of the Moscow Art Theatre in 1898.

Chekhov's own masterpieces were the principal Russian contribution to its early repertoire.

A few quotations from Chekhov's letters will be enough to show what he thought of the contemporary theatre. During the production of his *Ivanov* (1887) by the Korsch theatre, a private enterprise in Moscow, he wrote of the vanity of the actors, always fighting for the best parts, and of the purely commercial point of view of Korsch himself. A year later he expressed to Suvorin the opinion that it was not the public's fault that theatres were so bad, for the public had always needed proper guidance in matters of art. The same public would listen with pleasure to vaudevilles as to Shakespeare or grand opera. And to Shcheglov on the same date he wrote that the modern theatre was a foul skin disease that must be eradicated. It was certainly not a school for morals, as some claimed, for it was not higher but lower than the crowd. A little later, to the same friend, whom he was always urging not to write for the theatre, he said that if he occasionally had a play of his own performed, it was simply as an amusement, a gamble, like fishing. There was a glorious uncertainty about the result. Some of his trifles certainly proved quite profitable. In 1889, after a gay evening with the Korsch company, he again could not find much good to say of the men. Most of them had a good deal of the lackey about them; they had no 'purity of soul'. The women however seemed to him, writing on the morning after a very merry party, at which he had felt so much at home that he had kissed some of them on leaving, to have a certain distinction of temper. Though his views at that moment may not have been entirely unbiased, it must be said that his stories had already made a similar distinction between actors and actresses. With the talented producers and company of the Art Theatre when it was founded Chekhov was on the friendliest of terms. It was a partnership between dramatist and theatre that produced ideal results, results due to thought and good taste, as can be seen from Chekhov's letters of that time, especially those to Mme Knipper, his wife.

The early stories represent actors in general as men of little character and low social standing. *The jeune premier* likes to cut a dash in provincial drawing-rooms, and makes a considerable impression in a manufacturer's house until an unfortunate remark about a certain lady in another town, whom he claims to have conquered, arouses the wrath of a relative of hers who happens to be present, and the young man has difficulty in avoiding a duel.

In *A cure for drunkenness** an actor of some repute arrives in a provincial town and is warmly greeted by the manager as he steps from his first-class carriage—in which he has travelled only for the last stage of the journey. Before his much advertised first appearance on the stage he starts drinking, and as his bouts always last for two months, a most drastic cure has to be administered by the theatre hairdresser. Others quarrel and fight (*An actor's end*), steal and bully (*Boots*), and display in fact exactly the same moral defects as they had in similar circumstances in other countries, in eighteenth-century touring companies in Germany, for instance, for men of any education or refinement were rare at first in a career that promised so slight a reward, and the average actor took to the stage, as Katya told the professor in *A dreary story*, only as a last resource. In Germany his only alternative had often been to join the army, at that time the depth of degradation.

Katya, the professor's ward, had had a passion for the theatre from the age of fourteen, like many another Institutka, and on leaving school had insisted on becoming an actress. She had a most idealistic view of the stage and its influence on society. Like so many young enthusiasts in Germany when Goethe wrote the theatre novel which became *Wilhelm Meister's Apprenticeship*, she thought that 'the stage was a power uniting in itself all the arts, and actors were missionaries. No art and no science, taken separately, could have such a profound and serious effect on the human soul as the theatre, and it was no accident that the mediocre actor enjoyed much more popularity in Russia than the best of scholars or artists'. It is evident from Chekhov's many references that young Russians even in his day often looked on the theatre still as what Schiller called 'a moral institution'. Kuprin tells us how pleased Chekhov was with the anecdote (to be found in his note-books) about the Russian actor who after a rehearsal refused to whistle a tune on the stage for his mistress. 'What, whistle on the stage!', he said. 'Would you whistle in church? And isn't the stage the same as a church?'

It is interesting to find such ideas current in Russia a century after *Wilhelm Meister*, and tempting to explain their recurrence as mainly due to the presence in the political, social and cultural background of certain factors which had existed earlier in Germany. There was the system of absolutism, with all the trammels that it placed on men's activities, and especially on the free expression of opinion; energies which might have found another outlet in a free state were deflected into the arts, and in the art of the theatre there was always a possibility that the censor might be eluded. There was a new middle-class public emerging, which required its 'circuses' to keep it quiet, and as it grew more prosperous 'ordered its portrait' on the stage, to use Brunetiere's phrase. Above all there was the decay of orthodox religion among the intelligentsia, and its replacement by science, philosophy and literature, including the literary drama. German ideas on the religion of art, especially in their Romantic formulation, were readily accepted in Russia, just as German actors and managers, as well as innumerable German plays, had found a welcome there since the eighteenth century. Translations of Schiller were still on the repertoire in Chekhov's own day. 'The Robbers' is played for instance by a second-rate travelling troupe in *A tragic actor*. There are several other interesting features in this story, the warm welcome given to a troupe in a small town by the chief of police himself, who even invites some of the actors to his house, though not the actresses ('You see, I have a daughter'), the assurances of the manager over lunch of his profound respect for everyone in authority, and the elopement of the stage-struck daughter herself with the tragic actor, who marries her in the hope of gain and beats her when her father disowns her. Katya undergoes a similar disillusionment, and so does Nina in *The seagull*. The actor in *In the graveyard*, dying of drink, who comes to visit for the last time the grave of an older colleague who had filled him with illusions about the stage and led him to take up the wretched career, is a sort of male counterpart to these ladies.

Problems of the literary and theatrical life of his day, together with some other themes already touched upon in this chapter, were finally worked up into a complex pattern by Chekhov in *The seagull*, which more than any other of his plays is concerned with the intelligentsia in the wider sense. At Sorin's country house beside a lake of magic beauty, surrounded by big estates, where singing is still heard in the evening across the waters and something of the holiday atmosphere of more prosperous times still survives, the scene is laid of a play containing, as Chekhov wrote, 'much talk of literature, little action, and five poods of love'. There are links with the workaday world. Sorin is a high civil servant in retirement, his friend Dorn has been in his time a busy country doctor, Medvedyenko is a village teacher and Shamraev an ex-officer who, with his wife Polina and daughter Masha manages or mismanages Sorin's estate. But the four central characters belong to the world of literature and the theatre.

Sorin's sister Arkadina, a well-known actress, is visiting her old home, with her lover Trigorin, a successful writer. Her son Treplev, a young man of twenty-five with literary leanings, lives with his uncle and is in love with a neighbour's daughter, Nina, who is bent on a stage career.

There is no revolutionary talk among these artistic people. One of their defects is that their thoughts are entirely taken up with their own petty affairs, whether affairs of the heart or personal artistic triumphs. There is a hint of genuine devotion to an impersonal ideal in Treplev and Nina, the younger pair. Treplev had been obliged to leave the university half-way through his course, apparently for political reasons, and his literary efforts have the merit of sincerity, though vanity and a hopeless passion combine with external circumstances to make them ineffective. Nina too, when her infatuation with Trigorin has run its inevitable course, finds a true vocation in acting. Arkadina however, a popular favourite, is vanity and selfishness personified. All must listen to the story of her latest triumphs and admire her ever youthful charm, she is stingy, even with her son, jealous and incapable of real sympathy. Trigorin too, though in some respects he is simply the professional writer, always pursued, like Chekhov himself, by the thought of his unfinished work, and mentally filing every experience for future use, is a sleek, self-satisfied and unscrupulous worshipper of success and comfort. Selfishness and acute nervous sensibility lead to the storms that are as frequent in this 'heartbreak house' as in a nursery, for all are indeed, in the phrase already quoted of some others, 'spoilt children of life', none of them (except the contrast figure Medvedyenko) being compelled by economic, social or religious considerations to bridle their unruly desires. One of the unhappiest, and least attractive, is Masha, the frowsy would-be emancipated young woman with no particular gifts, who tosses off her vodka, takes snuff, and wears black 'in mourning for her own life'. With society as it was in that age, the ideas of life aroused in her by her reading, and by contact with Treplev and his family, have become incompatible with her opportunities as a half-educated officer's daughter.

It would clearly be a mistake to consider these characters as typical of Russians in general. They illustrate a particular set at a particular time, but they are no more representative of Russia as a whole at that time, as is evident from the rest of this study, than Aldous Huxley's characters in, say, *Point Counter Point*, were of England between the Wars. Like them, and like many similar figures in the European literature of the last century and more, from *La nouvelle Héloïse* and *Werther* onwards, with its disintegrating values and extreme individualism, they give to sexual love, in forms ranging from the romantic to the cynical, an importance which it could scarcely have had for so many in more stable ages, or even in Chekhov's own time in sections of society struggling with nature for a bare living, like his peasants. They seem to echo Perdican's words to Camille, in Musset's *On ne badine pas avec l'amour*, urging that though both men and women are depraved and contemptible 'il y a au monde une chose sainte et sublime, c'est l'union de ces deux êtres si imparfaits et si affreux'. This is perhaps the inner reason for the 'five poods of love', the semi-circle of linked triangles à la Racine which give the play its principal pattern—Arkadina, Trigorin, Nina; Trigorin, Nina, Treplev; Nina, Treplev, Masha; Treplev, Masha, Medvedyenko and, more in the background, Dorn, Polina, Shamraev. It would otherwise seem a little arbitrary that in this world love is never mutual and its possessiveness is always a source of suffering—except for a Trigorin, with whom it is chiefly a source of copy. The shot seagull laid at Nina's feet by Treplev in Act II, as if he should say: 'See what you have done to our love!', this thing of wild beauty wantonly destroyed, suggests to Trigorin an idea for a short story. 'A girl like you,' he says to Nina, 'has been living on the shores of a lake since childhood; she loves the lake like a seagull, and she is as happy and free as a seagull. But a man comes by chance, sees her, and having nothing better to do, ruins her, like this seagull.' The story of course comes true, partly because Trigorin himself is seeking material for some such story, and this not very original theme helps to hold the play together, but its main interest is the presentation in seemingly natural yet intensely poetical scenes, full of atmosphere, of a whole group of characters, each of whom has his personal tragedy, and of their constantly varying relations. Faguet's remark about Molière, that he puts just enough of a plot into his plays to give what is really a study dramatic form, could be applied to Chekhov too.

These characters are imagined by Chekhov with so much understanding sympathy that some might take the author to imply that their suffering is due to no fault of their own, but from what has been said in this chapter it is clear that he had a strong distaste for intellectuals of this stamp, though as an objective artist he aimed simply at drawing them convincingly. He shows them however in a significant setting. As so often in his stories, the pettiness and ugliness of human life are contrasted with the calm and beauty and vastness of nature, and in this play it is perhaps not fanciful to say that a vast span of time as well is suggested, for just as Treplev's stage, when the curtain is raised on his play within the play in the first act, reveals the broad lake as a natural background, so his expressionistic vision of an earth from which all life has disappeared puts into perspective in time the vanities of all these creatures of a day.

Not *The Sea Gull* alone, but all Chekhov's serious plays deal in greater or lesser measure with the world of the intelligentsia, and that is perhaps the main reason why those who know him chiefly from his plays find him a gloomy writer. Russian critics assure us that no one handling such a subject sincerely could be anything else, yet the subject had naturally a fascination for the intelligent public of those days. We have seen in earlier chapters that taken as a whole Chekhov's work shows much variety and that with the Russian public he actually made his name as a humorist. Of the plays already discussed, *The Three Sisters* deals mainly with one section of the educated class, the army officer and official, while *Ivanov* centres round a cultivated and liberal-minded landowner and *The Cherry Orchard* contains only one intellectual, the 'eternal student' Trofimov. The remaining play (apart from the farces) is *Uncle Vanya*, which has links both with *Ivanov* and with *The Sea Gull*. The first version of it, called *The Wood Demon*, was written in a great hurry for immediate performance a year after *Ivanov*, and the final version was not made until after *The Sea Gull*. It is a country-house drama of frustration with characters drawn from landowners and intelligentsia. The most interesting of them is Dr. Astrov in *Uncle Vanya*, who develops out of the title character in *The Wood Demon*. There he stands out among a company of country squires through his intelligence and his passion for forestry. In *Uncle Vanya* the centre of interest is shifted to one group of characters from the older play, the household of Professor Screbryakov, who has recently retired to the estate of his first wife in the country. The hardened old egoist who has developed out of a country priest's son, with his young and beautiful second wife and Uncle Vanya, his brother-in-law, who has managed the estate since it was first bought for his sister's dowry twenty years earlier, form the usual triangle, and the tension between them is increased by the professor's ingrained habit of putting his own interests first, in the name of the higher learning, and the disillusionment of his wife and of Uncle Vanya, who in his jealousy feels that he has wasted his life in serving the interests of a useless old bore.

Uncle Vanya is another Ivanov, without his idealism, and the other characters, apart from Astrov, are not outstanding. What is significant is the shift in the author's point of view between the two versions. In *The Wood Demon*, it is the private shortcomings of the characters which are made responsible for their fate. 'The world is going to ruin,' the professor's wife is made to say, 'not through thieves and robbers but because of the latent hostility or open hatred between decent people, all those little differences which are not seen by those who call our house a nest of the intelligentsia.' When the tension culminates in a violent quarrel between the professor and Uncle Vanya, the latter shoots himself, this shock brings people to their senses, and a change of heart in several characters (comparable with that of Laevsky in *The Duel*) brings about a happy ending. In the final version these Tolstoyan ideas are subordinated to a social interpretation of the evil, and the comedy becomes a drama, 'scenes from country life'. It is country life itself, in Russian conditions, so boring, stupid and dirty, as Astrov says, that drags intelligent people down to the level of the oddities around them. An improvement will be brought about, if at all, not by a change of heart but by the re-moulding of society as a whole, and the intelligentsia seem to him too petty and narrow-minded to attempt any such task. Uncle Vanya is prevented from shooting himself, and is seen at the close settling down again to his humdrum work with his niece, who in this version is also disappointed of her happiness, and can only console him with the faith that God will have mercy on them for all they have suffered. This note of resignation, characteristic of the 'eighties rather than the 'nineties, was not unnaturally criticised by activists like Gorky, though they did not dispute the truth of Chekhov's picture. In *The Three Sisters* and *The Cherry Orchard*, the two later plays, there are, as we have seen, at least hints of a more hopeful view of the future, in keeping with that often expressed by Chekhov privately in later years, though to his own generation he could still only offer the hard doctrine of altruism for the sake of coming generations.

CHAPTER VIII

INDUSTRY, COMMERCE AND TOWN LIFE

We have seen that in Chekhov's time Russia was still a decidedly agrarian country, 80% of whose population were officially classified as peasantry. Less than 13% of the population of European Russia lived in towns (to be compared with some 42% round about 1900 in Germany), but 13% meant twelve million people, and fifteen of the towns were large towns with over 100,000 inhabitants (to be compared again with Germany's thirty-three large towns, in a country with only two-thirds of Russia's population). The industrial revolution and capitalism had reached Russia late, but they had had very striking results since the Emancipation, though the capital employed was to a very great extent foreign. The total production in mining, oil and the heavy industries was indeed small, compared with that of the leading industrial countries, but it had grown from next to nothing in forty years, the production of coal, for instance, from .28 to 16 million tons between 1860 and 1900, oil from .027 to 10.4 million tons, pig-iron from .31 to 2.7 million tons.[1] Russia, like Germany, coming to capitalism later than Great Britain, and with more state control, the first large-scale industrial undertakings having been started in both countries to provide armaments for their forces, cloth for uniforms and so forth, had tended to develop very large concerns at an early stage, and there were particular regions where industries were very heavily concentrated, though there were others where there were none for hundreds of miles. There were survivals too on a large scale of every earlier kind of economy, from the primitive exploitation of virgin forests and the 'natural', self-sufficient economy on remote country estates to the domestic industries of village craftsmen, organised on a co-operative basis in their 'artels', and country factories (like those in *In the ravine*), employing free peasant labour, successors to the factories, belonging often to foreigners, to which bonded peasants had been 'ascribed' as forced labour in large numbers from as early as the seventeenth century. Similarly trade and communica-

[1] Sumner, *Survey*, p. 362.

tions showed a variety of forms which made of Russia at the end of the nineteenth century a veritable economic museum.

Of this infinite variety of activities we cannot expect to find more than a glimpse here and there in Chekhov, but what he does give us is again a valuable supplement to the formal historics, pictures in full perspective, without partisan bias, which bring home to us the fact that economic systems of every kind are worked by individual men.

One of the basic conditions of commercial and industrial development was of course the state of communications, and of this we obtain many clear impressions from the tales. The railway age had opened just before the Crimean War, and the growth of capitalistic industry had, as in Germany, been closely connected with railway development, but in the 'nineties the vast expanse was crossed as yet only by a few main lines. Chekhov's travellers, his architects, his examining magistrates and doctors going to inquests, his villagers going to hospital, his schoolmistress coming back to her village, have to go all or part of the way by road, in carriage or sledge, by the ordinary post, in a peasant's cart or on foot. As in the older Russian writers, we find vivid descriptions of abominable roads and conveyances, perilous fords and bridges, blinding snow-storms that blot out the road, and inns offering every degree of discomfort. We share for instance the feelings of the student who has begged a lift to the railway station (in *The Post*), sitting beside the surly driver of a post coach as the three horses take fright, and the coach jolts over roots of trees in the pitch darkness until it comes up against a wooden bridge, having thrown out the postillion, his rusty sword and the luggage, or of little Yegorushka on his long journey across the steppe to his new school (*The steppe*), first in an open springless britzka with his uncle and the priest and then, after tea at a lonely Jewish inn, amongst bales of wool on a waggon bound for market with a score of others. We follow the changing light, the sudden storms on the vast steppe, we hear the peasant drivers' racy talk and see them bathing and making their kasha at the midday halt.

The railway boom of the 'nineties is reflected in several stories where railways under construction are described. In *Lights* for instance we recapture something of the atmosphere prevailing at the birth of a railway when 'things are beginning to move'. They move in a very Russian way. We hear of engineers (in *My life*) who place a station five versts outside a town because the town council's bribe fell 10,000 roubles short of what they had demanded, a sum eventually more than required for the new road to the station. We see order emerging from chaos as embankments are made, rails laid and service trains with building material start running, but stations and bridges have still to be built. The engineer responsible for the bridge (*My life*) has had the foresight to acquire three estates near the new line. He is a different type from any we have met so far, with something of the American about him—clear-eyed, healthy, absorbed in work and money-making, a trained engineer who has worked for years with his hands and had experience abroad; but also something Russian— he is always receiving mysterious gifts and treats his subordinates like dirt. The crowd of ragged labourers, like the bridge builders in *The new villa*, are despised by settled townsfolk as rowdy riff-raff. *The cattle dealers* shows us the conditions on some of the railways in the 'eighties. We have already mentioned the endless series of tips that the cattle dealer finds necessary to get his cattle to their destination alive. At one point he also wires to the chief traffic controller. Even so, the journey takes several days instead of the advertised time of thirty-four hours. He and his son lie in one of the trucks with the cattle the whole way, eating their own provisions and buying hot water for tea at big stations. But the old man likes stronger drink, and has no difficulty in finding rail-way men to join him at the bar. On one of the stations an inspector mentions in the course of conversation that not long before this one railway company had simply stolen three hundred trucks belonging to another, and repainted them in its own colours, an anecdote heard by Chekhov himself on a journey in 1887 (see his letter of 2/4/1887). The scandalous state of the railways only escapes criticism, the inspector says, because there is no general background of good administration in the country to show it up. Many other stories throw incidental light on the railways and railway travel, *A happy ending* for instance (discussed above in connection with bribery), *Champagne* (an episode in the life of a station-master in the south-west, at a small station with not a single habitation for fourteen miles around), or the charming snapshot of a southern station in *The beauties*.

The contrast is most marked between the pictures of inns to be found in Chekhov and in nineteenth-century English writers. We hear of course of hotels of all sizes and sets of furnished rooms in the large towns, and these had evidently been much influenced already by western example, but country inns where the traveller might take his ease, if they existed, were not described by Chekhov.

Instead we find scenes such as the following, from the stage directions of the one-act play *On the main road:* 'The scene is Tikhon's tavern (in southern Russia). To the right the counter, and shelves full of bottles behind it. In the background a door leading out, with a greasy red lantern hanging above it outside. The floor and the benches round the walls are taken up by closely packed pilgrims and travellers. Many are sleeping upright for lack of space to lie down.' It was like the typical izba, and one is reminded of the conditions in eighteenth-century German country inns, for instance, where the traveller could usually only expect a 'Streu', a bed of straw on the floor. The better-class traveller in earlier days had to rely to a great extent on private hospitality, and if he had no friends in the neighbourhood, sought out at least a clean cottage. (See for instance the story *On official duty.*) But for an odd night he had to be content with the kind of accommodation described in *On the road*, where we see a gentleman and his little daughter sleeping in their clothes in the 'travellers' room' of a Cossack inn, in which they are later joined by a young lady, or in *The night before my trial*,* where a man spends the night on a couch covered with American cloth, in the waiting-room of a post station, a room with bare wooden walls, a big iron stove and a table with a smoky lamp on it. He politely offers the 'Persian powder' which he has had the forethought to bring with him in anticipation of bugs to two fellow sufferers whom he unexpectedly discovers behind a screen, with amusing consequences. These examples help us to understand why it was the normal practice for Russian travellers to take all their bedding with them. In out of the way places there were, no doubt, still inns where a man might find worse enemies than vermin, like the feldscher in *The horse-stealers*, a study of peasantry with dare-devil lawlessness in their veins.

There is little in Chekhov, except in letters, about travel by inland waterways, which had been the first to develop and was still considerable. Trade had followed such routes long before there were any made roads, a 'passive' trade at first, in the early middle ages, in the hands of Vikings, Greeks and Arabs. It was in those days that towns like Kiev, with its Byzantine connections, Smolensk, Polotsk, and Novgorod, the Hanseatic centre, became prominent, on the route between the Black Sea and the Baltic. 'The merchant had been together with the warrior the creator of the State because he was perpetually concerned with the outside world. The merchant was always dealing with foreign merchants, who were called guests. But by the time of Peter the Great the merchants were no longer politically the most important members of the community. They had fallen into their places as middlemen in a big, clumsy, agricultural community in which the landowners naturally took the lead. Peter made the merchants more important than they had been by opening a way out to Europe, and the importance of the merchant class had steadily risen in proportion as Russia had been steadily drawn into the movement of world trade. But many traces of the process of development still linger. The Russian merchant is not like those of other countries. In his mental make-up, in the traditions and conventions of his class there is something of the Moscow merchant who under the Tartar yoke was accustomed to trade chiefly with the East, and of that St. Petersburg merchant who was as often as not a German, and at any rate was strongly influenced in all his dealings by Germans and Swedes. It is the latter type that has been the means of slowly modernising the others, and the process of modernisation is still going on, is not yet complete, and is centred not in St. Petersburg but in Moscow, the heart of the Empire.' So H. W. Williams wrote in 1914.

His description of the Russian merchant's way of life explains many details that might otherwise be puzzling to English readers in, for instance, Chekhov's *Three Years*, for merchants play a very small part in the chief Russian novels known to the West, though a big one in Ostrovsky's comedies. 'The English word merchant has a slightly incongruous sound,' Williams wrote, 'as applied to members of the Russian trading class. In England the word seems suggestive of a city man in silk hat and frock-coat, of an alderman, of the Tabard Inn, or of the portly head of some mediæval Venetian firm. The Russian merchant is a different being, although he certainly has many mediæval characteristics. He is called a *kupiets*, or buyer, which is a word having the same root as the German Kaufmann or our "chapman". Not so many years ago most members of the class wore a characteristic costume, a long kaftan of dark cloth, hooked, not buttoned, up to the neck, a belt around the waist, baggy trousers, top-boots, neckcloth, and peaked cap. A beard was worn and the hair cut so as not to hang lower than the nape of the neck. This costume may be still frequently seen in the smaller towns, and the way in which its various elements are combined with modern articles of clothing indicates the extent to which the process of Westernisation has developed. The peak cap and top-boots often linger on when the kaftan has given way to a humdrum jacket. Starched shirts and collars are adopted last of all. The merchants have their own peculiar modes of speech, their quips and cranks, their own elaborate etiquette. They are punctilious in their observance of church ritual—not a few of them are Old Believers—pay serious attention, in contrast to the intelligentsia, to the details of eating and drinking and the mere process of living generally, are very hospitable within their own circle, and make much of festivals and family events such as births, marriages, and deaths. The typical merchant of the not distant past could hardly read or write. He kept no books—the word for bookkeeper in Russian is borrowed from German—but had a peculiarly retentive memory for figures and facts.'

Chekhov's *Three years* (1895) is a small-scale *Buddenbrooks*, written six years before Thomas Mann's masterpiece, and eleven years before the first part of the *Forsyte Saga*. In his epigrammatic way, the author gives us in 130 pages, and the story of just three years, the same feeling for the inevitable differentiation of successive generations which Mann and Galsworthy elaborate at much greater length. His story centres round the marriage of Laptev, the younger son of a rich Moscow merchant, with the daughter of a doctor in a provincial town. The theme of the love story is rather like that of *Evgeny Onegin* with the rôles reversed— it is the man who loves passionately at the beginning and the woman at the end, but Chekhov's picture of three years of their marriage looks before and after, showing us what they have come from and what they will grow into, together with their immediate circle, against a Moscow as well as a provincial background. The superb skill with which this feat is accomplished, and the national and stylistic differences between these three authors, would repay full study, but here we are only concerned with the impression of the Russian merchant that is to be obtained from the story.

Like Thomas Mann, Chekhov sees a process of degeneration at work in the life of a merchant family, and there are obvious resemblances between the two authors due to the general 'climate of opinion' of the age and their common models among the French naturalists, particularly their insistence on the force of heredity and their questioning attitude towards the bourgeoisie. They have nothing of the time-serving complacency which Chekhov found for instance in *The Family of the Polonetskys* by Sienkievicz, which he read about this time (letter of 13/4/1895). This he described as 'Polish Easter curd cake with saffron . . . inspired by

Bourget's *Cosmopolis*, by Rome, and by marriage. . . . The object of the novel is to lull the bourgeoisie to sleep in its golden dreams. Be faithful to your wife, pray with her over the prayer-book, make money, love sport, and all is well with you in this world and the next. The bourgeoisie is very fond of so-called positive types, and novels with happy endings, since they soothe it with the idea that one can both accumulate capital and preserve innocence, be a beast and at the same time be happy.'

It is clear that Chekhov had no love for the bourgeoisie, but he interprets the degeneration of his merchant family less subjectively than Thomas Mann, and perhaps with more sociological insight. The German author can never get away from the problem of the artist, who is for him a typical late product, overripe and biologically unsound compared with the normal bourgeois, so he makes his merchant family gradually 'degenerate' into artists, and finally die out. Chekhov's Laptev family have a different history. The old man is not unlike a type of business man who occurs in protestant literature, inflexibly self-righteous characters, whose whole personality, however religious externally, is integrated round the instinct of self-assertion. Laptev senior is a domestic tyrant, a little God in his own eyes, whose one joy in life is to exercise power. He has no particular ability, but in his day, according to his son, given a certain start, a merchant could make a fortune almost automatically. 'The money comes to him of itself,' in this case no less than some six million roubles, all from wholesale dealings in trimmings, fringe, buttons and so on. He never leaves his warehouse, just because he enjoys ordering his assistants about and making fun of the customers. 'He is an elder at church because he can lord it over the choir and make them bend the knee before him'—he even stands in front of all in church and criticises the priest if he does not perform every rite according to his notions. He is a curator of a school for a similar reason. 'What a merchant likes is not trading, but exercising authority, and your warehouse is not a commercial establishment, but a torture chamber.' Coming back after some months' absence, Laptev sees the boys still being whipped and punched on the nose as he was himself as a boy. When they grow up, he says, they will do the same to their juniors. The fifty assistants are exploited mercilessly, living under conditions which are evidently exceptionally bad, as they are the talk of the market quarter. They live in, packed three or four in a room in the basement or a lodge of their master's house. They eat from one dish at dinner, though each has his own plate, for it is typical that liberties are allowed in theory which they seldom or never dare to take in practice. They do not marry, for instance, and seldom go out in the evening, for they must be in by nine, and know that the old man will notice if their breath smells of vodka next morning. They are obsequious to a degree, Uriah Heeps every one of them, and therefore potential tyrants too.

What Chekhov is castigating here is the tradition of the 'khozyain', the patriarchal head of a household, exercising his unlimited authority in an inhuman fashion, this time in a mercantile milieu, just as we found him earlier in the peasant joint family. It is a crass instance, but typical in so far as unlimited power always corrupts. The present generation, because of the more general diffusion of the feeling for human freedom in the world, have not reacted in the same way as their predecessors. They know that their grandfather was beaten by squires and petty officials, and that he beat their father in his turn, but they have not borne blows gladly in the assurance that their turn will come. Instead their life has been poisoned by fear. Conceived in fear, by a mother who at seventeen had been married to a man of forty-five and trembled at his nod, they have been 'educated' with the whip, nauseated with family prayers and church and set to work in the warehouse from the age of eight, working half a day there even while attending the gymnasium. Chekhov had of course experienced something of this kind himself. The result has been, Laptev says, to break his will to live. He has an inferiority complex, as we should say now, even with concierges and gendarmes. The brother, when his unconscious attempts to conceal his unhappiness under a mask of piety or of social vanity have failed, becomes a nervous wreck, and Laptev hopes that their 'distinguished merchant family' will die out with them.

While at the university, Laptev, encouraged by a friend, had made a bid for independence, taken a flat and reduced his share in the work of the firm to a minimum, though still deriving from it an income of 2500 roubles a month. To the age of thirty-four he had led a gay bachelor's life in Moscow, with intelligent friends and a mistress, in a circle with artistic and musical interests and the individualistic point of view of the intelligentsia, though his means allowed him to be generous in his charities. He had no religion and no particular aim in life, living from impulse to impulse, with an overhanging vague fear. Now he falls deeply in love, but his relationship with Julia is poisoned from the outset by the thought, prompted partly by his self-distrust, that she married him for his money, though in reality it was to escape from her father and to live in Moscow. When after three years she has really grown to love him, his own love is dead, and there is a hint of the usual triangle of frustration developing, with his best friend Yartsev in love with Julia. Meanwhile he has become head of the firm, and finds himself a prisoner of the wealth that could bring him freedom. 'He was convinced that the millions and the business, for which he had so little liking, would spoil his life and make a slave of him once and for all; he pictured to himself how he would gradually get used to his position, gradually enter into the rôle of head of the firm, find his sensibilities blunted, grow old and in the end die the sordid, soured death of the ordinary philistine, after being a weariness to all around him.' Yet he could make no attempt to escape. 'And he was annoyed both with himself and with this black dog on the stones at his feet, that did not run away to the fields, the woods, where it would have been free and happy. The same thing, clearly, prevented them both from leaving this courtyard, mere force of habit, reconciling them to captivity, to the life of a slave.'

What is the underlying cause of this sense of frustration that we find everywhere in Chekhov? Is it, in his view, something given with life itself, something metaphysical, or is it the product of social maladjustments, which could be changed by a sufficient effort of will? We shall return to this question in the last chapter. The cause is evidently a force that at least works through particular social conditions, plainly drawn here for the merchant class. As a picture of manners the story is vivid and convincing, bringing in many of the characteristics of the *kupiets* singled out by H. W. Williams. Some external features have gone or partly gone by this time in Moscow, the costume, for instance, but we still see the punctilious observance of church ritual, the quips and cranks and peculiar idioms, the elaborate etiquette—particularly in the solemn reception of the son's bride in the family mansion, with elaborate religious ceremonial—and the absence of book-keeping, and therefore of the impersonality and strict rationalisation usual in western firms of this size.

Yet business ethics were certainly no higher than in the West. Old-fashioned firms like this probably made little use of advertisements, for their wares were in constant demand, and they could dispense with the 'air of European civilisation' which hung about the tea merchant in *The writer**, for instance, with his cigar and

7

his fashionable suit. In this sketch the intelligentsia and the commercial world meet. An old, red-nosed 'writer', with pangs of conscience at deceiving all Russia, produces a very literary advertisement with no snap in it, and is paid for it by the young tea merchant in tea and sugar. To any customer who spends fifty roubles this smart firm already (in 1885) offers a free gift, either a tea-pot, a hundred visiting-cards, a plan of Moscow, a tea-caddy shaped like a naked Chinese girl, or a book, 'The wooer surprised, or The bride under the trough'. The trick of paying for services in kind is also mentioned in *In the ravine*, where Tsybukin pays the dress-makers in candles and sardines. Though a sympathetic character compared with his daughter-in-law, he cheats whenever he can, sells rancid oil and bad beer and receives stolen goods, just as the assistants in *Three years* laugh at their own cleverness when they have palmed off out-of-date goods on some country customer. In these circles 'you can walk about a whole day', as young Tsybukin says when his own conscience is pricking him, 'and not meet a single man with a conscience. The reason is that they don't know whether there is a God or not.'

A better type of merchant is drawn for us, with obvious sympathy, in Lopakhin (*The cherry orchard*), who is contrasted, as we saw, in his energy and enterprise, as a decent self-made man, with the aristocratic landowners. The son of a coarse village shopkeeper, he has had little education and writes an appalling hand, but he has gained some polish by mixing with people, 'behaves like an educated man, with no quips and cranks', and is not a mere money-grubber (letter of 30/10/1903). The fact that he occurs in Chekhov's last play, written eight years later than *Three years*, when under Witte's leadership industrialisation was beginning to show good results, is perhaps significant, though it is more likely that Chekhov would never have denied that there were plenty of good men in the merchant class, like his own relatives.

Handicrafts are comparatively seldom mentioned by Chekhov, not because they were unimportant in Russia, but no doubt because he knew little about them. We hear of a few village craftsmen, as we have seen, some of them itinerant, and one or two stories give shocking examples of brutality in the treatment of children by their employers in towns. In *Vanka*, for instance, a nine-year-old orphan boy apprenticed to a shoemaker writes a Christmas letter to his grandfather in his village, where he had been so happy, begging him to take him away, or he will die.

His master beats him with a boot-stretcher for falling asleep over the cradle, or knocks him down with a last. 'The workmen laugh at me and send me for vodka, they tell me to steal the master's cucumbers for them, and then the master beats me with anything within reach. And there is nothing to eat. For breakfast they give me bread, for dinner "kasha" and in the evening bread again; but if there is tea or cabbage soup, the master and mistress keep it to themselves. And I am made to sleep in the cold passage, and when their brat cries I have to rock the cradle and get no sleep at all.' The contrast between his memories of the village and his present life is imagined with a vividness and pathos in which every note rings true. *Sleepy*, a short story much admired by Tolstoy, is on a similar theme, about the tortures suffered by a thirteen-year-old nursemaid, again in a shoemaker's house.

These sketches are great art, but they do not tell us very much about the craftsman class, except that in Chekhov's view it was not untypical to find amongst them the same coarse manners and insensitiveness as amongst the peasantry, their social equals, and that child labour was a commonplace. According to *My life*, the house-painters with whom the hero worked were easy enough to get on with, but they considered him a freak because he did not steal the master's oil and paint, as they all did. They would beg shamelessly for tips and say anything to please a customer. The trouble here, as in the villages, was that there was no one to set the 'black' worker a better example or to encourage him in habits of self-respect.

The problem of big industry occupied Chekhov much more, because he realised it was becoming more pressing every day. Two short stories, *A doctor's visit* (1898) and *A woman's kingdom* (1894), show that Chekhov had kept his eyes open on his infrequent visits to factories, and that he was very much alive to the social questions raised by the growth of capitalistic industry. Here again, however, he merely states the question, he does not claim to know the answer, and as in *Three years*, the question is for him fundamentally a moral one. For the young doctor called out from Moscow to a big cotton-mill in the country there is something sinister about the whole atmosphere of the place, about the workmen timidly taking off their caps to his carriage, the workers' cottages with the washing outside, the bare enclosed court-yard, like a prison, with its five factory buildings, warehouses, workers' huts, all covered with a grey film, and the uncanny metallic noises made by the watchmen as they beat the hour from each building in turn. From what he has read and seen he does not like such places, and after visiting his patient, the heiress to all this, whose father has recently died, he feels that even the owners are no happier for their wealth, and that some two thousand people are slaving to make bad cotton goods in order to enable a complacent governess, the only person he has met who is thoroughly at home in these surroundings, to eat sturgeon and drink madeira. ' "But that is only in appearance, she is only a lay figure here. The chief person for whom all this is being done is the devil." And he thought of the devil, in whom he did not believe, and looked at the two windows in which a light was shining (in a factory whose chimney belched smoke and flame). It seemed to him that the devil himself was looking at him through those blood-red eyes, that unknown power which determined the relations between the strong and the weak, the immense wrong which it seems impossible to put right. It is a law of nature that the strong should interfere in the life of the weak, but it is only in newspaper articles and text-books that this is understandable and easily accepted by the mind, as part of the same hotch-potch presented in daily life, the tangle of petty circumstances which are the stuff of human relations. It is no longer a law, but a logical contradiction, when both strong and weak alike fall victims to their mutual relations, submitting themselves without a will of their own to some unknown, non-human directive power that stands outside life.'

This is a protest in the name of morality and common-sense against the assumption of an economic necessity behind the capitalistic system, considered from the side of production. It is because the daughter of the low-browed, self-satisfied manufacturer, whose portrait hangs in the drawing-room, through her reading and brooding over modern literature, can no longer accept this idea, that she has her fits of nerves. It is an illness, the doctor says, that does her credit. He is one of Chekhov's optimists, and believes that in fifty years the system will be abandoned and the question settled, though he does not know how, and that then it will again be good to be alive.

In the earlier and longer story, *A woman's kingdom*, the central figure is again a young woman, who has inherited an engineering concern employing 1800 men. It was perhaps because his theme was the ethical aspect of big business, a question of conscience for the factory owner, that Chekhov draws family concerns, not joint stock companies, and does not show us a man, building them up, but a woman of some refinement who has inherited them, and is likely to be more open-minded and sensitive in such matters. Seen through Anna's eyes, the works and their sur-roundings again inspire fear and loathing, the ugly buildings, the terrifying power and noise in the engineering shop, the crowds of rough but obsequious workmen, living in tenements and huts, with nothing but vodka to cheer their drab lives. The ruler of this kingdom, a natural, good-hearted woman of twenty-five, has more questions on her mind than she can deal with, and no disinterested advisers. Sometimes she wishes herself back again amongst the working class, whose life she had shared until her uncle, three years before his death, had taken her father into partnership, or she longs for a husband to relieve her of it all. One great problem is how best to use her money, and particularly how to dispense her bounties among the hundreds who clamour for them. She finds this almost insoluble, though she soon repents of a rash resolve to give a large sum to one applicant chosen at random, instead of frittering it away among many. It is not only in this respect that she has far more power at her disposal than she relishes. There is something unnatural, she feels, in deriving a large income from a business about which she understands nothing. Her managing director cannot entirely relieve her of responsibility for working conditions, the state of the workers' huts, for example, which some say are damp, full of bugs, worse than a prison, though thousands of roubles a year are spent on them. One of the worst blots on Russian industrialism, by all accounts, was the most squalid, insanitary housing, much of it of a temporary kind, though many companies, like Anna's, spent large sums on workmen's settlements.[1] The first factory law had indeed been made in 1882, but this and later measures were subject to many exceptions and not efficiently enforced in Chekhov's time.[2]

Anna's main problem, however, and the main theme of the story, is the conflict between her natural desire for marriage and the limitations imposed by her social position. Like the hero of *Three years*, she is ill at ease in her world, a prisoner of her own wealth. Her uncle, who had apparently built up the firm's prosperity, and her father, had been two brothers of very different natures. The one was hard as flint, strict in religious matters, with a tendency towards Old Belief, an ascetic of power again like old

[1] Mavor, *Econ. History of Russia*, II, chap. 3.
[2] *Ibid*, chap. 4.

Laptev and some familiar Calvinist types of business man, content to live in one room in his office quarters and make no use of his mansion except on special occasions. For the Russian capitalist, as for the rest, 'The duty of saving became nine-tenths of virtue and the growth of the cake the object of true religion', in the words of J. M. Keynes' famous analysis. Anna's father, on the other hand, was easygoing, rather a dreamer, not interested in money or power or religion, but only in making things with his hands, and therefore despised by his elder brother and kept for most of his life in the position of an ordinary workman at sixteen roubles a month. He lived with his wife and daughter in a tenement, where Anna had dusted and ironed contentedly, amidst the sounds of neighbours laughing or shouting, children crying, of accordions and lathes and sewing-machines. She still does not feel that she quite belongs to the world of the privileged, so it is not surprising that the idea should occur to her of marrying a workman, one of her foremen, for instance, who takes her fancy. But she finds she is too far committed to her new world to carry the plan through, and has to admit that she prefers it now to the other.

In these two stories we were shown two reputable firms in the heart of Russia. What might go on in the remoter regions, further from the control of a by no means grandmotherly government, is suggested by a story put into the mouth of the eccentric *Pechenyeg* in the steppes, about a landowner who had mines on his estate, where he employed only men without passports, all sorts of vagabonds who had nowhere to go to. When they went for their pay on Saturday, they would be told by the foreman that there was none for them. They would kick and beat him senseless, but he was a tough who had been promised ten roubles a week if he would stand this treatment, and was glad to do so. When the men had gone away, the master would have some water poured over him and give him his ten roubles. On the Monday he would take on a fresh set of down and outs. It is hard to believe that things would really work out quite like that, and one wonders what sort of work would be obtained from men treated in this way, but this is the kind of reputation some mine owners had; it is a mine almost as bad to which the long-suffering traveller in *On the road* is going as manager. He is warned by the lady whose acquaintance he makes in the inn that her uncle, who owns the mine, is a maniac, a despot, a bankrupt, who will not even give him his salary.

We have had evidence from several other stories that the new forms of industry and commerce took a particular colouring from the age-old habits of Russian social life. Village capitalists, as we have seen (Chapter III), revealed peasant ways of thought and action in their enterprises, the Russian merchant, even if he was a millionaire, was still deeply affected by the traditions of his class, and the ignorance and slackness of the provincial philistine, the absence of any social standard of honesty and decency, made him often incapable of feeling, like the self-respecting early capitalist in the West, that honesty was the best policy. This point emerges clearly in the story *In trouble*, where the merchant Avdyeyev, though he had known for two years that there was something wrong with the affairs of the local bank, had continued to sign any accounts that were put before him as a member of the auditing committee, and had even accepted a big loan from the manager. He knew nothing about book-keeping, he protested when examined, and everyone in the town had known as much about what was going on as he had. It was with a look of injured innocence on his face that he faced the court, and the story describes how very slowly it dawned on him that in the eyes of the world he was guilty, and a ruined man.

This is of course only a fraction of the truth about Russian industry. As we have seen, economists for the most part agree that the best hope of improving the material well-being of the mass of the Russian people lay at that time in the further industrialisation of the country, and that this was necessary, for instance, in order that agriculture itself might flourish (see page 73). But industrialisation could have been carried through, as it is being at present, without the indefinite retention of the system of free enterprise and an autocratic political constitution. Chekhov's sketches give a convincing impression of some highly undesirable social consequences of the system of free enterprise, viewed in the light of what he most valued in life. The industrial system was for him, quite rightly, a means, not an end, and he helped men to realise what the effects of the unchecked pursuit of wealth were on individual beings and their relations with each other, the ultimate test of the success or failure of the system, and a guide to future action.

A woman's kingdom reminded us that the old order of society, by which it was divided into 'conditions', nobles, clergy, merchants and peasantry, based on hereditary status, was being replaced by one based on classes in the Marxian sense, differing from each other in wealth measured in money. The abject adulation of wealth, even by so-called educated people, is illustrated in *The mask* and *Drunk*. In the former, during a charity masked ball in the social club of a certain town, the quiet of the reading-room, where five leading intelligents are deep in their newspapers, is suddenly disturbed by a masked figure, accompanied by two 'ladies', who begins to turn the quiet room into a bar, sweeping the papers from the table and treating the indignant non-dancers, who are bank directors and the like, with the utmost contempt. When they try to have him ejected, he takes off his mask with a flourish, and an electrifying effect is produced. They creep out on tip-toe and leave him in peace, for he is the local millionaire. In *Drunk* we see another rich manufacturer enjoying his power and contemptuously making everyone, from his lawyer down, dance to his tune. The scene is a high-class restaurant, from which, late in the evening, all other guests have been excluded at the great man's request. Dining there with his lawyer, the manu-facturer, who, though half drunk, is no fool, does his utmost to discover a limit to the bland servility of the waiters, who look like professors, earn 200 roubles a month and send their daughters to high schools. One of them brings a sauce-boat to the table. ' "What is that you are serving?" asked Frolov. "Sauce provençale for the herring, sir." "What? Is that the way to serve it?" shouted the manufacturer, not looking into the sauce-boat. "Do you call that sauce? You don't know how to serve things, idiot!" Frolov's velvety eyes flashed. He wound a corner of the table cloth round his finger, pulled it slightly, and with a tinkle and a swish, the hors d'œuvres, the candlesticks, the bottles crashed to the floor. The waiters, long accustomed to tavern catastrophes, ran up to the table, and coolly and seriously, like surgeons at an operation, began to pick up the fragments. "How well you know how to treat them," said Almer (the lawyer), laughing. But— come away from the table a bit or you'll put your foot into the caviare." ' This is how Frolov enjoyed a night out, that might cost him nearly a thousand roubles, and at the same time got his own back on the world for the domestic unhappiness that was partly a consequence of his wealth, for like the hero of *Three years* he could never free himself from the gnawing suspicion that his wife had married only for his money.

The general character of town life is well conveyed to us in a great number of stories about the average philistine, the principal butt of Chekhov's satire. The uniformity of provincial towns, of which he complains in his letters, was due no doubt partly to similar conditions of life, and partly to the control, of public building, for instance, exercised by St. Petersburg. Of course there were differences in size and importance. There were semi-rural small towns like the one in the first chapters of *Three years*, where the cattle were driven through the streets night and morning, raising clouds of dust, to the sound of the herdsman's horn; medium-sized towns with sixty or seventy thousand inhabitants, like the one in *My life*; and some provincial capitals with over a hundred thousand of a population. Moscow and St. Petersburg, owing to their history, both had a highly individual character, different from each other and from all the rest, as we noted in Chapter II.

The town in *My life* is represented as an average type, not distinguished by any special form of industry. It did not go in for samovars and rifles, like Tula, or tailoring, like Odessa, and it was hard in fact to know how most of its citizens made a living at all. In the Bolshaya Dvorianskaya ('Great Street of the Nobility') and two other streets they were rentiers and officials, but goodness only knew what they were in the other eight streets, which ran in parallel lines for three versts. Their manner of living anyhow was a disgrace to any town. There was no town park, or theatre, or respectable orchestra. The city and the club library were used only by young Jews, and books and magazines would lie there uncut for months. Even well-to-do people and the intelligentsia slept in stuffy little bedrooms, in wooden beds full of bugs, their nurseries were filthy, and their servants, however old and respected, slept on the floor in the kitchen, covered with rags. On ordinary days their houses smelt of beetroot soup and on fast days of sturgeon fried in sunflower oil. Their cooking and their drinking water were equally bad. They talked and talked about a loan of 200,000 roubles for an aqueduct but never did anything about it, although there were some thirty really rich people in the town who squandered whole fortunes at cards. As to their moral character, we have already heard how they took bribes. The young girls were attractive in their innocence, but the rest, though they went to church, had no principles and no spiritual life, but lived in the same mental atmosphere, the same horror of freedom, as three hundred years before. *Fellow citizens** shows how public affairs were conducted in such a town, how the firemaster got a scheme approved by the town council for raising the height of the watch tower—and incidentally putting money into his own pocket. When a fire broke out however there were no horses and only one of the six firemen available, the rest being busy about the firemaster's or their own private affairs, but the firemaster was still talking, as in the council, about how they did things in Paris. There is a very similar situation in *Minds in ferment*.

Chekhov is inexhaustible in genre pictures of the everyday life of rich and poor. In the larger towns, only comparatively well-to-do people seem to have lived in separate villas. We see something of the lighter side of their life in *My life* (amateur theatricals), *A duel* (parties and a picnic) and particularly in *A teacher of literature*. We see the two daughters and their friends riding through the city park, where all are hurrying in to hear a military band, out along the main road to the suburban park, with its swings and refreshment booth, and on to the family's farm, then home as the sun is setting to tea in the garden, eager talk and arguments, parlour games and supper. 'It was not only at the Shelestovs that people were enjoying themselves. Nikitin had not gone two hundred yards before he heard the sound of a piano from another house. A little further on he saw a peasant at the entrance to a courtyard playing the balalaika. In the park the band was blaring out a pot-pourri of Russian songs'—though it was after midnight.

But such pictures of the domestic happiness of the well-to-do are never more than incidental. The 'man with a hammer' (p. 86) soon knocks at the door of the author's mind, and he remembers how the happiness of the few is bought at the cost of the suffering of the many. Nadya in *Betrothed*, for instance, suddenly realises the truth of what Sasha, who as a bohemian artist has escaped from middle-class values, has been telling her for years, that there is something wrong with the life of business families like hers, where they live in comfort and idleness but treat their servants still as everyone had treated them twenty years before. Four of them sleep amidst dirt, bugs and beetles on rags on the kitchen floor (cf. *My life*, similarly in *In the coach-house* the coachman sleeps on the floor in a corner of the coach-house). Yet Nadya's mother is a sensitive, even sentimental woman, who speaks French, acts in plays and philosophises about religion. The great cleavage between the privileged and the 'black' classes was illustrated in every such household, and below stairs, as we see again in *The cook's wedding*, the servants led uncomplainingly the life to which they had always been accustomed in their izba in the village.

The average citizen in these towns lived in a flat, and the discomforts of life in flats are frequently stressed, particularly the lack of quiet and privacy, as in *Home*, or *The misfortunes of life**. Professional men in particular in these larger towns, imitating the aristocracy, liked to have a 'dacha', a week-end or summer cottage for their family, which might be their own or might be hired furnished for a month or two. At seven o'clock on a June evening you might see 'a crowd of dacha dwellers who had just come out of the train at the small station Khilkovo and were making their way towards the dacha colony, most of them fathers of families, burdened with shopping bags, brief cases and hat-boxes. They all looked worn out, hungry and in a bad humour, as if the sunshine and the green grass meant nothing to them' (*Not wanted*). Several stories remind us that the dacha habit was so widespread that the usual cottage was not something idyllic in a country village, but a small house in a colony put up by speculative builders—Lopakhin's plans for *The cherry orchard* will be remembered. In *A nest of kulaks** we see a peasant letting wretched converted huts and barns on a tumble-down estate and making extortionate charges even for permission to pick mushrooms. The colonies were sometimes so much alike that it was easy to mistake one for another, as we see from *Gone astray*, the amusing adventures of a man who tries to get into the wrong house. Chekhov makes much comic play in the early tales with the hardships suffered by the men and the gay goings-on among their wives while they are away. According to Zaikin in *Not wanted*, dacha life was the invention of the devil—and women. 'Back in town you have no furniture, no servants—all are out at the dacha. You feed on the devil knows what, have no tea to drink because there is no one to heat the samovar, you can't get a proper wash, and when you come out here, into the lap of nature, you have to walk from the station in the dust and heat. . . . It's a wonder we are still alive.' Dymov in *The grasshopper* might have echoed his sentiments, but *Bad weather* shows us the other side of the picture, the wife and her mother at the cottage, waiting for a husband who is enjoying himself in town. It is probably no accident that the families in these dacha stories are mostly childless; family men would not so easily afford such a luxury. But love of the country was evidently a marked trait of townspeople of all classes. We have noticed evidence of its existence among the less fortunate already in *Bird market*, and have seen that the dream of the average bourgeois was to live in the country on his own estate (*Gooseberries*, and also *The lottery ticket*). Scenes from proletarian life in tenements occur for instance in *A woman's kingdom*, *A father* and *The old house*. In the first tale we hear of a dark, evil-smelling outer gate and court-yard and 'narrow stone stair, dirty, steep, with a landing on every storey and greasy swinging lanterns; on the landings near each door were water troughs, chamber pots, rags. One door was open and through it you could see Jewish tailors wearing caps, sitting on a table, sewing'. In *The old house* a clerk with thirty-five roubles a month sublets one of his three rooms in this tumble-down rabbit-warren of a building to a locksmith, for a rent of two and a half roubles. We hear of all sorts of craftsmen plying their trade in similar conditions. Four children and the clerk's old mother sleep in another room and he and his wife in the third. The story describes how he goes downhill through drink after the death of his wife, in spite of the devotion of the old mother. In the same house there is a laundry, where in the evening people foregather and drink beer, three rooms let to neatly dressed 'ladies' who receive a great many guests, and one that had been let to a street singer for ten years, where after his death twenty thousand roubles were found in his feather-bed.

Chekhov's great stand-by in his early work for the comic papers had been family events in all classes, the trials of parents with daughters on their hands, of young men with mothers-in-law, proposals, marriages, curtain lectures and similar subjects of universal appeal, and he frequently returned to them later. It would be tedious to summarize them here, but nothing could convey better the atmosphere of Russian home life than these brilliant little sketches. It is interesting to compare for instance with regard to marriage customs, stories like *The wedding** (of the daughter of a lieutenant colonel) or *The teacher of literature*, with *Marriage for money**, lower down the social scale, where a dispute about the dowry at the wedding breakfast leads to a procession to the magistrate the next morning. The second of these deals particularly with the service in church, and the other two with the celebrations in the bride's home. Intermediate socially between these two grades is *A slander*, at the wedding of a teacher's daughter, and below them come the peasants' weddings, as in *In the ravine* or *The cook's wedding*. The blessing of the bride 'with bread and salt' by her parents, who do not go to the church, the music and further blessings on the young pair's return from the ceremony, the feasting and dancing until late into the night, are common to all, for the young couple do not usually 'drink a glass of champagne, change and drive to the station', as in *Anna on the neck*, where 'instead of enjoying a gay wedding ball and supper, music and dancing, they went off to a shrine two hundred versts away'. In all alike there is much talk of the dowry, and several other stories show the part it played in the preliminary stages, the troubles of parents with daughters to wed (*A blunder, Suitor and papa, At the baths**), the rôle of the marriage-broker (*A happy ending*), the barrier of rank and wealth (*A lady's story*).

It would be rash indeed to generalize about married life in Russia from Chekhov's writings, for like all realists, and like Maupassant in particular, whom he so much admired, he finds the best material for his art in marriages that go astray and irregular relationships. As a doctor moving in literary and artistic circles he naturally had no lack of models, as will have been clear from the chapter on the intelligentsia. But about the relation of the sexes in general in Russia there is little to be said here, except that his picture does not err on the side of optimism. The stranger with the radiant smile, who comes up to the carters' fire in *The steppe*, so happy that he does not know which way to turn or what to do to keep himself from being overwhelmed by the profusion of his delightful thoughts, has only been married eighteen days. He is a rare exception among Chekhov's husbands, and he is a peasant. The infinitely complex and ever changing relations of man and woman display better than any other subject that 'disharmony between people's moods and circumstances' from which, as Mr. Edward Garnett so well says, 'springs the peculiar, subtle sense Chekhov conveys of life's ironic pattern of time and chance playing cat and mouse with people's happiness'. He has the ironist's delight in unmasking the unconscious insincerities of married people, the play-acting of Lizochka when she has a chill (*Martyrs*), the absorption of *The darling* in the interests of each object of her devotion in turn, or the more complex studies already discussed in *The grasshopper, The wife, Ivanov* and several other works.

The relations of parents and children are the theme of many other tales. *The head of the family* and *Difficult people* show the family tyrant, *A father* a remarkably devoted (and surely peculiarly Russian) son, *Volodya* the trials of an adolescent with a frivolous mother, and *Home* a father's attempt to reason with his seven-year-old son. Other stories, like *A trifle from life* or *Three years*, reveal with subtle sympathy the sufferings of the children of unhappy marriages. Among the most delightful stories are the studies of children at play, like *Children*, a nursery scene, or *Boys*, about the Wild West enthusiasms of two youngsters home from boarding school. It is a favourite device of Chekhov's to draw familiar things from an unfamiliar angle by imagining them as seen through the eyes of a child, as in *The cook's wedding* and several other tales in the same volume of Mrs. Garnett's translation, *Grisha*, *The runaway*, *Oysters*, *An incident* and so on. The setting in all these is Russian, but what interests us particularly is the purely human, and the impressionistic skill with which Chekhov conveys to us a sense of the differentness of a child's world, and indirectly of the conventionality of our own. How meaningless geographical boundaries and historical barriers become when one reads: 'To a grown up attentively observing him, Seryozha might have seemed abnormal. For him it was possible and reasonable to draw people taller than houses, and to express in pencil not only objects, but his own sensations. So he would depict the sounds of an orchestra in the form of blobs of smoke, and a whistling noise like a spiral thread. In his mind sound was closely connected with form and colour, so that when he was painting letters, he always made L yellow, M red, A black, and so on. Leaving his drawing, Seryozha wriggled about again, found a comfortable position and began playing with his father's beard. First he carefully smoothed it, then he parted it and began combing it into the shape of side-whiskers. "Now you are like Ivan Stepanovich," he murmured, "and in a minute I'll make you like—our porter. Papa, why do porters always stand about doors? So as not to let in thieves?" ' (*Home*). This little boy reminds us that children are much the same in every land, and the affectionate sympathy and truth with which he is portrayed fill us, no less than more ambitious pictures, with confidence in Chekhov's artistic integrity and the essential rightness of his values.

CHAPTER IX

CHEKHOV'S VALUES

In spite of Chekhov's conscious objectivity as an artist, every page of his work reveals that he was no dispassionate observer, coolly registering impressions. He wrote only of subjects which he knew at first hand, aspects of the life of his day which evoked in him as man and artist a direct response. It is true that he never addressed the reader in his own person; any opinions that may be found, even in his stories, are expressed dramatically, through the mouth of one of his characters, and the primary purpose they serve is to bring this character vividly before us. His first aim, his only conscious aim, was to present convincingly a scene formed in his imagination. But there was no divorce between his imagination and his mind and heart as a man. He had in high measure a 'talent for humanity'. The imagined scene shows some recurrent aspect of life, made transparent and interpreted by the mind of an artist who discriminated sensitively between the better and the worse in man and in society, in the light of his own ideals, his own well-pondered system of values. That is no doubt what Mr. Gerhardi means when, quoting the passage about good writers 'going towards something and summoning you towards it' (see p. 18) he adds the comment: 'This is the precise quality of Chekhov's own writing—not less so because in a moment of depression, in his letter he laments the absence of these laudable characteristics from the writings of himself and his contemporaries. He, even more distinctly than his predecessors, makes us feel that he is going out and drawing us "towards something" transcenden-tal'—though 'transcendental' is perhaps hardly the right word for the creed of an agnostic.

As the letter in question itself reminds us, it was peculiarly difficult for writers of Chekhov's time and country to arrive at a satisfying philosophy of life. In religion, philosophy, social and political thought, the most diverse views were held by leading minds, and the babel of doctrine, which we have come to regard as typical of modern times, was more confusing than ever because of the violence of the conflict between science and religion, in our day somewhat abated, because their boundaries are better defined, and the acuteness of the social and political tension in Russia. Through the absence of an old-established intellectual tradition and the consequent lack of a common background among the intelligentsia, the Russians had long been in the habit of accepting on trust from the West the most extreme and contradictory doctrines, and believing in them, like the hero of *On the road*, 'po russki', with all their heart. So the rationalism of the Age of Enlightenment, which had affected France and Germany far more deeply than England, made almost a clean sweep of religion among the Russian intelligentsia, and was strongly reinforced by the scientific materialism which had developed out of it in the West in the nineteenth century. Similarly, socialistic ideas moved thousands of Russians to subordinate everything else in life to work for the good of the 'people'. The desperate attempts of the autocracy to foster orthodoxy and loyalty by compulsion only made the opposition to Church and State more extreme.

Chekhov's personal history made it perhaps more difficult for him than most to achieve a unified view of life, for he was a spiritual aristocrat, brought up among shopkeepers and descended from serfs. The sufferings of the peasantry and the poor town workers never ceased to fill him with pity and indignation, yet through his university education and his contacts with the landed aristocracy and intelligentsia he early became an admirer of the literary, artistic and scientific culture introduced by the aristocracy from the West. He knew the peasant too well to idealise him in the manner of the 'narodniki' and Tolstoy, and he believed too firmly in the spiritual achievements of western culture and their enrichment of life to practise the cultural asceticism of the narodniki and those who sympathised with them. Another source of conflict within him was the difficulty of reconciling his filial respect for the simple orthodoxy of his parents, with whom he lived in one house for most of his life, and the scientific outlook produced in him by his medical studies, not to speak of the atheism current among the educated generally.

It is not surprising then to find Chekhov saying in his letters, even down to about his thirtieth year, that he had no 'philosophy of life'. To Grigorovich (9/10/88) he writes: 'I have no political, religious and philosophical Weltanschauung yet, I change it every month, and so I have to restrict myself to describing how my heroes love, marry, have children, die, and how they talk.' When

he was criticised for ending *Lights* (a story which he did not re-
publish in his collected works) with the phrase 'You will never
understand anything in this world', he defended it not only as
suitable in the mouth of the speaker, but also on the ground that
he believed it to be true. Honestly to confess one's ignorance, like
Socrates and Voltaire, was better than to imagine one knew
everything, like the common herd. Yet in a letter (28/11/1888)
about an apparently unpublished story, in which a very ordinary
man finds himself unable to answer some of the commonest
questions about his relations with others if he has no philosophy
of life, he says that the last reflexion from his hero's diary expresses the very old truth that for a thinking man life without a
philosophy is a burden and a horror.

Chekhov could find no dogma that would save him the trouble
of thinking for himself, and he was too fully conscious of the complexity of the religious, philosophical and political problems of
his time to arrive at clear-cut ideas that could be expressed in
systematic form. His profound mistrust of broad generalisations
comes out repeatedly in his comments on Tolstoy, Dostoievsky
and others. 'Tolstoy's philosophy touched me profoundly and
took possession of me for six or seven years,' he wrote (27/3/1894),
'and what affected me was not its general propositions, with
which I was familiar beforehand (cf. earlier in the letter, "I have
peasant blood in my veins, and you will not astonish me with
peasant virtues"), but Tolstoy's manner of expressing it, his
reasonableness, and probably a sort of hypnotism. Now something
in me protests, reason and justice tell me that in electricity and
steam there is more humanity than in chastity and vegetarianism.
. . . I am sick of theorising of all sorts.' For Tolstoy as a creative
artist, on the other hand, he had a boundless admiration, as is
clear from the criticisms in his letters of *War and Peace, Anna
Karenina, Resurrection*, etc., criticisms unsurpassed in their sureness
of judgment. Dostoievsky he spoke of as a fine writer, but long-
winded, indiscreet and pretentious (5/3/1889). Of Nietzsche he
wrote: 'I should like to meet a philosopher like Nietzsche somewhere on a train or steamer, and to spend the whole night talking
to him. I consider his philosophy won't last long, however. It is
more showy than convincing' (25/2/1895). Max Nordau was a
'bounder' who filled him with disgust. A similar hatred of abstractions comes out in what he wrote of Bourget's *Disciple*, with its
tirades against materialism, or Merezhkovsky's attempt at a
scientific criticism of literature.

Chekhov's horror of rash generalisations and his sense of humour are amongst his most attractive qualities for an English reader. They were of a piece with the 'prostota' or unspoiled simplicity of heart of which Gorky speaks, which made him capable of a direct human relationship with all sorts of men and evoked a like sincerity in others. In his presence people 'tried to be simpler and more sincere, and to avoid bookish phrases and catchwords'. He had a knack of drawing out his visitors and divining their real interests, often quite ordinary material ones or hobbies, though they might assume intellectual airs in his presence. Mme. Korolenko too said that in Chekhov's face, in spite of its unmistakable intellectuality, there was a certain trait reminding one of a simple-hearted country lad, which was particularly attractive. The unassuming simplicity of his movements, gestures and speech was the predominant feature of his personality, as well as of his writings. And Tolstoy seems to have admired the same quality in him. In Gorky he found something not quite Russian, but 'turning to Chekhov, he said: "Now *you* are Russian! Yes, very, very Russian." And smiling affectionately, he put his arm round Chekhov's shoulders. Chekhov, embarrassed, began to talk about his dacha, or the Tartars. Tolstoy loved Chekhov, and whenever he looked at him he seemed to caress his face with his glance'. He was as modest and quiet, he said, as a girl.[1]

It was Chekhov's spiritual integrity which made him so acutely sensitive to every kind of meanness, or 'poshlost', as the Russians call it. 'Poshlost' is a word as common in the mouths of intellectual Russians as 'Kitsch' with Germans, and equally untranslatable. It implies everything that is reprehensible morally, socially or aesthetically, the ignoble, caddish, shabby in every form. Gorky, Nemirovich-Danchenko the producer, and most Russians who have written about Chekhov see in him above all the enemy of 'poshlost'. 'Chekhov showed up all the horror of Russian actuality,' writes B. Lvov, for instance,[2] 'he branded the slavishness of soul of his time, and to a society suffering from psychic blindness, a society which saw and did not understand, he said with unparalelled force: "You cannot go on living like this!" '

This is to ascribe to Chekhov the superior moral insight of a latter-day prophet, and undoubtedly he possessed something of this quality. One can well imagine that in an earlier age he might

[1] Gorky, *Reminiscences of Tolstoy.*
[2] In the essays on Chekhov edited by N. Pokrovsky, Moscow, 1906.

have been a monk, like his Nicolai in *Easter Eve*, whom he defended against the charge of being a 'superfluous man', though he himself would probably not have remained content with the ecstatic contemplation and praise of the Divine Essence. He would have felt too profoundly the need for guidance of his brothers in the world. As he said in a letter (4/5/1889) praising the calming influence of nature, he had a measure of detachment, the 'equanimity, which enabled him to see things clearly, to be just and to work'. It was not rapt contemplation or the indifference of the egoist, however, but the artist's faculty of putting the necessary distance between himself and his work. Gorky understood that, gentle and ironic as he was by nature, he could be stern and resolute in fighting a hostile principle. But what he instinctively avoided was any attempt at self-dramatisation. To set himself up as a prophet would have been to take himself too seriously, and any kind of high falutin' was anathema to him. He even felt uncomfortable as soon as people began to talk solemnly about Art or Morality, and was reminded of the scholastic disputations of the Middle Ages. He knew what was good and bad conduct, and good and bad art, for him, but like a true artist he had the impulse to express himself concretely, in characters and situations.

It is not easy then to describe Chekhov's system of values, though he undoubtedly had one. The difficulty is both illustrated and explained in the following passage from Goldenveizer's *Talks with Tolstoy*.[1] Tolstoy had been praising Chekhov's mastery as of the highest order, and went on: 'And yet it is all a mosaic; there is indeed no directing inner link. The most important thing in a work of art is that it should have a kind of focus, i.e. that there should be some point where all the rays meet or from which they issue. And this focus must not be able to be completely explained in words. What indeed makes a good work of art important is that its fundamental content in all its entirety can be expressed only in itself.' If one may dare to disagree with Tolstoy, it seems as if he had failed to apply to Chekhov the profound insight expressed in his last sentence, and had looked for ideas 'completely explained in words' such as are found in most of his own works. Chekhov 'poses problems and does not solve them', certainly, but his works do seem to have a focus, genuine artistic unity, and indirectly they express a consistent outlook on life.

[1] Trans. in Hogarth Press, 1923.

The core of it was made up of certain ethical convictions, fundamentally Christian, which he owed no doubt in the main to the example and precept of excellent parents of peasant stock. Many of them are to be found in a devastatingly candid letter which he wrote to his too bohemian artist brother Nicolai in 1886. It is Nicolai's own fault, he tells him, if he feels himself to be misunderstood. He has very good qualities. He is unselfish, almost too kind, free from envy and malice, simple-hearted, full of pity and trust, and he has genuine talent. But he is 'misunderstood' by well-bred people, because he does not behave as a cultivated man should.

Chekhov then outlines his conception of the principles of an 'educated man' (what we should call a gentleman). (1) He respects human personality, and therefore he is always kind, gentle, polite and ready to meet others half-way. (2) He does not bestow his sympathy merely on beggars and cats, but uses his imagination to divine the needs of others. He will sit up at night to pay for his brothers at the university, or to buy clothes for his mother. (3) He pays his debts. (4) He avoids every kind of insincerity and lying even in small matters. (5) He does not give way to self-pity. (6) He is not conceited, but self-effacing. (7) If he has talent, he respects it and makes sacrifices for it. (8) He develops his aesthetic sense, so that he cannot sleep in his clothes, or tolerate bugs, bad air, dirty floors, haphazard cooking. He tries to restrain and ennoble his sexual impulses. If he is an artist especially, he likes a woman to be fresh, to have good taste, and the human feeling of a good mother, not the qualities of a cocotte.

This is clearly the positive ideal, in the light of which Chekhov wrote his satirical sketches of the intelligentsia, 'spoilt children of life', most of them, not trained in the grammar of civilised life in society which the European has worked out in the last two thousand years. It will be noticed that there is nothing specifically Russian in these elementary ideals. They owe a good deal in fact to the West. The basis is Christian respect for personality and love of one's neighbour, common to Russia and the West. Sincerity and self-respect are perhaps even more widely respected virtues, certainly not exclusively Christian. But the aesthetic considerations (no. 8) are more Western than Russian in origin, aristocratic borrowings, the absence of which in certain Russian circles Chekhov often referred to as 'Asiaticism'. He himself would owe them to education rather than to nurture.

There are two other passages in particular in the letters which throw light on Chekhov's general philosophy. The first occurs when he is discussing the novel which he began in 1889 but later apparently abandoned. His aim was, as he wrote to Pleshcheyev (9/4/1889), to paint life truthfully, and incidentally to show how it differed from 'the norm'. 'The norm is unknown to me, as it is to all of us. We all know what a dishonourable act is, but what honour is we do not know. I shall keep to that framework which is nearest to my heart and has long been tested by people stronger and wiser than I am. It is the absolute freedom of man, freedom from violence, from prejudice, from ignorance, from the devil, from passion and the like.' The spiritual freedom of the individual is the ideal expressed here, a more inclusive form of that personal freedom which he once described as the birthright of the aristocrat, as we saw in Chapter I, and which had to be painfully acquired by plebeians like himself. He was to show how far his characters, as victims in varying degrees of oppression, inherited prejudices, ignorance and their own passions, fell short of attaining this supreme good, a free personality. The inspiration here is Greek and Christian, continued in the tradition of the European gentleman and inherited by the liberal thought of the German classics and nineteenth century thinkers like J. S. Mill. The three stories, *The man in a case*, *Gooseberries* and *About love*, which are exceptions in Chekhov's work in being loosely connected by a common framework story, may have been a part of this novel, and the reflexions put into the mouth of Ivan Ivanich at the end of *The man in a case* indicate why Chekhov's ideal made such a strong appeal to the men of the 'eighties: 'To have to see and hear how they all lie—though they call you a fool for putting up with it—to suffer insults, humiliation, not to dare to declare openly that you are on the side of the honest, free people, and to lie to yourself, to wear a smile on your lips, and all for the sake of a crust of bread, for a warm corner, for some sort of official rank not worth a farthing—no, we can't go on living like this!'

The second passage is in a letter to the same friend a few months later, about *A dreary story*, in which he is sure people will look for a 'tendency', although there is none. His only desire is to be a free artist, and he regards trade-marks and labels of all kinds as a superstition. None of them fit him, nor has he a preference for any class or calling, whether gendarmes, butchers, scientists, writers or the younger generation. 'My holy of holies' he writes, 'is the human body, health, intelligence, talent, inspiration, love and the most absolute freedom—freedom from violence and lying, whatever forms they may take.'

What Chekhov seems to be saying is: 'I am an artist, not a propagandist, and I am not trying to uphold any social or political cause, or giving good or bad marks to any class of the population. I am interested in them all as men, and my aim is to present my characters and situations convincingly. But even if I am not a party man, I naturally have views about what things make life worth living. For me they are vigorous bodily health and quick intelligence, love (including friendship, which I put higher), complete freedom of thought and expression, the power to enjoy art, philosophy and science and, best of all, to add to them creatively myself.' The answer implies individualism of the type considered for example by Ivanov-Razumnik to be characteristic of the Russian intelligentsia, as opposed to the bourgeois philistine, aiming at 'the physical and mental, social and private freedom of the individual personality'. Russian literature is their gospel, he says, and for their history Pushkin or Chekhov are just as important as Shestel or Bakunin. But Chekhov, as an artist, emphasises not only freedom *from* interference, but freedom *for* creative activity.

These views, at which he arrived before the age of thirty, are as Professor Elton says 'a good working creed on what are called naturalistic lines', but Chekhov was well aware of their philosophical deficiencies, for 'no one has a sharper sense that all things are mysterious, than the born agnostic' (Elton). In spite of his belief in reason and science, Chekhov was alive to the limitations of the human intellect, and he anticipated the Freudian school in his understanding of the influence of unconscious motives on conduct. Similarly he realized the impossibility of 'explaining' beauty in terms of reason, or developing a scientific literary criticism such as Merezhkovsky as a young man had attempted (cf. letter of November 1888 to Suvorin). Many of his stories suggest too, as we shall see, that he was still strongly attracted by religion, however much his reason rebelled. The conflict that resulted seems to be of great importance for the understanding of the tone of much of his work.

The theme of the story *Lights* (1887), which concludes with the sentence about the impossibility of understanding life, is precisely the inadequacy of the current philosophy of nihilism, with its reliance on analytic reasoning, as a guide to life. A middle-aged engineer tells how experience has modified the confident rationalism of his youth, when, like the young colleague to whom he is speaking, he had seen no aim or meaning in existence and prided himself on his disillusionment. They are working, it may be noted, on one of the new railways which are opening up Russia for the new age of science and industry. An amorous episode that turned into real love had taught him for the first time to think seriously about what he was doing, to acquire, as he says, the technique of thinking. His philosophy had been one of pure egoism, and he had lived from impulse to impulse, but through love and family life he had learnt the necessity of a longer view for anyone who really cares for others involved in his actions. 'It would be all right if, with our pessimism, we went to live in a cave, or made haste to die, but as it is, we live, feel, love women, bring up children, construct railways.' Life in society, in short, is impossible without sympathy and fairness, but these do not, it is implied, involve the supernatural, They require a certain insight and power of reflection, but 'it is only the finer and most expert development of these powers that is uncommon in the course of nature'.[1]

As a student, the engineer had combined 'the loftiest ideas (about the powers of man) with the lowest prose'. Thoughts of the darkness of the grave had not reduced his interest in the other sex, and his attitude to women had been more than crude. 'One who knows that life is aimless and death inevitable is not interested in the struggle against nature or in the conception of sin: whether you struggle or not, you will die and rot just the same. Secondly, our philosophy instils even into very young people what is called reasonableness. The predominance of reason over the heart is simply overwhelming amongst us. Direct feeling, inspiration— everything is choked by petty analysis. . . . Thirdly, our philosophy denies the significance of each individual personality. It is easy to see that if I deny the personality of some Natalya Stepanovna, it is absolutely nothing to me whether she is insulted or not. To-day one insults her dignity as a human being and pays her *Blutgeld*, and next day thinks no more of her.'

Though the artistic form here again is dramatic, and Chekhov in a letter[2] deprecates the identification of any character with the author, emphasising his Socratic or Voltairian agnosticism, the feeling behind the story is clearly the same as is expressed for

---

[1] cf. J. Laird, *Mind and Deity*, London, 1941, 254.
[2] See above, p. 199.

example in *A nervous breakdown, The duel* and many other stories, even in *A dreary story*, as Chekhov interprets it in the letter already quoted: 'If the professor had been a different sort of man, Liza or Katya might not have come to grief.' Respect for human personality is the keynote, a Christian idea, but one which Chekhov evidently thought capable of standing alone, as a direct moral intuition, without supernatural sanctions. Though an individualist in his desire for complete freedom from historical and traditional restraints, he knew that no one can live as a discrete individual in any society, even in a single family. To liberal individualism we must add Christian charity as a fundamental constituent of his point of view, and a third main element was his aesthetic craving for beauty and order in the world around him. The whole comes very near to the undogmatic humanistic religion of the German classics, as expressed for example in Goethe's poem, *The Divine*, 'Edel sei der Mensch, hilfreich und gut'.

In the society of his day in Russia, Chekhov was repelled by the coarse, hard life of the peasant and 'black' worker on the one hand, and by the self-satisfied lazy life of the bourgeois intelligentsia on the other. He had much in common therefore with Tolstoy, lived under his influence for several years and became a close personal friend. 'I have never loved any man as much as him,' he wrote in 1900 to Menshikov. 'I am not a believer, but of all beliefs, I consider his the nearest and most akin to me.' But he differed from him in two principal regards. He rejected the authority of Christianity, even as interpreted by Tolstoy—see for instance his criticism of the conclusion of *Resurrection*: 'To settle it all by a text from the Gospel is as arbitrary as dividing the convicts into five classes. He must make us believe in the Gospel first.' And he rejected the methods of social reform advocated by Tolstoy. 'The question is not what kind of community life is best,' said Tolstoy, 'but what are *you* going to do as a reasonable being appearing for a brief moment in the world, who may depart at any moment? I know nothing of the result, I only know what one must do.' This seemed to Chekhov an over hasty attempt to salve one's own conscience, unlikely to influence events. He shared in the moral bewilderment of his age, but he saw that it was largely due to the collapse of respect for Orthodoxy, because of its association with reaction on the one hand, and its apparent incompatibility with scientific thought on the other, and further to the endless complexity of the social situation. As Professor

Morris Ginsberg has pointed out in an analysis of the 'moral bewilderment' of our own day,[1] moral questions in social matters are closely interwoven with questions of fact, and lack of accurate knowledge obscures the ethical aspects for intelligent men. As a good doctor, Chekhov wanted a thorough study to be made of the diseases of society before remedies were attempted, and he clearly regarded Tolstoy's successive cures, vegetarianism, physical work for all and other forms of self-perfectionism, as quack remedies.

So much is clear from *My life*, for instance, as we have seen, or *Ward no. 6*. In the latter story Chekhov puts into the mouth of Ivan Dmitrich strong arguments against self-perfectionism, or the cultivation of a philosophic detachment in the face of life's evils. It was possible to be a Diogenes in the climate of Greece, says Ivan Dmitrich, but we are not really free from the influence of our environment, and it is dishonest to pretend that we are. Nor is the Stoic ideal a desirable one. To cultivate indifference to suffering is to aim at a living death, for to feel is to live. Moreover there is a kind of selfishness in thinking too much of one's own salvation or one's own peace of mind. The discussion of the meaning of life, the theme of so much of Russian literature, is continued in *The duel*, for this story turns round a conflict of philosophies as well as personalities. Stories of ideas like this, or *Ward no. 6*, or *An artist's story*, must have had the same kind of interest for the Russian educated public as, let us say, Lowes Dickinson's *A modern symposium* for ours, but the argument is conveyed as much by incident and description as by speeches, and the characters are more fully developed, in keeping with the fictional form. We have seen how the self-indulgent laxity of the young intellectual Laevsky brings him to an impasse of insincerity, from which he is finally delivered by the shock of facing death. His opponent Von Koren, the scientific reformer, is allowed to develop his ideas at some length, but it is obvious from the tone of the whole, as well as from what we know of Chekhov, that he is not simply the mouthpiece of Chekhov, as Merezhkovsky for instance rather unfairly represents him to be. Von Koren's coldly rationalistic desire for order and tidiness, without any feeling for human personality, is fed by pride and love of power, one feels, and he proves a bad psychologist in the end. The germ of right in his view is that he reasserts in an extreme form the claim of society on the individual, like those Nazi philosophers

[1] In *Scrutiny*, autumn, 1944.

who rejected all individualism and liberalism in order to re-establish loyalty to the group. The army doctor in the story shows perhaps how far mere good nature and an instinctive response to one's fellow-creatures can take one, but he is often bewildered by the subtleties of the situation. Chekhov draws with sympathy too the deacon, a happy trustful nature with the laugh of a child, a poor parish-clerk's son, sharing the disillusioned wisdom and charity of the Church, and fortified by direct acquaintance with the coarseness and cruelty of the common people, so that the faults which Von Koren and Laevsky find in each other seem to him trifles. But he has a very limited view of what can be done for society and seems to be principally concerned about his own future in the little self-contained world of the church, though he knows even from his seminary that orthodoxy can hide much uncharitableness. 'No one knows the real truth,' Laevsky concludes at the close ('You will never understand anything in this world'). He sees a symbol of human destiny however in the struggle of the small boat that is taking Von Koren out to his ship. 'In their search for truth men advance two steps, and fall back one, like the boat in the waves, but their thirst for truth and their determination are superior to the suffering, the mistakes and the weariness of life. And who knows? Perhaps they will reach the real truth in the end.'

If we ask what kind of truth Chekhov contemplates as the goal of man's efforts, it is clear from *The three sisters*, *The cherry orchard* or his last published story, *Betrothed*, that it is an entirely secular one. He looks forward to a state of things when the moral sciences will have caught up with and been co-ordinated with the natural sciences, and a society can be established in which men will be delivered from want, injustice and fear. 'Everything in the town had grown old, out of date, and was only waiting for, was it the end, or the beginning of something young and fresh? Oh would that that new, brighter life would come quickly, when it would be possible to look one's fate boldly in the face, know oneself to be right, and be happy and free! And such a life would come sooner or later' (*Betrothed*). In such passages the phrase 'in three or four hundred years' occurs with the regularity of a refrain, and Chekhov even used it, says Kuprin, in conversation. Dreaming of the future happiness of others, he 'was eagerly interested in new and original buildings, steamers, inventions, and was not bored by specialists. He said that crimes such as murder, theft and adultery were decreasing and believed that in the future true culture would ennoble mankind'.[1] He shared, in his later years at least, the belief of his age in progress. 'The Russian intelligentsia loved Chekhov and Gorky,' says Merezhkovsky, 'because they taught them to believe in the triumph of progress, science, human reason, everything that is summed up in the phrase "humane ideas".' Chekhov himself wrote in 1902 to Dyagilev: 'Of the cultured classes of our society we may say that they have moved away from religion and will continue to move further and further away, whatever may be said about it, and whatever philosophico-religious societies may be founded. Whether this is a good thing or a bad thing I will not try to decide. I will only say that the religious movement of which you write is one thing, and the whole culture of to-day is another thing, which it will never be possible to bring under the former. Modern culture is the beginning of work for a great future, a work that will perhaps continue for tens of thousands of years in order that, even if only in the remote future, humanity may come to know the truth about the real God: not guess at it, that is, or look for it in Dostoevsky, but know it clearly, as it knows that twice two are four. Modern culture is the beginning of this work, but the religious movement in question is a survival, almost the last trace of something that has ceased or is ceasing to exist.' As if this were not explicit enough, he says in a later letter that he has long ceased to believe, and that any intelligent believer is a puzzle to him.

For all that, the sympathy and understanding with which Chekhov treats religious subjects is, as Chapter VI indicated, remarkable. There is none of the irony of an Anatole France in his pictures of the orthodox clergy, from village priests to bishops, and no one could be more sensitive to the beauty and impressiveness of the rites of the church. Particularly striking is his understanding of the monk who wrote songs of praise in *Easter Eve*, and of the bishop, so lonely as a man and so strong in the spirit through prayer and worship. No one would know that these things were not the work of a believer, and in view of his treatment of officials, for instance, one feels that he must have gone out of his way to avoid anything derogatory to the church, though by all accounts he would not have lacked material if he had chosen otherwise. The only explanation seems to be that though his intelligence made him doubt, his heart and imagination were still held captive by the traditional religion of his country.

The student, a favourite with Chekhov, reinforces this im-

[1] A. Chekhov, *Literary and Theatrical Reminisces*, 51.

pression. We are told here how simple people in a remote village are moved to tears, on the eve of Good Friday, by a student's artless narration of what had happened nineteen centuries before on this same night in the High Priest's courtyard. 'The story he had just told,' the student thought, 'had some relationship to the present, to this desolate village, to himself, to all men. The past was linked to the present by an unbroken chain of events proceeding one from another. And it seemed to him that he had just seen both ends of the chain: he had touched one, and the other had stirred. The truth and beauty which had guided human life there in the high priest's yard had continued without interruption to this day, and had clearly always been the chief thing in human life and indeed in the whole world.'

There is no logical contradiction between this and the letter to Dyagilev, for again, we must not identify Chekhov with his characters. That is how a theological student may well have thought, but Chekhov, though fully conscious of the great good wrought by Christianity while men could sincerely believe its message, could no longer accept it fully himself, much to his regret, one seems bound to add, for he did not lie at ease on his pillow of doubt. Like Faust listening to the Easter bells, he looked back with longing to the days when he shared the common faith, and he was filled with that post-Christian nostalgia for faith so common since Romantic times, though like many others he often concealed his feelings under a mask of irony.

This sense of something lacking is surely one source of that hopeless sadness which broods over almost all of Chekhov's serious work. In the preceding chapters we have been concerned with the other cause of it, the hopeless state of Russia. Politically, economically and morally there was little indeed, as we have seen, that gave ground for hope to one with Chekhov's ideas of the good life. But even when, in the later 'nineties, he began with his contemporaries to take a rather more cheerful view of the material and political prospects for Russia, the general tone of his work did not change markedly, for it had been influenced from the beginning by his sense of the transitoriness of all that is good and beautiful in life and its lack, for him, of a central meaning. In the same story *Lights*, from which we have quoted, the engineer who protests against the pessimism of the young, as a mere intellectual fashion, admits that 'thoughts of the transitoriness of life, its lack of meaning and aim, of the inevitability of death, of the shadows of the grave, are good and natural in old age, when they come as the product of years of inner travail'. They are in fact 'the highest and the final stage in the realm of thought'. Perhaps Chekhov was trying to reason himself out of such paralysing reflections, in this story written at the age of twenty-seven, but they repeatedly recurred in his work. We found them, in the first chapter, in *The Beauties*, in that feeling for the preciousness of beauty, combined with and enhanced by the consciousness of its fragile hold on life, which lent a truly tragic atmosphere to these two slight episodes. They are a marked feature of his plays, from *Ivanov* to *The cherry orchard*, which one and all, in spite of flashes of comedy, seem to repeat the refrain 'the pity of it!' And they occur so regularly in the stories as to throw over them, as Gorky says, the atmosphere of 'a melancholy day in late autumn, when the air is so clear, and the bare trees, narrow houses and grey people stand out in sharp outline. All is strange—lonely, motionless, exhausted'. Nature itself, whether through the work of man's hand, as in *The pipe*, or without his agency, as in *The steppe*, often seems to Chekhov to proclaim this same message, of beauty and sadness inseparably joined, one which had been sounded so frequently in Russian nature poetry from Pushkin and Lermontov onwards, in striking contrast to the Deistic poetry of the eighteenth century.

It is a spiritual malaise then, in addition to a sense of social and political frustration, that Chekhov finds in himself and depicts in his characters, and there is clearly a connection between the spiritual disharmony and the other. As one of the characters in *In the ravine* says: 'You can walk about a whole day and not meet a single man with a conscience. The reason is that they do not know whether there is a God or not.' Or as the husband in *Terror*, when asked what he is so afraid of in life, replies to the friend who is so soon to deceive him: 'I am afraid of everything. I am afraid, because I do not understand what is the use of all this to anyone. I do not understand anyone or anything.' Lacking this understanding, 'l'homme moyen sensuel' acted in accordance with his passing personal interests, or at most with those of his family or class, and the result was the chaos that Chekhov depicts so well. In their present poverty of the spirit they were still haunted however by the memory of better days. Religion had provided them with an all-inclusive meaning and aim in life, and though so many looked upon it now as an illusion, or even as something devised by men to deceive their fellows, century-old habits of thought were not easily broken.

Like the hero of *On the road*, some sought and found ever new aims in life, and accepted each belief for the time with all the energy of the 'broad' Russian nature, so that it became a kind of religion, though perhaps not a good one. Defending the legitimacy of Comte's Religion of Humanity, J. S. Mill himself had written: 'Candid persons of all creeds may be willing to admit that if a person has an ideal object, his attachment and sense of duty towards which are able to control and discipline all his other sentiments and propensities, and prescribe to him a rule of life, that person has a religion.' In short, a man has to be *possessed* by his moral ideas to be a really good man, and that is religion, not ethics, to quote Professor Laird's paraphrase of Mill's dictum, but he points out that secular emotions like patriotism or vengeance may similarly possess a man.[1] It is in some such sense as this that communism has been called a religion, and that Nazism could have been called one too.

Among the movements centred round ideal objects which served in some measure as substitute religions, we find reflected in Chekhov above all the social revolutionary movement, eventually to bear fruit in the transformation of Russian society that we have witnessed in our own day, then the Tolstoyan movement, Slavophilism, and even such things as spiritualism (*Nerves* and *A terrible night** and homœopathy (*Malingerers*). A small minority found an absorbing aim in natural science (*A dreary story*) or humanism (*The black monk*). The hallucination taking the form of a black monk, which expressed a young scholar's deepest longings, assured him that he was one of the few who are justly called the chosen of God, who serve eternal truth, in a life dedicated to the rational and the beautiful, to the eternal. To them immortality is granted, an immortality of influence. But however much these scientists and scholars might hasten the progress of civilization (incidentally we may note that they did not examine critically enough, for our modern ideas, the assumption that their influence was always for good), their personal lives, as imagined by Chekhov, proved the inadequacy of their science or scholarship, absorbing though it might be, as a guide to life. Their creator found a more satisfying meaning and aim in life himself through his devotion to his art, but as early as 1888 we find him writing to his brother Alexander: 'We cannot escape death, we have not long to live, and for that reason I do not attach serious importance to my writing, or my fame, or my literary mistakes. I recommend

[1] *Mind and Deity*, London, 1941, 255.

the same to you' (24/9/1888). And we read in his private note-book: 'In the next world, I should like to be able to think this about our present life—there were lovely visions in it,' a characteristically modest wish.

It may be objected that in this analysis of Chekhov's view of life we have not taken sufficient account of his physical health. It might be held that his early humorous work was that of a normal healthy man, but that after 1885, when the first symptoms of consumption appeared (not acknowledged as such by him), his outlook became increasingly that of a man doomed to a pre-mature death. The state of Chekhov's health must inevitably have influenced the tone of his work, but it was almost certainly not the main cause of the increasing seriousness that we notice from about 1886. His artistic conscience was already pricking him, as we have seen, in 1883, and there seems to be no reason to doubt his own explanation, that it was only about 1886, through being taken seriously by Grigorovich and Suvorin, that he began to take himself seriously, and to despise work which did not freely express his own personal reactions to life.

Temperamentally he was quiet and gentle, but exceedingly gay and buoyant, quick to see the comic side of human situations and fertile in amusing ideas. His early work is the product of this temperament and his immense talent for writing, for finding the right words, uneven, hasty work, most of it, because of the conditions under which it was done. In it Chekhov usually accepts the ordinary conventional values of his public and is content with 'flat' figures, figures not drawn in the round, but what is so enter-taining is the verve that rings endless comic changes on everyday situations. He will show us a young man trying to wriggle out of an engagement, who tells the girl's father that she does not share his ideas, that he is unworthy of her, that he is too poor, a hereditary drunkard, charged with embezzlement and forgery, that he is an escaped convict and finally that he is mad. When the father, determined to marry off his daughter at all costs, insists on a doctor's certificate, the young man's doctor friend will not give him one, because to refuse to get married is the mark of a sane man (*Suitor and papa**). Or a twenty-six year old girl who at last gets a young man to look at her, finds that he is a bashful artist who never goes further than mute admiration. When her father has entertained him, his brother and a friend for three months, and he seems at last to have been brought to the point of declaring himself, all he says to the girl is: Will you be my—model? (*A nasty story**). Young men are always marriage-shy, cashiers always dishonest, no one refuses a bribe, and so on The conventions, one might say, are those of the music hall, and most of the sketches not included by Chekhov in his collected works are products of the head only. The ones he did include have a character interest or a poetic atmosphere which link them with the later stories, though a considerable number of them are decidedly humorous in tone. There are some he simply seems to have overlooked in making his selection. One can think of no other reason for the exclusion of *Other people's troubles** (about a young couple buying an estate, and what they see of the life of the seller), *By the river** (a picture of the breaking up of the ice, and life on a timber raft), *A wretched night** (a village fire) and several others included in Mrs. Garnett's last volume.

As Chekhov matured, his works were marked then by ever increasing truth, truth to nature and truth to himself, but the development was a gradual one. Something like what Tolstoy imagined to have happened in the case of *The darling*, that the author came to understand and admire a character whom he had intended to ridicule, may have happened in many stories. Certainly Chekhov was not content now with conventional valuations. All his characters have their interest for him as men, and not simply as pieces in a pattern. The pattern perhaps suffers sometimes, or at any rate it becomes far less obvious. Some tales remind us of those reproductions of details from a great master which are now so popular, but however slight the subject, there is 'a feeling of the human mass out of which the figures have come, and atmosphere and background'. The old humour keeps breaking in, in sly touches of irony, comic comparisons, and minor characters verging on caricature. It was still more apparent in his conversation and his delightful letters, in playful exaggeration and banter, witty and amusing turns of phrase, and in the impish delight he took in pricking bubbles of conceit and pretence, by contrasting people as they saw themselves and as others saw them.

In his acute analysis of Chekhov's development as an artist Prince Mirsky has shown how, out of the many elements still present in the stories written between 1886 and 1888, descriptive journalism (*Uprooted*), ironical or tragi-comical anecdote (*The first class passenger, Vanka*), the lyrical expression of atmosphere (*The steppe, Happiness*), psychological studies of morbid experiences (*Typhus*), there emerged the typical Chekhovian art of *The party* (1887) and especially *A dreary story* (1889), which trace the biography of a mood, produced in the hero by the action of the pinpricks of life on some deep-lying physiological or psychological process. In *The party* it is pregnancy, in *A dreary story* the professor's incurable illness and waning powers. 'No writer excels him,' he says, 'in conveying the mutual unsurpassable isolation of human beings, and the impossibility of understanding each other. This idea forms the core of almost every one of his stories.' It is of course particularly well seen in his plays, where we find the opposite of that over-careful dovetailing of speeches that marks the dialogue of inexperienced dramatists. Instead of keeping more closely than in real life to the one line of thought and feeling, 'each speaks of what interests him or her, and pays no attention to what the other people in the room are saying'.

In spite of this obstinate separateness, Chekhov's characters, in Prince Mirsky's view, are 'singularly lacking in individual personality'. This is perhaps not very happily expressed. Chekhov's characters certainly live, but like the classical dramatists Chekhov makes little use of characteristic speech, and he is interested in the generic features in man, he is, in fact, as we have suggested above, more than a little of a sociologist, like the great French novelists who influenced him. 'His characters cannot be recognized, as Tolstoy's and Dostoevsky's can, by the mere sound of their voices,' and he is 'a student of man in general, of the genus homo.' It would be truer to say that he is a student of social types, never losing sight of the social background of his characters, seeking always to give his pictures, as we have urged, a representative quality. That he was conscious of this himself is indicated by his remark (in a letter of 23/12/1888): 'To men who devote themselves to the study of life I am as necessary as a star is to an astronomer.' Here we see how his interest as an artist in the unique, the new, the purely individual, was modified by his desire to understand, to bring new experiences under general laws, the desire that made him so susceptible to scientific influences. In this again he closely resembles Goethe. Readers whose taste inclines towards the romantic feel the same disappointment with some of his work as do those critics of Goethe who hold, with J. G. Robertson, that 'when he renounced the naive for the reflective, the high lights of his genius went out'. And most would admit that his studies are occasionally, as Professor Elton puts it, 'over-clinical'. It is this aspect of his work that Tolstoy had in mind, no doubt, when he said to Gorky that Chekhov would have written still better if he had not been a doctor. There are others again who particularly relish the 'astringent' quality of his writing, and praise him as an anti-romantic, seeing in *The lady with a dog* for instance a subtle 'depoetization of adultery', and in innumerable other stories an ironic treatment of romantic passion.

To discuss Chekhov's style at any length would be foreign to the purpose of this book, and it has been very well done already, especially by Prince Mirsky. His appreciation of the form of Chekhov's stories, a musical form in the sense that each is a pattern carefully constructed out of themes which are emotional experiences of the central character, is very convincing. 'Chekhov excels in the art of tracing the first stages of an emotional process; in indicating those first symptoms of a deviation when to the general eye, and to the conscious eye of the subject in question, the nascent curve still seems to coincide with a straight line.' The style of drawing is never linear, however, for the stories are 'at once fluid and precise', like a painting by Rembrandt, one might say. 'The constructive lines are complicated by a rich and mellow atmosphere, which he produced by the abundance of emotionally significant detail. The effect is poetical, even lyrical: as in a lyric it is not interest in the development the reader feels, but "infection" by the poet's mood.'[1]

In this and earlier chapters an attempt has been made to explain the prevailing mood, one of melancholy sympathy with the sufferings of the victims of life. The passive hopelessness of Chekhov's principal characters is apt to depress English readers, with their more active temperament and happier lot, but it is understandable if we remember the circumstances of the time, the baffled spiritual longings of the educated classes, and perhaps we should also add, a certain literary tradition, going back to Lermontov and Byron, of self-dramatization in an attitude of despair, the attitude with which Chekhov makes ironic play in *Lights*, when he makes his engineer say:

'As I sank into a doze, it began to seem that it was not the sea murmuring, but my thoughts, and that the whole world consisted of nothing but me. And concentrating the whole world in myself in this way, I forgot cabmen and town and Kisochka and gave myself up to the sensation I liked so much, the sensation of terrible loneliness, when you imagine that in the whole universe, dark and formless, nothing exists but you. It is a proud, demonic sensation, only possible to Russians, whose thoughts and sensa-

[1] *Contemporary Russian Literature*, 90 ff.

tions are as broad, unlimited and gloomy as their plains, woods and snow. If I had been an artist, I should certainly have tried to paint the expression of a Russian's face when he sits motionless on his crossed legs and, clasping his head in his hands, gives himself up to this sensation. . . . And together with this sensation he has thoughts of the aimlessness of life, of death, of darkness beyond the grave. . . . The thoughts are not worth a brass farthing, but the expression on his face, I am sure, is very fine.'

It will occur to every reader that nothing could be less like one's conception of the young Russian of to-day than this Asiatic romanticism. 'Sviridov's novel *Komsomolites* describes the struggle of young Communist peasants against the old farmers, and above all the rich ones, and also against their own reactionary contemporaries. It is winter. Sergey and his Komsomolites leave their native village for the forest to increase the production of the lumbermen, which is lagging a long way behind the figures of the Plan. They nearly lose courage more than once on account of the heavy work amid snow and frost, the miserable accommodation, and the unfriendly bearing of the workers. But Sergey and a few other activists are successful in carrying the rest with them each time. Shock-brigades and Socialist competitions are introduced. Production begins to climb. The Komsomolites equal the output of the old and proved lumbermen. Then they outstrip it. This is more than the workers can endure, a feverish race begins. With ever-increasing speed the different gangs eat their way into the forest. By the spring the lumber Plan has been fulfilled in spite of every kind of outrage on the part of the frantic kulaks and their accomplices. The river ice melts; the timber begins to move towards its destined place in the structure of the Soviet Union. With the money they have earned in the forest the Komsomolites set up their commune.'[1]

Not a rather self-conscious despair, but an unshakable sense of superiority, of self-assurance, is characteristic of the young Soviet citizen of to-day, according to Mehnert, writing in 1932. 'It is the superiority felt by a healthy man among a crowd of sick, by one who can see among a crowd of blind. The superiority felt by a man who is convinced that he alone has a clear course before him, while all the rest are moving senselessly towards insanity.' This pride in hard-won experience was accompanied, Mehnert said, by a missionary idea, a feeling of obligation to lead the rest of the suffering world towards salvation. One might compare it,

' K. Mehnert, *Youth in Soviet Russia*, 96.

we may add, with the feeling of the Populists in earlier days, the fortunate few who experienced a moral urge to go out among the people and put them on the right road. 'If they succeed in combining, as they dream of doing, their fanaticism, their readiness to stake everything, their disdain for life and earthly goods, with the technical efficiency of the West, including the technique of war, then unimaginable prospects will be unfolded,' prospects unimagined certainly in 1932, or 1942, by Germany.

The transformation of Russia that has already taken place was itself unimaginable in 1904, but it is not unprofitable all the same for citizens of to-day to study attentively the older Russia, as we have tried to do with Chekhov's help in these pages. The past lives on in the present, even in 'young' countries like Russia, and a knowledge of the past can in some measure contribute to our understanding of the present, and guide our expectations for the future. We may conclude with some general considerations about the bearing of the topics discussed in earlier chapters on our understanding of Russia to-day.

We realize in the first place that political and social changes of a very far-reaching kind were already long overdue in Chekhov's Russia. It was indeed 'impossible to go on living like that', and none of the remedies applied in Chekhov's day promised satisfactory results. As to the period between then and 1917, we have had no evidence, but Maynard's statement seems to be well supported, that 'the administration of 1914, with some qualifications, was absolutely better than that of twenty years earlier, but not better relatively to the expectations of the Russian people'.[1] The pitiable state of the vast mass of the people, the peasantry, the inefficiency and corruption of the government machine, the insignificant contribution of free capitalistic enterprise by 1904 to the general well-being, the sceptical resignation of the average educated citizen to police rule, to wide-spread social injustice and to the moral degeneration brought about by social and intellectual influences and the decay of religious belief—all these things are plainly indicated.

We find good evidence further to support Sir Ernest Barker's contention[2] that a dictatorship of some kind was inevitable, when the shock of war finally brought down the tottering state, because of the traditions of tsarism and the impossibility of arriving at an agreed policy by the democratic methods of discussion and com-

[1] *Russia in Flux*, 74.
[2] *Reflections on Government*, Oxford, 1942, 313.

promise, where history had made such broad gulfs between the various factors concerned: the Tsar, the bureaucratic aristocracy and the Orthodox Church; the slowly rising and deeply divided middle class; the 'hypocritical, false, hysterical, uneducated, lazy' intelligentsia; and the ignorant and wretched peasantry. There is less evidence in our data, but still some, for Professor Barker's further conclusion, that the imposed scheme was bound to proceed from the urban proletariate, 'the one social element which, entrenched in the urban centres, could gather itself together and collect and enforce its ideas'. It is perfectly clear however that Bolshevism did not mean the pulling down of a system based on consent and the erection in its place of one based on force. Even with the Duma grafted on to autocracy, there had never been a system based on consent.

We can see too (after the event, of course) a pre-disposition towards the continuance, at least for a long transition period, of highly centralized bureaucratic methods of administration and the extensive use of the political police, the inevitable alternatives to rule by discussion and compromise. The new autocrats, in conditions of class warfare, naturally turned to the tools already to hand. But we can also see, in the village communities, and in a rather different way in the zemstvos, the seeds of that system of direct and omnicompetent democratic organs for local and provincial government, still subject to the over-riding control of the central government, that has grown up in the hierarchy of soviets. The village soviets correspond more closely to the village communal councils than any of the higher soviets do to the zemstvos, in that the village communes already excluded the gentry, but the zemstvos, dominated by the gentry, had shown better what could be done in the way of practical government by means of discussion and compromise in the common interest.

The Soviet solution of the land problem, the greatest economic problem of Chekhov's Russia, becomes far more intelligible through what we have learnt about peasant life and work. We have seen the effects on daily life of an inefficient system of small-scale agriculture. Incidentally, the picture closely resembles that drawn by a recent observer[1] of the Eastern European peasantry of to-day, amongst whom the same system of open-field husbandry still prevails and where the rule holds good: 'the smaller the holding, the lower the productivity of the soil'. The same problems occur as in the older Russia, over-population and

[1] Hugh Seton-Watson, *Eastern Europe between the Wars*, Cambridge, 1945.

under-employment, and land reforms on an individualistic basis have left the situation in many parts worse than before. There seems to be an inherent weakness in small-scale agriculture in modern conditions. When we see how hopelessly uneconomic it has proved, the drastic action taken in Russia to end it appears in a different light. In many ways the new system continues features of the old, that are strange to us but long familiar in Russia. 'The peasant invited to pool holding and equipment,' as Maynard says, was not 'a free yeoman accustomed to deal as he pleased with his own.' He had been subject for centuries to the common rules of cropping and so forth necessitated by the open-field system, so that collective work according to a Plan was not a novelty.

In judging the effect of Soviet rule on the life of the workers, whether in agriculture or in industry, we ought in fairness to compare their present standard of living, not with that of advanced Western countries, but with that of the older Russia, and here again Chekhov has been of value by reminding us how low this standard long had been in such essentials as food and housing. Similarly with the question of personal freedom. Quite apart from the ingrained habit of obedience to directions from above and the effects of military service, the 'direction' of workers to distant places in accordance with the needs of the Plan must have seemed far less of an outrage than it would have been here in peace-time, to peasants accustomed to large-scale seasonal migrations and the semi-permanent separation, sometimes of even husband and wife, that the search for work involved. One whole sex has been given quite new opportunities since the revolution. We have found how true are Maynard's words: 'Woman's life, except for a limited class, has been a domestic slavery.' Only now, he says, it begins to emerge from this, with a measure of economic as well as of social liberty. Above all, hereditary privileges that told against the worker have been abolished and he has been given an entirely new status. Only some acquaintance with the older Russia can bring home to us the full meaning of this revolution.

About the reversal of values and of general habits of thinking that have produced and accompanied these changes volumes could be written. A brief reference has been made above to the change in the tone of literature. Scepticism, lazy indifference, boredom, fear of life are no longer tolerated. The general note is pride in human and especially in Russian achievement, confidence in the future, lack of interest in the other-worldly. 'The fear of the Lord is no longer the beginning of wisdom. It is Man himself who is set upon the pinnacle. Vladimir Mayakovsky, in his *Mystery Bouffe*, showed us the Host of the Unclean clambering upwards into the Seventh Heaven and defying the lightnings that threatened them there.'[1] This is the culmination of the humanism and faith in science typical already of Chekhov's age, but it is not a shame-faced humanism now, with a sense of spiritual malaise. It is Nietzschean in its insistence on pride and courage and the power of the will. Through the group of writers who called themselves 'Scyths', and who rejected the small and petty deed, Nietzsche may well be in the spiritual ancestry of Bolshevism, but it is in the main no doubt the philosophy of an age of expansion in a vast undeveloped country.

Among the young, Mehnert tells us, the old Church had been made to appear so ridiculous and antediluvian by the Anti-Religious Movement that in 1932 any thought of its revival seemed out of the question. Their religious needs were largely satisfied through the process of establishing Socialism. 'For Socialism too is a doctrine of grace, which meets the Russian's desire to surrender himself to a power lying outside his own person and, if need be, to sacrifice himself for it.' We have seen above how far back this attitude goes in the revolutionary movement. The new priesthood, it has often been suggested, is the Party. Yet Orthodoxy is far from dead, it may even have gained in some ways through persecution. 'The formal State adherence of all in Tsarist times was gone, and it was nothing that need be greatly missed. The inner core of the spiritual life of Russian Christianity was probably never stronger than now, when sufferings for the faith were common to all believers. The Commissary of Education, Lunacharsky, who as such had led the attack, made the damning admission: "Religion is like a nail, the harder you hit it the deeper it goes into the wood".' 'Yaroslavsky (the president of the Union of the Godless) in his report of the work of his Union in April 1937, reckoned up the results of all his attacks; one third of the townspeople and two-thirds of the country people were still religious, which means more than half of the whole.'[2]

So many aspects of Russian life are touched upon in Chekhov's work that there is no end to the comparisons and contrasts it suggests to readers whose imagination has been stirred by the

---

[1] Maynard, *The Russian Peasant*, 15.
[2] Sir Bernard Pares, *Russia* (Penguin), 1941, 163, 168.

immensity of the social changes that have been wrought in modern Russia, the energy and will-power that have gone to their making, and their incalculable importance for the whole of humanity. One question that we cannot but ask ourselves finally is: What has become of the old aristocratic and bourgeois culture of Russia since the Revolution, and in particular, in the present connection, what do Russians really think of Chekhov now, the last of the classics? Mr. Desmond McCarthy, in his review [1] of Mr. Kornei Chukovsky's recent book on *Chekhov the Man*, found the portrait drawn of Chekhov in that work difficult to reconcile with the impression of Chekhov which he has received from Chekhov's own writings. How can modern Russia, he asks, really like Chekhov and the 'superfluous men' of his generation, sensitive artists, some of them, but sceptical observers, full of pity and longing, not hopeful and self-confident men of action? Yet there is no question that they do like him. His plays are still splendidly acted and enthusiastically received, and his stories are issued in popular editions sold by the hundred thousand. Does it simply show 'how genuine admiration of an artist can be stimulated and supported by misconceptions'?

To speak of misconceptions surely begs the question. It is certain that everyone is influenced in his attitude towards any author by conceptions, by the ideas and feelings that his own particular development has made dominant in him at the time. These will be called misconceptions of the author by people with a sufficiently different background. This is not to deny of course that there are genuine misconceptions too, that we often entertain quite false ideas, and completely misunderstand other people. But still more frequently A's attitude towards an author differs from B's in that A sees one aspect of him, supplying a little perhaps from his own experience or emotional needs, and B is sensitive or over-sensitive to another. So Mr. McCarthy finds Chekhov himself in the weak and dreaming intellectuals whom he drew so well, not allowing enough perhaps for the fact that Chekhov was constantly criticizing them in his work, and was at least sufficiently different from them to be capable of criticism, though admittedly so close to them that he knew them through and through. Our study of Chekhov in his background has suggested that this is a one-sided and perhaps typically foreign view of Chekhov. Mr. Chukovsky on the other hand, who, if he is the pre-revolutionary Kornei Chukovsky (b. 1883), the Russian

[1] *Sunday Times*, 26/8/45.

G. K. Chesterton, has been writing about Chekhov since 1910 at least, is really saying to the young 'Komsomolites' who are still suspicious of bourgeois literature: 'You see, we were not so bad as you imagine. Here is Chekhov, for instance, the 'poet of futility', who can be proved on the evidence of his letters and the testimony of his friends to have had a social conscience as sensitive as yours, and energy and will-power equally great. He did all a man could in his day for the good of his fellows and, living against the grain of his time, showed heroic strength of purpose in moulding his own personality in accordance with his ideals of freedom.'

There is a basis of truth in this view, as we have seen, though it is expressed here with some exaggeration. Chekhov would certainly not have thought of himself as a hero, though he was equally certainly not a weakling. But it is clear that the young Russian of to-day can be taught to appreciate Chekhov best from this angle, because he is a hero-worshipper, and to possess a social conscience is for him the very essence of culture. We may be sure that there are other conceptions of Chekhov which may also be reconciled with current Russian ways of thinking. For some he is no doubt a pathetic victim of the old system, for others a mine of warning examples of its effects, for others again the author of some of the funniest stories in the language, and for a small number simply a great artist, whose point of view they can still imaginatively share at least as well as we can that of, say, Dickens.

When all this has been said, there is still no denying the contrast between Chekhov's Russia and that of to-day, and one element we particularly miss in his picture, as is clear from earlier chapters, is the type of man capable of leading a successful revolution. He seems to give us all the material for a revolution except this. There is one character in a tale of his whom he refers to in a letter[1] as 'a born revolutionary'. This is the dare-devil peasant Dymov in *The steppe*, the incarnation of reckless energy that finds no proper outlet, whom we first see beating a snake to death with his whip, only to be told a moment later that it was no viper but a harmless grass-snake—a symbolic condemnation of anarchist activities? 'There will never be a revolution in Russia,' was Chekhov's comment in 1888, 'and Dymov will end by drinking himself to death, or be thrown into gaol. He is a superfluous man.' Yet seen from another angle, Dymov has in him the makings of Gorky's Nil, the 'unmistakable anticipation of the Bolshevik attitude to life'. There is no clearer indication of the amazement that Chekhov

[1] of. 25/9/1888.

would feel if he could see what changes have been wrought, and by whom, not two to three hundred, but twenty or thirty years after his day, in the Russia that he knew and loved so well.

   To read Chekhov then is to be reminded that his Russia has indeed changed into something very different, but that the successful revolution has been carried through, not by an abstract proletariat against an abstract bourgeoisie, but by creatures of flesh and blood in a country with its own unique character and traditions. One may see in the passion for justice and the faith in science which we have found in his pages the inspiration of what is best in the Russian society of to-day, but one realises too that the system of government, through the instrumentality of which these ideals have been translated into reality, is itself a historical product. It is not only the ideas of Marx and the intellectuals, but the political habits of an old autocracy, with its police rule and its fear of freedom of speech, which have gone to the making of the new Russia. It is good therefore to know that such a decided Westerner as Chekhov, for whom 'humane ideas', the watch-word of the intelligentsia of his generation, meant not only justice and science, but human kindness and good will, and an amused scorn for self-important officialdom, is genuinely popular, and can hardly be considered a corrupting influence by a Soviet of People's Commissars which has initiated the first really complete edition of his works.

BIBLIOGRAPHY

(Titles of Russian books are preceded by 'r'.)

I. WORKS AND LETTERS OF CHEKHOV.

r. *Complete Works* in 14 volumes, Marks, St. Petersburg, from 1902 (vols. 12 to 14 contain stories not included by Chekhov in the *Collected Works*).

r. *Complete Works and Letters*, ed. Baluchaty, Potemkin, Tikhonov (Moscow, 1944).
(Of this, the first critical edition of all the known works and letters, only Series I, vol. 1 (*Works to 1883*) was available.)

Works, translated by Constance Garnett, 15 vols. (London, 1916–1923).

r. *Letters*, ed. with biographical introductions by Michael Chekhov, 6 vols (Moscow, 1912–16).

r. *New Letters*, ed. B. L. Modzalevsky (Leningrad, 1922).

r. *Letters to O. L. Knipper* (Berlin, 1924).
(English translation by Constance Garnett, London, 1926.)

r. *Uncollected Letters*, ed. N. K. Piksanov (Moscow and Leningrad, 1927).

Letters of A. Tchehov to His Family and Friends, translated by Constance Garnett (London, 1920).
(A selection in one volume from the 6-volume Russian edition, with a biographical sketch based on Michael Chekhov's.)

Life and Letters of A. Tchehov, translated by S. S. Koteliansky and P. Tomlinson (London, 1925).
(A different selection, but overlapping considerably with Mrs. Garnett's, with essays by various authors.)

r. *Notebooks*, ed. Grossmann (Moscow, 1927).
(English edition, abridged, with Gorky's *Reminiscences of Chekhov*, London, 1921.)

II. CRITICAL WORKS ON CHEKHOV.

A. L. WOLYNSKI, *A. P. Chekhov* (German translation), (Berlin, 1904).

r. N. Pokrovsky (editor), *Chekhov in His Importance as a Writer and Artist* (Moscow, 1906).
(A selection from the Russian criticism of Chekhov, mainly from periodicals.)

r. *Chekhov Jubilee Volume*, ed. M. Semenov and N. Tulupov (Moscow, 1910).
(Critical essays and reminiscences by many hands.)

r. D. S. MEREZHKOVSKY, "Chekhov and Gorky", in *Collected Works*, vol. 2 (St. Petersburg and Moscow, 1911).

L. SHESTOV, *A. Chekhov and other Essays*, translated by S. Koteliansky and J. Middleton Murry (Dublin and London, 1916).

W. GERHARDI, *Chekhov*, a critical study (New York, 1923).

A. Chekhov, Literary and Theatrical Reminiscences (by Sobolev, Korolenko, Kuprin, Bunin, Andreyev, etc.), (London, 1927).

O. ELTON, *Chekhov* (The Taylorian Lecture, 1929), (Oxford, 1929).

r. M. GORKY, "Reminiscences of Chekhov and of Tolstoy", reprinted in *Selected Critical Essays* (Moscow, 1941).

r. S. BALUKHATY, Chekhov, in *Classics of the Russian Drama* (Leningrad and Moscow, 1940).

r. V. VILENKIN, vl. I. Nemirovich-Danchenko (Moscow, 1941).

r. N. TELESHOV, *An Author's Memoirs* (Moscow, 1943).

KORNEI CHUKOVSKY, *Chekhov the Man*, translated by Pauline Rose (London, 1945).

III. HISTORY OF RUSSIAN LITERATURE.

HON. MAURICE BARING, *An Outline of Russian Literature* (London, 1914).
JANKO LAVRIN, *The Russian Novel* (London, 1942).
P. MILIUKOV, *Outlines of Russian Culture*, Part II, Literature (Philadelphia, 1942).
PRINCE D. S. MIRSKY, *Contemporary Russian Literature* (1881–1925), (London, 1926).
— *A History of Russian Literature to 1881* (London, 1927).

IV. THE INTELLIGENTSIA.

For the concept 'Intelligentsia':
KARL MANNHEIM, *Ideology and Utopia* (London, 1936).
— *Man and Society in an Age of Reconstruction* (London, 1940).
R. H. TAWNEY, *Equality* (London, 1931).
r. IVANOV-RAZUMNIK, *History of Social Thought*, 2nd ed., 2 vols. (St. Petersburg, 1908).
r. D. N. OVSYANIKO-KULIKOVSKY, *History of the Russian Intelligentsia*, 3 vols. (St. Petersburg, 1911).
r. *Landmarks* ('Viekhi'), 2nd ed. (Moscow, 1909).
(Essays by various authors after the 1905 revolution.)

V. POLITICAL AND SOCIAL BACKGROUND.

General:
R. BEAZLEY, N. FORBES, G. A. BIRKETT, *Russia from the Varangians to the Bolsheviks* (Oxford, 1918).
D. FOOTMAN, *Red Prelude* (*Life of Zhelyabov*) (London, 1944).
M. KOVALEVSKY, *Russian Political Institutions* (Chicago, 1902).
A. LEROY-BEAULIEU, *L'empire des Tsars et les Russes*, 3 vols. (Paris, 1881–89).

r. P. LYASHCHENKO, *History of the National Economy of the USSR*, vol. 1 (19th century), (Moscow, 1939).
SIR D. MACKENZIE WALLACE, *Russia*, 2 vols., revised ed. (first edition 1877), (London, 1905).
SIR BERNARD PARES, *A History of Russia*, revised ed. (London, 1926).
— *Russia* (Penguin Special), (London, 1941).
M. N. POKROVSKY, *Brief History of Russia*, translated Mirsky, 2 vols. (London, 1933).
A. RAMBAUD, *Histoire de la Russie* (Paris, 1878).
S. STEPNIAK, *Russia under the Tsars*, 2 vols. (London, 1885).
B. H. SUMNER, *Survey of Russian History* (London, 1944).

Social history:
HON. MAURICE BARING, *The Russian People* (London, 1911).
— *What I Saw in Russia* (London, 1913).
— *Mainsprings of Russia* (London, 1914).
EUGEN HÄUSLER, *Der Kaufmann in der russischen Literatur* (Königsberg, 1935).
SIR JOHN MAYNARD, *Russia in Flux* (London, 1941).
— *The Russian Peasant and other Studies* (London, 1942).
PRINCE D. S. MIRSKY, *Russia* (London, 1931).
H. W. WILLIAMS, *Russia of the Russians* (London, 1915).

The peasant question:
BARON VON HAXTHAUSEN, *The Russian Empire*, 2 vols. (London, 1856). (German edition, 1847.)
G. PAVLOVSKY, *Agricultural Russia on the Eve of the Revolution* (London, 1930).
G. T. ROBINSON, *Rural Russia Under the Old Regime* (London, 1932).

Education:
Board of Education Reports on Special Subjects, vol. 23; Thos. Darlington, *Education in Russia* (London, 1909).
N. HANS and S. HESSEN, *Educational Policy in Soviet Russia* (Introduction and chapter 1, Pre-Bolshevic), (London, 1930).

Postscript, 1970. The bibliography may be supplemented, especially on the biographical and critical side, from the studies of Chekhov by R. Hingley (1950), D. Magarshack (1952), E. J. Simmons (1962), and from the successive volumes of *The Oxford Chekhov*, translated by R. Hingley, from 1964.

INDEX OF REFERENCES TO CHEKHOV'S WORKS

(Works to be found in Mrs. Garnett's translation are referred to by her title. All others are marked with an asterisk.* Titles of plays are printed in capitals.)

GENERAL INDEX

Academies, ecclesiastical, 144 f.
Actors, 168 ff.
Administration, 104 f.
Aksakov, Sergei T., 14, 23, 79.
Aksakov, Ivan, 32.
Alexander I, Tsar (1801-1825), 31, 152.
Alexander II, Tsar (1855-1881), 32, 113, 152 f.
Alexander III, Tsar (1881-1894), 33.
Angling 39 f.
Army, 123 ff.
Artists, 166.

Baring, Hon. Maurice, 20, 163.
Barker, Sir E., 218 f.
Barristers, 156 f.
Bolshevist revolution, 35 f.
Bourget, Paul, 199.
Bribery, 97 ff.
Bureaucracy, see Officials.

Cantonal elder (starshina), 55 f.
Capitalism, 175 f., 185 ff., 192.
Catherine II (1762-1796), 27, 31, 78, 152, 155.
Chekhov, Alexander, P., 21.
Chekhov, Anton, P.:
  Early life, 1 ff.
  Student days, 4.
  As doctor, 4 f.
  Early literary life, 5 ff.
  Journey to Sakhalin, 8 ff.
  Travels in Europe, 10, 13.
  At Melikhovo, 11 ff.
  At Yalta, 13.
  Artistic aims, 14 f.
  Influence of medical studies, 15, 215.
  Temperament, 15, 213.
  Artistic objectivity, 16.
  Realism, 16 ff.
  Lack of a message, 17 ff.
  Landscapes, 21 ff.
  Attitude to religion, 128 f., 206, 209 ff.
  Attitude to theatre, 167 f.
  Values, 197 ff.
  Simplicity of heart, 200.

Ethical convictions, 202 ff.
  Individualism, 204.
  Attitude to Tolstoy, 206 ff.
  Hopes for the future, 208 f.
  Source of his melancholy, 211.
  His humour, 213 f.
  Development as artist, 214 f.
  Relation to present-day Russia, 217 ff.
Chekhov, Ivan P., 4.
Chekhov, Michael P., 2, 11, 119.
Chekhov, Nicolai P., 7, 202.
Chekhov, Paul J., 3, 12.
Children in Chekhov, 195 f.
Chinovnik, see Officials.
Chukovsky, Kornei, 2, 222 f.
Church, Orthodox:
  Fasts and feasts, 63 f.
  In the village, 64 ff.
  And state, 127 f.
  In Russian life, 129 f., 221.
  And cultured classes, 130 f.
  Rites, 131 ff.
  Clergy (parochial), 136 f.
  Clergy (monastic), 137 ff.
  Sectarianism, 140 f.
Committee of ministers, 104.
Communications, 176 f.
Council of state, 104.
Craftsmen, 184 f.

Decembrist revolt, 31, 78, 143.
District Committee for Peasant Affairs, 111 f.
Doctors, 157 ff.
Dostoievsky, F., 199, 209, 215.

Economic Development, 175 ff.
Education:
  Primary, 60 f.
  Ecclesiastical, 143 ff.
  Of the gentry, 145 f.
  University, 146 ff.
  Secondary, 152 ff.
  Of women, 155 f.
Elton, Professor Oliver, 204, 215.
Emancipation of the serfs, 32.
Engineers, 177.